ARAGON
ISSUES IN
PHILOSOPHY

D1559419

PARAGON ISSUES IN PHILOSOPHY

THE PARAGON ISSUES IN PHILOSOPHY SERIES

At colleges and universities, interest in the traditional areas of philosophy remains strong. Many new currents flow within them, too, but some of these—the rise of cognitive science, for example, or feminist philosophy—went largely unnoticed in undergraduate philosophy courses until the end of the 1980s. The Paragon Issues in Philosophy Series responds to both perennial and newly influential concerns by bringing together a team of able philosophers to address the fundamental issues in philosophy today and to outline the state of contemporary discussion about them.

More than twenty volumes are scheduled. They are organized into three major categories. The first covers the standard topics—metaphysics, theory of knowledge, ethics, and political philosophy—stressing innovative developments in those disciplines. The second focuses on more specialized but still vital concerns in the philosophies of science, religion, history, sport, and other areas. The third category explores new work that relates philosophy and fields such as feminist criticism, medicine, economics, technology, and literature.

The level of writing is aimed at undergraduate students who have little previous experience studying philosophy. The books provide brief but accurate introductions that appraise the state of the art in their fields and show how the history of thought about their topics developed. Each volume is complete in itself but also complements others in the series.

Traumatic change characterizes these last years of the twentieth century; all of it involves philosophical issues. The philosophy editor for Paragon House, Don Fehr, has worked with us to develop this series. We hope it will encourage the understanding needed in our times, which are as complicated and problematic as they are promising.

John K. Roth   Frederick Sontag
Claremont McKenna College   Pomona College

AFRICAN PHILOSOPHY
THE ESSENTIAL READINGS

TSENAY SEREQUEBERHAN

HAMPSHIRE COLLEGE
AMHERST, MASSACHUSETTS

AFRICAN PHILOSOPHY THE ESSENTIAL READINGS

PARAGON
ISSUES IN
PHILOSOPHY

PARAGON HOUSE • ST. PAUL, MINNESOTA

FIRST EDITION, 1991

PUBLISHED IN THE UNITED STATES BY

PARAGON HOUSE
2700 UNIVERSITY AVENUE WEST
ST. PAUL, MN 55114-1016

FRONTISPIECE IS AN ORIGINAL PAINTING FROM THE ART GALLERY OF
THE ERITREAN PEOPLE'S LIBERATION FRONT IN SAHEL LIBERATED
ERITREA, 1987. USED WITH THE PERMISSION OF THE ERITREAN
PEOPLE'S LIBERATION FRONT, WASHINGTON, D.C., 1990.

SERIES DESIGN BY KATHY KIKKERT

LIBRARY OF CONGRESS CATALOGING-IN-PUBLICATION DATA

AFRICAN PHILOSOPHY : THE ESSENTIAL READINGS / TSENAY
SEREQUEBERHAN, EDITOR. — 1ST ED.
     P.   CM. — (PARAGON ISSUES IN PHILOSOPHY)
    INCLUDES BIBLIOGRAPHICAL REFERENCES.
    ISBN 1-55778-309-8 : $13.95
    1. PHILOSOPHY, AFRICAN. 2. PHILOSOPHY—AFRICA, SUB-SAHARAN.
  I. SEREQUEBERHAN, TSENAY. II. SERIES.
  B5375.A47   1990
  199'.6—DC20   90-35405
                                              CIP

MANUFACTURED IN THE UNITED STATES OF AMERICA

10 9 8 7 6 5 4 3

THE PAPER USED IN THIS PUBLICATION MEETS THE MINIMUM
REQUIREMENTS OF AMERICAN NATIONAL STANDARD FOR INFORMATION
SCIENCES—PERMANENCE OF PAPER FOR PRINTED LIBRARY MATERIALS,
ANSI Z39.48-1984.

DEDICATION

TO THE ERITREAN PEOPLE'S LIBERATION FRONT AND
TO ALL THOSE WHO, SACRIFICING LIFE AND LIMB, HAVE
FOUGHT FOR AND ARE STILL FIGHTING FOR THE COMPLETE
EMANCIPATION OF THE AFRICAN CONTINENT. IT IS IN LIGHT
OF THEIR ENDURANCE AND SACRIFICE THAT OUR
INTELLECTUAL EFFORTS HAVE ANY SENSE OR MEANING.

CONTENTS

ACKNOWLEDGMENTS

Onyewuenyi, Innocent. "Is There an African Philosophy?" *Journal of African Studies*, vol. 3, no. 4, pp. 513–28, 1976–1977. Reprinted with permission of the Helen Dwight Reid Foundation. Published by Heldref Publications, 4000 Albemarle Street, N.W., Washington, DC 20016. Copyright © 1976.

Oruka, Henry Odera. "Sagacity in African Philosophy." Reprinted by permission of the *International Philosophical Quarterly*, from vol. 23, no. 4, issue no. 92, December 1983, pp. 383–93.

Bodunrin, Peter O. "The Question of African Philosophy." *Philosophy*, vol. 56, no. 216, April 1981. Reprinted with the permission of Cambridge University Press.

Wiredu, Kwasi. "On Defining African Philosophy." Reprinted with the permission of the author, August 1989.

Hountondji, Paulin J. "African Philosophy: Myth and Reality." Extract taken from *African Philosophy: Myth and Reality* by Paulin Hountondji, reproduced by kind permission of Unwin Hyman Ltd. First published in French, 1976. Copyright © François Maspero, Paris 1976. First published in English, 1983. Copyright © Paulin Hountondji 1983. Translation copyright © Hutchinson & Company (Publishers) Ltd.

Keita, Lansana. "Contemporary African Philosophy: The Search for Method." Reprinted with the permission of *Praxis International*, vol. 5, no. 2, July 1985.

Owomoyela, Oyenka. "Africa and the Imperative of Philosophy: A Skeptical Consideration." Reprinted with the permission of *African Studies Review*, vol. 30, no. 1, March 1987.

Towa, Marcien. "Conditions for the Affirmation of a Modern African Philisophical Thought." Reprinted in translation with the permission of *Présence Africaine*, nos. 117–18, 1st and 2nd quarterlies, 1981.

Okolo, Okonda. "Tradition and Destiny: Horizons of an African Philosophical Hermeneutics." Reprinted in translation with the permission of *Présence Africaine*, no. 114, 2nd quarterly, 1980.

Wamba-Dia-Wamba, E. "Philosophy in Africa: Challenges of the African Philosopher." Reprinted with the permission of *Mawazo*, vol. 5, no. 2, December 1983.

PREFACE

It gives me great pleasure to acknowledge all the help that was extended to me by friends and colleagues in the process of putting together this anthology. I thank Jay Garfield for first suggesting and encouraging this work and for some very helpful and insightful discussions on African philosophy. I thank Lucius Outlaw for encouraging this project when I first mentioned it to him and for a long and fruitful discussion at his home when I first started working on this book. I thank Jill Lewis for meticulously checking and double-checking the two French translations that were prepared for this collection and for generously giving of her time. I also would like to thank Nuhad Jamal for countless discussions on African philosophy and related subjects.

I am deeply indebted to Kango Lare-Lantone, a co-African and an economist with a philosophical bent. Throughout the duration of this project, he generously gave of his time and assisted me in every respect. Be it in conversations on African philosophy or in selecting the pieces for this anthology, I have benefited from Kango's constant and generous assistance. In addition to the above, Kango also translated Okolo's contribution to this collection. I also thank Aster Gashaw for translating Towa's piece with great care at short notice and for double-checking Wamba's translated contribution to this collection.

To all those whom I pestered by mail, by telephone, and in person in the process of completing this work, especially to Olabiyi Yai, Kwasi Wiredu, Mahmood Mamdani, and Rowland Abiodun, I express my thanks and appreciation. I also would like to thank Mark Feinstein and Jay Garfield for helping me to make sense of a particularly difficult French phrase in Towa's piece. Last but not least, I would like to thank Lenore Bowen and Ruth Hammen for all kinds of assistance.

Tsenay Serequeberhan
Hampshire College, 1990

TSENAY SEREQUEBERHAN

INTRODUCTION

Metaphysics—the white mythology which resembles and reflects the culture of the West: the white man takes his own mythology, Indo-European mythology, his own logos, that is, the mythos of his idiom, for the universal form of that he must still wish to call Reason.

—Jacques Derrida

Munene, one of my younger brothers, had been one of these. He had been away a long time, and when he came back he wore clothes like a Pink Cheek and he came with one of them, in a box-on-wheels, which is called motorcar, along the new road.

The Pink Cheek called a Council together and when all, both Elders and the young men, were assembled and sat round, he spoke. He spoke of Munene; he told us of his learning and of his knowledge of the customs of the Pink Cheeks and of his cleverness at organizing.

"Because of this," he said, "and because he is a wise man, the Government, the Council of Muthungu that meets in Nairobi, have honored him and, in honoring him, are honoring you all."

He paused and looked at us. Beside him Munene stood smiling.

"He has been appointed Chief of this district and he will be your mouth and our mouth. He will tell us the things that you want to say and he will tell you the things that we

want to say to you. He has learned our language and our laws and he will help you to understand and keep them."
We Elders looked at each other. Was this the end of everything that we had known and worked for? What magic had this son of my father made that he who was not yet an Elder should be made leader over us all who were so much older and wiser in the ways of our people? It was as if a thunderbolt had fallen among us.
—Chief Kabongo, of the Kikuyu

I

This anthology of African philosophy aims to make available to the interested reader a representative selection of important texts from a literature dispersed in specialized journals on both sides of the Atlantic. As a field of study, African philosophy is situated at the intersection of philosophy and African studies. Thus, this anthology will be useful for courses in African philosophy, for more general courses in African and African-American studies, and for any course of studies surveying contemporary developments in philosophy. Beyond the classroom, the audience for this volume includes all those who have an ongoing interest in Africa and African intellectual productions.

Even though there are important non-African contributors to the discourse of African philosophy, this volume is composed only of African contributions. The reason for this is to document in one volume a variety of views articulated by African scholars in and on African philosophy, simply to hearken to what Africans have to say for themselves!

In my view, this exclusionist approach is necessary—at least at this time in the development of African philosophy—precisely because African philosophers need to formulate their differing positions in confrontation and dialogue and on their own, that is, minus foreign mediators/moderators or meddlers. African philosophers must engage in a theoretical threshing of their philosophical formulations in order to separate the wheat from the chaff in their own discourse. Thus, African philosophy will find its own theoretical space from within African problems and concerns that are felt and lived.

II

The eleven papers in this anthology represent a variety of philosophical positions that are interior to the debate—in and on African philosophy—as it has developed thus far. This debate, in one form or another, has been a reaction to Father Placide Tempels's book *Bantu Philosophy* (1945). As V. Y. Mudimbe has observed, thus far "[i]mplicitly or explicitly, the most inspiring trends in the field still define themselves with respect to Tempels."[1] In other words, as presently constituted, African philosophy is a body of texts directed at philosophically engaging African concerns and on the other hand, documenting the implicit philosophies and worldviews of ethnic Africans. This duality of purpose has been the area of contention around which the debate is focused.

As is well known, Tempels's aim in writing his *Bantu Philosophy* was to supply a documentation of the African's mentality and therefore to assist the European colonialist venture in Africa. Disregarding his colonialist intentions and motivation, his African disciples have continued the documentary orientation of his work. This orientation has been polemically characterized by Paulin J. Hountondji as the school of ethnophilosophy, that is, philosophy deriving from the study of ethnic Africans.

In opposition to Tempels and his African disciples, one finds a number of philosophers who stand united against this documentary orientation while simultaneously articulating a variety of differing positions. The one thing that these diverse thinkers share is the deeply felt commitment that, beyond documenting the philosophies of ethnic Africans, African philosophy has to be concretely engaged with the contemporary lived concerns and problems of the African continent. Within this oppositional stance to the documentary orientation in African philosophy, one finds two trends: a scientistic and a historico-hermeneutical trend. Let us now take a quick glance at the contributions that constitute this anthology and represent these two trends.

III

The paper that opens the anthology is an essay I prepared specifically for this collection. In this paper, "African Philosophy: The Point in

Question," I explore what might be questionable in the question of African philosophy. I do so by engaging in an overall discussion of the historical, political, and existential context within which the question is framed. The intent of the paper is to give the reader a sense of what is at stake in the discussion in and on African philosophy.

"Is There an African Philosophy?" (1976–1977), is the work of Innocent Onyewuenyi (University of Nsukka, Nigeria) and is representative of the documentary orientation. Onyewuenyi starts by presenting us with a programmatic statement and defense of this orientation. He then goes on to give us brief resumes of African metaphysics, epistemology, and ethical theory.

I have placed this essay at the beginning (following my own exploratory piece) of the anthology precisely because it states clearly and concisely the case for the trend which is a continuation of Tempels's work. I thus invite the reader to enter into the debate in the manner in which it was historically initiated, that is, as a polemical confrontation with the disciples of Father Tempels.

The papers that follow—"Sagacity in African Philosophy" (1983), by Henry Odera Oruka (University of Nairobi, Kenya); "The Question of African Philosophy" (1981), by Peter O. Bodunrin (University of Ibadan, Nigeria); "On Defining African Philosophy" (1981), by Kwasi Wiredu (University of South Florida); "African Philosophy: Myth and Reality" (1973), by Paulin J. Hountondji (National University of Benin, Cotonou); and "Contemporary African Philosophy: The Search for a Method" (1985), by Lansana Keita (University of Ibadan, Nigeria)—all attempt, in differing ways, to articulate positions that reject ethnophilosophy and in so doing emphasize the universality of philosophy as a discipline and the importance of a scientific (scientistic?) approach in philosophy.

Oruka's paper is an attempt to formulate a position distinct from ethnophilosophy and yet grounded in the traditional wisdom of African sages. This is an ambivalent position, caught between the claims of traditional African wisdom (sagacity) and the claim that philosophy is a culture-neutral universalistic dicipline. Bodunrin, Wiredu, and Hountondji, on the other hand, reject African traditional wisdom and, in affirming the universality of philosophic discourse, insist that

African philosophy can only be an "orientation," to use Wiredu's formulation, a "geographic" designation, to use Hountondji's words. Along these lines, Keita's piece highlights the practical contributions that philosophy can make in assisting scientific pedagogical developments in Africa.

The concluding four papers that form the anthology—"Africa and the Imperative of Philosophy: A Skeptical Consideration" (1987), by Oyenka Owomoyela (University of Nebraska); "Conditions for the Affirmation of a Modern African Philosophical Thought" (1981), by Marcien Towa (University of Cameroon); "Tradition and Destiny: Horizons of an African Philosophical Hermeneutics" (1980), by Okonda Okolo (National University of Zaire); and "Philosophy in Africa: Challenges of the African Philosopher" (1983), by E. Wamba-Dia-Wamba (University of Dar Es Salaam)—all attempt to articulate philosophical positions that are methodologically informed by the historicity of the African situation.

These last four authors critically engage the critique of ethnophilosophy and in so doing emphasize, in differing ways, the importance of a serious and concrete engagement with the traditional, historical, and contemporary situation of the continent. Philosophy, for these authors, is not only and merely a methodologically rigorous undertaking but, and more fundamentally, it is a serious engagement with one's own historicality and tradition, that is, with the African situation. These authors, to be sure, do not articulate a single position but stand together in emphasizing the importance of the historicity of the African situation for the methodologically rigorous and reflective project of African philosophy.

As should be clear from my own contribution and from what I have said in this introduction, it is with these last four authors that I align myself in the debate in and on African philosophy. For me as for them, philosophy—and specifically African philosophy—is a historically engaged and politically committed explorative reflection on the African situation aimed at the political empowerment of the African people. Beyond this admittedly vague but foundational formulation, we all speak with differing voices, articulate differing positions, and are ultimately responsible for our own views and commitments.

IV

As evinced by the two quotations at the beginning of this introduction, the latest deconstructive wisdom of the West coincides with the robust awareness our grandparents had of the implications of the European presence on African soil for African existence. This similitude of opinions, expressed from within the context of two fundamentally and radically different worlds—in the last quarter of the twentieth century, a hundred years after the European scramble for Africa—mocks the imperious/imperialistic European claim to be Reason Incarnate. Thus, from within and without Europe, is assailed!

To explore the historicity that has produced this unlikely confluence in mockery and assault reflectively—this is, among other things, the task of African philosophy and the *calling* of the African philosopher. This call comes to us from a lived history whose endurance and sacrifice—against slavery and colonialism—has made our present and future existence in freedom possible. The reflective explorations of African philosophy are thus aimed at further enhancing and expanding this freedom—at thinking the origins of its possibility and the deficiencies of its actuality and thus aiding in its further development and growth.

NOTES

1. V. Y. Mudimbe, "African Gnosis: Philosophy and the Order of Knowledge," *African Studies Review*, vol. 28, nos. 2–3, June–September 1985, p. 194.

AFRICAN
PHILOSOPHY
THE ESSENTIAL
READINGS

TSENAY SEREQUEBERHAN

AFRICAN PHILOSOPHY: THE POINT IN QUESTION

Any discourse on philosophy is necessarily implicated in an already presupposed conception of philosophy. As Martin Heidegger and Hans-Georg Gadamer tell us, reading or interpreting a text (compiling an anthology!) means being already involved with it. What needs doing then, is not to try to avoid this unavoidable "circle" of interpretation/philosophy, but to engage it fully. In other words, to bring to the fore—as much as possible—the operative pre-judgments at work in one's philosophical engagement.

In what follows, I will present a broadly historical, political, existential discussion of the question of African philosophy. My purpose will be to expose and legitimate my own prejudgments in terms of the historicopolitical horizon within and out of which African philosophy originates as a discourse. In doing so, I will stake out a critical position in the debate on and also within African philosophy.

I

The closing years of the nineteenth century witnessed the consummation of European imperial ambitions in the complete dismemberment and colonization—except for the kingdom of Abyssinia—of Africa.[1] Colonial conquest and the imposition of violent European rule on the partially destroyed and suppressed indigenous societies and the insertion of Africa into the modern European capitalist world as a dependent appendage to it effected decisive breaks and distortions in the previous patterns of life prevalent on the continent at large.[2] As Basil Davidson points out:

The colonial period, in *European mythology*, was supposed to have effected that particular transition [from pre-colonial to modern society]. Generally however, it did nothing of the kind. Historically . . . the colonial period was a hiatus, a standstill, an interlude when African history was stopped or was forced to become, for that period, a part of European history.[3]

African historical existence was suppressed and Africa was forced to become the negative underbelly of European history. What is paradoxical in all of this is the fact that Europe undertook the domination of Africa and the world not in the explicit and cynical recognition of its imperial interests but in the delusion that it was spreading civilization. In the poetic words of Rudyard Kipling:

> *Take up the White Man's burden*
> *Send forth the best ye breed*
> *Go bind your sons to exile*
> *To serve your captives need;*
> *To wait in heavy harness*
> *On fluttered folk and wild*
> *Your new-caught, sullen peoples,*
> *Half devil and half child.*[4]

This first stanza of Kipling's *The White Man's Burden* depicts concisely the European conception of itself and of the non-European. This conception unhesitatingly sees itself as the proper embodiment of human existence *as such* and goes on to impose itself on the non-European, who is viewed as "half devil and half child." This conception was not an isolated image concocted by Kipling. Rather, it is an accurate articulation of European colonial consciousness, which was amply represented not only in the popular literature of the day but also in the enduring conceptions and speculations of modern European thought.[5]

In the name of the universality of values, European colonialism violently universalized its own singular particularity and annihilated the historicality of the colonized. In this context, Western philosophy—in the guise of a disinterested, universalistic, transcendental, speculative discourse—served the indispensable function of being the ultimate *veracious buttress* of European conquest. This service, furthermore, was rendered in the name of "Man" and the emancipation of "Man." In the words of Immanuel Kant, European modernity saw itself as "man's release from his self-incurred tutelage."[6]

James Schmidt has pointed out that "the question of enlightenment" in modern European thought was a politically oriented struggle against superstitious beliefs (as distinct from established Christian doctrine) aimed at the "release" of "Man" from darkness and ignorance through the employment of Reason.[7] As Antonio Gramsci correctly observes, this orientation of modern European thought "presupposes a single culture, a single religion, a single global 'conformism,' "[8] that is, a singular globalized cultural totality.

It is important to notice that such a homogenizing globalization of the historical, political, and cultural horizon of European modernity inevitably sees the "world" as nothing more than a homogenate replica of Europe. Given this orientation, the *subjugation* of the non-European world—"half devil and half child"—by Europe, understood as the historical embodiment of Reason, has to necessarily be seen as the *emancipation* of "Man" on a global scale. Thus, victorious over superstition and the darkness of ignorance, Europe spreads the light of Reason!

In this manner, colonial "European mythology" found, in the speculative discourse of Western philosophy, its highest pinnacle and ultimate justification. For, as Enrique Dusell has correctly observed, Western philosophy has always been the "philosophy of the center" which designates the periphery and frames it as such.[9] Let us now take a quick glance at some choice samplings of the philosophical underpinnings of this colonial "European mythology."

Hume and Kant held the view that Africans, in virtue of their blackness, are precluded from the realm of reason and civilization. As Hume puts it, "I am apt to suspect the negroes, and in general all the other species of men (for there are four or five different kinds) to be naturally inferior to whites. There never was a civilized nation of any complexion than white." Kant, in agreement with Hume, asserts that "[s]o fundamental is the difference between the two races of men, and it appears to be as great in regard to mental capacities as in color."[10] Making a subtle observation on the intellectual capacities of a black person, Kant astutely remarks that "this fellow was quite black from head to foot, a clear proof that what he said was stupid."[11] In the same vein, but now reflecting on history, Kant asserts that "if one adds episodes from the national histories of other peoples insofar as they are known from the history of the *enlightened* nations, one will discover a regular progress in the constitution of states on our continent (which will probably *give law*, eventually, to all *the others*)."[12]

Expressing the same "enlightened" view in the *Philosophy of History*, after describing the Negro as beyond the pale of humanity proper, Hegel categorically affirms that Africa "is no historical part of the world; it has no movement or development to exhibit. Historical movements in it—that is in its northern part—belong to the Asiatic or European World."[13] As Lucius Outlaw points out:

This orientation to Africa so poignantly expressed by Hegel was widely shared by many of its earliest European visitors (explorers, missionaries, seekers after wealth and fame, colonizers, etc.), whose travelogues and "reports" served to validate the worst characterization as the European *invention* of Africa and Africans out of the racism and ethnocentrism infecting Europe's project in its encounter with Africa as a different and black other.[14]

In the *Philosophy of Right*, Hegel systematically presents this same perspective as the unfolding of Reason in its world-historical process of self-institution. What the "explorer" and the "colonizer" express as a crude Eurocentric racism, Hegel and modern European philosophy articulate as the universality of Reason, the trademark of Europe. In fact, for Hegel, the possibility of "ethical life" in the context of modernity is predicated on the necessity of colonial expansion.[15]

In like manner, the Marxist critique of idealist philosophy and European capitalism sees the possibility of the actualization of its critical project as directly linked to the colonial globalization of Europe. Marx and Engels—the self-proclaimed radical critics of nineteenth-century European capitalism—articulate this same Eurocentrism as an integral part of their philosophicohistorical position. For both, the colonial Europeanization of the globe was a prerequisite for the possibility of true human freedom, that is, communism.[16]

The very hope for the possibility of human emancipation anticipated and articulated out of European history—the Marxist project—is itself predicated on the subjugation and obliteration of non-European histories and cultures. As Marx points out, commenting on the world-historical role of European colonialist expansion:

England has to fulfill a double mission in India: one destructive, the other regenerating—the annihilation of old Asiatic [African] society, and the laying of the material foundations of Western society in Asia [Africa].[17]

In the same vein, but more forcefully, Engels states that:

Then there is also the case of the conquest and brutal destruction of economic resources. . . . Nowadays such a case usually has the opposite effect, at least among great peoples [nineteenth-century colonialist Europe!]: in the long run the vanquished [the African, the Asiatic, the non-European] often gains more economically, politically and morally than the victor.[18]

It is important to note that, behind and beyond the differing Eurocentric views of the above thinkers—and the modern tradition of Western philosophy as a whole—lies the *singular* and grounding metaphysical belief that European humanity is properly speaking isomorphic with the humanity of the human *as such*. Beyond all differences and disputes this is the common thread that constitutes the unity of the tradition. Philosophy, furthermore, is the privileged discourse singularly rooted in European/human existence *as such*, which articulates and discloses the *essence* of the *real*. Thus, European cultural-historical prejudgments are passed off as transcendental wisdom!

European colonialism established the material and cultural conditions in which this self-aggrandizing and grounding metaphysical delusion could be institutionally embodied and incarnated in the consciousness of the colonized. Simultaneously, this same delusionary metaphysical belief also provided the evidence—in its material instantiations and inculcation in the consciousness of the colonized—

for its own "veracity." The very fact of conquest was taken as metaphysical proof of the unhistoricality—the lack of humanness—of the colonized. In Hegel's words, the "civilized [European] nation is conscious that the rights of *barbarians* are unequal to its own and treats their autonomy as only a formality."[19]

As Edward Said correctly points out, the result of colonialism in the colonized world was "a widely varied group of little Europes throughout Asia, Africa and the Americas."[20] The "little Europes" constituted on the African continent required the replication of European institutions and forms of life and the simultaneous depreciation and suppression—as barbaric, savage, nonhuman—of African institutions and culture. They also required the systematic inculturation of urbanized Africans, whose very formation as a section of the dominated society was predicated on the rupture of African historical existence in the face of European violence.[21] Thus, the Europeanized sections of colonized Africa were physically and culturally disinherited. The non-Europeanized sections, on the other hand, were forced to submit to a petrification of their indigenous cultural and historical existence.

This is not to suggest that the urbanized and—at various levels—Europeanized African consciously and in these very terms endorses the European metaphysical prejudices cited above. Nor is it to argue that indigenous cultures were completely obliterated by colonial conquest. Rather, it is to indicate and strongly emphasize the fact that the Europeanized African's internalized negative disposition toward his own indigenousness and his estrangement from African cultures and traditions has deep roots and finds its ultimate "veracious" justification in the delusionary metaphysical belief articulated in and out of the tradition of Western philosophy. On the other hand, the cultural-historical stagnation of the indigenous non-Europeanized African is itself the result of European conquest, which ironically is used to justify this same conquest.[22]

Encased between these two contradictory and complementary forms of estranged existence, one finds contemporary Africa. The estranging dialectic of these two broad segments of society constitutes the existential crisis of the continent. In a paradoxical and distorted manner, these two segments of African society, mimic and replicate the estranged and estranging violent dialectic of the colonizer and the colonized described so well by Albert Memmi. But in this case the roles of colonizer and colonized are played by the native, cast on both sides of this antagonistic relation, by reference to the culture of the former colonial power. Power or empowerment is thus a function of European culture which manifests itself in and legitimates the power of the neocolonial elites of postcolonial Africa.

As Davidson points out, the African anticolonial struggle did not only expel the physical presence of colonialism but it also put in "question the smoothly borrowed assumptions of the social hybrids [Europeanized Africans] about the opposition of 'European civilization' to 'African barbarism.' "[23] Indeed, beyond the political and historical combat to expel colonialism, contemporary Africa finds itself confronted and hindered, at every turn, by that which this combat has put in *question* without fundamentally eradicating.

Present-day African realities are thus constituted partly by the ossified remnants of European colonialism/neocolonialism—as embodied at every level in the institutional forms of contemporary Africa and in the conscious self-awareness of Europeanized Africans—and by the varied forms of struggle aimed at actualizing the possibility of an autonomous and free Africa in the context of the modern world. The hope, in other words, is of actualizing the real but unactualized possibilities of the African anticolonial struggle.

It is in and out of this overall historical-political-existential *horizon* that the discourse of African philosophy carves out and secures a space in which, and out of which, it can articulate itself as a viable and pertinent undertaking. African philosophy is thus a reflective supplement to the concrete efforts under way on the continent. As is evinced by the papers collected in this volume and in the field at large, in *differing* ways, the concerns of African philosophy and the efforts of African philosophers hover around this central point: the historical-political-existential crisis of an Africa saddled with a broken and ambiguous heritage.

In the poetic words of Aimé Césaire, "more and more the old negritude is turning into a corpse."[24] But the new "negritude" is yet to be born and in and out of this historical interlude—this absence, this lack, this impasse—African philosophy finds its problems and concerns. Whether these problems are expressed in explicit political terms or as questions regarding science and its importation, this impasse, this felt need, today calls forth and motivates the varied struggles on the African continent and simultaneously engenders and makes possible the further elaboration and development of African philosophical questioning.

As Theophilus Okere puts it:

[W]hether it is a Plato from Greek antiquity, a Hegel from modern philoso-phy, or a contemporary philosopher like Heidegger himself, the conclusion is the same, namely, that their thought is inscribed and their problematic dictated by the non-philosophy which is their own cultural background, especially by their religious beliefs and myths.[25]

The basic and most fundamental fact in Africa today is the misery the continent is immersed in and the varied struggles—in different arenas—to overcome this wretched condition. In response to this grim reality, this somber "nonphilosophy," philosophical reflection has become relevant in the present African situation.

To be sure, African thinkers can also reflect on their traditional "religious beliefs and myths." But if African thinkers are really to engage actual problems, then it is clear that African philosophy has to—at some level or other—be connected with the contemporary struggles and concerns facing the continent and its diverse peoples. For it is not the "beliefs and myths" of the peoples of Africa—in their intricate magnificence—that are mindboggling, but the concrete misery and political insanity of the contemporary African situation.

It is necessary to note that Placide Tempels's book, *Bantu Philoso-phy*, published in 1945—which provoked and served as both the positive (ethnophilosophy) and negative (professional philosophy) point of departure for the contemporary exchanges in African philosophy—was not a book innocent of politics.[26] The basic intent of Tempels's work was to explore and appropriate by subversion the lived world outlook of the Bantu in the service of Belgian colonialism, that is, the European "civilizing mission" in the Congo. In fact, Tempels's work, is an exemplary effort aimed at the expropriation of the interiority of the subjugated in the service of colonialism.

Bantu Philosophy articulates the need to expose and appropriate the intellectual productions of the Bantu/African in order to better anchor the European colonialist project in the consciousness of the colonized. For Tempels, one had to recognize the humanity of the colonized in order to better colonize and Christianize them! But is not colonialism itself predicated on the absence of humanity—as Western philosophy affirms—in the "savage," who thus needs to be colonized in order to be "humanized"?

The fruitful ambivalence of Tempels's position, from the perspective of the colonized, is rather obvious. Inadvertently and in the service of colonialism, Tempels was forced to admit—against the grain of the then established "knowledge"—that the Bantu/African is not a mere beast devoid of consciousness, but a human being whose conscious awareness of existence is grounded on certain foundational notions. Thus, the positive response to Tempels's work (ethnophilosophy) is an attempt to capitalize on this ambivalence—the recognition of the humanity of the colonized. The negative response to his work (professional philosophy) on the other hand is a scientistic attempt to expose and guard against the colonialist ambivalences utilized to placate, minimize, and bypass the obdurate political-cultural resistance of the colonized.

In either case, these philosophical responses are inherently political precisely because they are provoked by the politics of colonialism in the realm of philosophy. At this point, it is necessary to note that Tempels's singular effort in philosophy can best be understood for what it is only if it is seen as the practical and de facto implementation of the grounding metaphysical prejudice embodied in the Western tradition of philosophy as a whole. As was indicated earlier, this is the delusionary metaphysical belief that European existence is isomorphic with human existence *as such*. As V. Y. Mudimbe has observed, the colonizing and the missionary/evangelic "work" of Europe in Africa has always been and cannot help but be (two sides, spiritual and earthly, of) a single project of domination.[27]

Viewed in this light, the political imperative of African philosophy is rather clear. For, as E. Wamba-Dia-Wamba has observed, "[i]n today's Africa, to think is increasingly to think *for* or *against* imperialism."[28] That is to say, "to think for or against" the Eurocentric metaphysics of Western philosophy and the perpetual subordination—at all levels—of Africa.

II

The period of world history that begins with the end of the Second World War has been for Africa not a period of relative calm and peace, but rather a period of accelerated war and political turmoil. To be sure, these conflicts have not been futile. By the end of the 1960s, most of Africa had achieved the status of political independence, and the early 1970s witnessed the end of Portuguese colonialism, the oldest European colonial empire in Africa.

To this day, however, armed political conflicts rage on—in the midst of famine and "natural" calamities—in both independent and nonindependent Africa. Grim as this picture may be, it is important to remember that it constitutes the African people's varied and differing struggles to define and establish their freedom. But what are the people of Africa trying to free themselves from and what are they trying to establish?

This is the basic question, as we noted earlier—formulated in a variety of ways—out of which the differing concerns of African philosophers are articulated and which constitutes the basic concern of African philosophy. As Okere correctly observes, the discourse of African philosophy is located within the "movement in both artistic and intellectual life to establish a certain [African] identity."[29] It is an effort, on the plane of theoretical struggle, to explore reflectively and supplement theoretically the concrete emancipatory efforts—at various levels and in differing arenas—concretely under way on the continent. It is a concrete engagement with "Africa in metamorphosis."[30]

In being so, it institutes itself in the context of and by concretely engaging the contemporary problems and questions pertinent to the

African situation. Furthermore, this is not a question of "choosing" or "preferring" one set of questions as opposed to another, as if one could choose what needs to be thought! It is, rather, a question of being *open* to that which *needs* to be *thought* in contemporary Africa. As Okanda Okolo puts it, this is the hermeneutical situation of the "formerly colonized, the oppressed, that of the under-developed, struggling for more justice and equality."[31]

For philosophers, as Marcien Towa has observed, are

beings of flesh and bones who belong to a continent, to a particular culture and a specific period. And for a particular philosopher, to really philosophize is necessarily to examine in a critical and methodic manner the essential problems of his milieu and of his period.[32]

In the differing formulations of the papers presented in this collection—and in the varied works of African philosophy at large—there is a dispute as to how these "essential problems" might best be engaged. This dispute, however, is grounded on a shared understanding that it is the present-day African situation as it arises out of the ambiguous and broken heritage of the African past that calls for thinking. Thus, these "essential problems" are the lived concerns, the questions and issues, embedded in a concrete existential-historical-political *horizon*, that evoke questioning, that is, the discourse of African philosophy.

As Heidegger points out, philosophy or "meditative thought," does not just happen; rather, it is interior to and arises out of the region/horizon that is originatively its own.[33] In each case, and for philosophical reflection *as such*, it is the lived life concerns of a culture and of a tradition, as they are disclosed by questions posed from within a concrete situation, that serve as the bedrock on which and out of which philosophical reflection is established. Or, as Okolo puts it, "hermeneutics [philosophy] exists *only* in particular traditions."[34]

Thus, the fact that African philosophers have been concerned with and have made the problems of their own, that is, Africa's own lived historicality and broken heritage/tradition, the focal point of their reflections is as it should be. For ultimately, whether we are aware of it or not, it is out of a lived heritage or tradition that we speak; and even when we deny this, it is a particular tradition (scientism?) that *speaks* and utilizes our voice.

III

Given what has been said thus far, what then is the point in question in the question of African philosophy? In the history of philosophy and presently, ethnic qualifiers have been and are still operative with regard to designating specific philosophical perspectives. Jewish, Arabic/Islamic, Medieval/Christian, European, German, Greek, Oriental, American, and so forth—all these ethnic, religious, continental qualifiers designate the specificity of a philosophical perspective in terms of the background culture or tradition within which and out of which a particular philosophical discourse is articulated. The latest addition to this list of ethnic qualifiers in philosophy is "Contemporary French Philosophy," which Vincent Descombes describes as "coincident with the sum of the discourses elaborated in France and considered by the public of today as philosophical."[35]

In short, what has to be noted is that the designation "African philosophy" has behind it a long list of precedents and thus needs no justification. And yet, the justification of this label or conversely the attempt to reduce it to an external, merely geographic[36] designation has been a basic preoccupation of much of the literature to date.

To be sure, African philosophy does present problems for the established tradition of Western philosophy. Okere convincingly argues that the possibility of African philosophy as a legitimate field of discourse presupposes the weakening, if not the demise, of the absolutist and Eurocentric paradigm of thought dominant in Western philosophy thus far. Indeed, it is no accident that the discussion of African philosophy is taking place in the context of the increasing contemporary importance of hermeneutics, deconstruction, and, in general, context-oriented modes of doing philosophy in the discipline at large. The "historicity and relativity of truth—and this always means truth as we can and do attain it—is one of the main insights of the hermeneutical revolution in philosophy,"[37] which is substantiated and in turn substantiates the efforts embedded in African philosophy.

In this regard, African philosophy is an added questioning voice in the varied current discourses of contemporary philosophy. For as Outlaw pointedly observes, at a deeper philosophical level the methodological "issues involved" in the question of African philosophy "are only immediately concerned" with philosophy as an intellectual discipline.

> The deeper issue is one with much higher stakes: it [the question of African philosophy] is a struggle over the meaning of "man" and "civilized human," and all that goes with this in the context of the political economy of the capitalized and Europeanized Western world.[38]

On the other hand, for Lansana Keita, Kwasi Wiredu, Peter O. Bodunrin, and Paulin J. Hountondji, the concerns of African philosophy are centered on questions of methodology focused on the role that philosophy can play as the "handmaid" of science in the context of Africa.[39] In order to better understand how these (scientistic?) concerns are superimposed on the substantive politico-philosophic questions articulated thus far in our discussion by Okere, Outlaw, Wamba, Towa, and Okolo, it is necessary to begin by taking a quick glance at the diversified literature that presently constitutes African philosophy.

Thus far, African philosophy has been an exploratory meta-philosophical discourse that simultaneously harbors and is articulated out of substantive philosophical positions and concerns. Following Henry Odera Oruka, one can classify African philosophy into four basic trends: ethnophilosophy, philosophic sagacity, nationalistic-ideological philosophy, and professional philosophy.[40] In his more recent work, without substantially changing this order of classification, Oruka recognizes an added hermeneutical-historical trend in African philosophical thought. This orientation is, broadly speaking, basically concerned with interpretatively engaging and thinking through the concrete politico-historical actuality of the present African situation and its future possibilities.[41]

Oruka's classificatory schema has pedagogic merit insofar as it presents a concise overview of the field at large. But this merit is offset by the fact that this ordering gives the false impression that these trends are somehow independent of each other. Thus, while utilizing Oruka's schema, we will supplement it with V. Y. Mudimbe's and Kwame Gyekye's more accurate conceptions.

For Mudimbe, the works of African philosophy can be viewed as extending on a continuum. On one extreme of this continuum, one would place all those efforts aimed at documenting the philosophies of African peoples. On the other extreme, one would place the work of those who have insisted that African philosophy is basically the work of Africans trained in the Western tradition of philosophy.[42] This schema has the merit of placing these seemingly contradictory perspectives on the same spectrum and presenting them as differing refractions originating from the same source, that is, "Africa in metamorphosis." In like manner, for Gyekye,

a distinction must be made between traditional African philosophy and modern African philosophy: The latter, to be African, and have a basis in African culture and experience, must have a connection with the former, the traditional.[43]

In other words, the literature of African philosophy is a body of texts produced by Africans (and non-Africans) directed at philosophically engaging African problems and/or documenting the philosophies of African peoples. The hesitation expressed by the conjunction/disjunction in the previous sentence is the hesitation on which the question of African philosophy hangs and on which the methodological and politico-philosophical issues indicated above are focused. As Oruka points out:

Early writers on the subject of African philosophy such as Fr. P. Tempels, J. Mbiti, Alexis Kagame and to a lesser extent Prof. W. Abraham, have all fallen into the pitfall of considering African philosophy to be a philosophy only in the unique and debased sense. By saying this I am not saying something new. It has been said before; and we now have various philosophical articles that point out the danger of this pitfall.[44]

By the "unique and debased sense" of philosophy Oruka means the effort to document the philosophies and worldviews of African peoples—that is, ethnophilosophy. The "various philosophical articles" he refers to are the works of Hountondji, Wiredu, Bodunrin, and himself, which he collectively designates as the school of professional philosophy. On Mudimbe's schema, these two trends—ethnophilosophy and professional philosophy—would constitute the two extremes of the continuum of African philosophy. In like manner, for Gyekye, these two trends represent the "traditional" and the "modern" aspects of African philosophy.

Without in any way sharing Oruka's prejudice, let us now look at how this confrontation is articulated, for it is the polemic out of which the discourse on and in African philosophy is constituted in its inception.

Ethnophilosophy

This orientation is basically aimed at systematizing and documenting the differing worldviews of African peoples, which are viewed—by the proponents of this trend—as properly constituting African philosophy. For the proponents of this trend, African philosophy is incarnated in the mythical/religious conceptions, worldviews, and lived ritual practices of ethnic Africans, which can and should be documented by Europeans and Africans with a Western education.

The basic direction and motivation of this orientation is to expose the "mentality" of the African to the European missionary or to those engaged with the task of "civilizing"/colonizing and/or modernizing the African. This is, at least in its inception, the motivation of this current as documented in Tempels's work, *Bantu Philosophy*.

The disclosing of the "mentality" of the African for modernizing purposes is still viewed—by the African followers of Tempels—as the basic task of African philosophy. Without making a clear distinction between philosophy and religion, John S. Mbiti puts it thus:

These religions [and the philosophy they embody] are a reality which calls for academic scrutiny and which must be reckoned with in modern fields of life like economics, politics, education and Christian or Muslim work. To ignore these traditional beliefs and practices can only lead to a lack of understanding African behaviour and problems.[45]

While lacking Tempels's colonialist orientation, Mbiti's aim is to expose the interiority of the African to the subversive gaze of the Christian, Muslim, or modernizing Europeanized African. The basic aim is to document the

philosphical understanding of African peoples concerning different issues of life. Philosophy of one kind or another is behind the thinking and acting of every people, and a study of traditional religions brings us into those areas of African life where, through word and action, we may be able to discern the philosophy behind.[46]

Thus, the designation "ethnophilosophy" (coined by Hountondji); that is, philosophy deriving from the ethnological study of ethnic Africans. In its own positive self-designation, this perspective calls itself "cultural philosophy" or African philosophy without qualifications.[47]

The basic criticism that has been directed against this orientation is that philosophy is not equal to the worldviews and or religious conceptions of ethnic peoples. African philosophy, if it is to be philosophy properly speaking, must be capable of being subsumed under a common notion of philosophy understood as the critical self-reflection of a culture engaged in by specific individuals in that culture. Politically, it has been criticized as part of the European colonialist discourse aimed at disarming and subjugating the African. Indeed, this is the explicit intent of Tempels's work. His *Bantu Philosophy* is aimed at the "colonizer of good will," who, according to Tempels, needs to know the Bantu/African in order to better "civilize" and convert him to the "true" faith.

In a more charitable tone, Outlaw and Oruka observe that in its inception Tempels's work served—even if inadvertently—a positive function. It challenged the then common notion that the African was completely sterile in intellectual and moral-spiritual productions of his own.[48] But even in this edifying role, the singular development of this current can have no further function than to abstractly assert the existence of a static African culture and civilization predating the colonial conquest. As Frantz Fanon remarks, commenting on similar edifying quests for the African past:

> Let us be clearly understood. I am convinced that it would be of the greatest interest to be able to have contact with a Negro literature or architecture of the third century before Christ. I should be very happy to know that a correspondence had flourished between some Negro philosopher and Plato. But I can absolutely not see how this fact would change anything in the lives of the eight-year-old children who labor in the cane fields of Martinique or Guadeloupe [or, for that matter, any part of contemporary Africa].[49]

In other words, documenting the traditional philosophies and worldviews of African peoples is fruitful only when undertaken within the context of and out of an engagement with the concrete and actual problems facing the peoples of Africa.

Philosophic Sagacity

Philosophic sagacity, the position advocated by Oruka, is an attempt to carve out a middle ground between the opposing positions of ethnophilosophy and professional philosophy. For Oruka, in spite of the fact that Africa has predominantly nonliterate cultures, it has had in the past and has presently indigenous wise men sages/philosophers who critically engage the established tradition and culture of their respective ethnic groups and or societies. In contrast to ethnophilosophy, these sages inhabit a critical space within their cultural milieu, which allows them to reflect on it instead of merely being the trusted preservers of tradition. In view of this fact, the task of a modern African philosopher is to dialogically extract the philosophical wisdom embodied in these sages. Thus the designation philosophic sagacity.[50]

Oruka has been criticized for failing to recognize the facticity of the interpretative situation in which the modern African philosopher finds himself in when engaged in dialogue with an African sage. These dialogues and interviews are indeed works of African philosophy. But they are the joint products of the sage and the modern African philosopher, whose questions elicit the responses and thus direct the sage in the articulation of his wisdom. Oruka's strong claim of uncovering "authentic African philosophy," in some primordial "uncontaminated" form, is thus made questionable—for the claim of philosophic sagacity is that beyond the collective myths (ethnophilosophy) of African peoples, the African past and present has traditional (non-Western educated) sages/philosophers in critical dialogue with their respective traditions.

National-Ideological Philosophy

This trend is embodied in the assorted manifestos, pamphlets and political works produced by the African liberation struggle. The writings of Nkrumah, Toure, Nyerere, Fanon, Senghor, Césaire, and Cabral, and the national liberation literature as a whole, harbor differing politico-philosophical conceptions that articulate the emancipatory possibilities opened up by the African anticolonial struggle. A critical interpretative engagement with these texts is thus a properly philosophical and historical task, since the critical examination and exploration of these texts promises the possibility of developing an African philosophical discourse on politics.

More importantly, as Wamba correctly observes, this discourse— which is the theoretical offshoot of the African anticolonial struggle—has to be taken as the grounding point of departure of African philosophical engagement. In this respect, Wamba points to the work of Amilcar Cabral, who represents the zenith of this politico-philosophical undertaking.[51]

But beyond particular thinkers and their contributions, the political and philosophic output of the African anticolonial struggle as a whole has to be understood as the originative grounding that is—implicitly or explicitly—presupposed by contemporary African intellectual work *as such*. To explore and examine the emancipatory possibilities embedded in this lived political and historical presupposition of contemporary African intellectual production is thus a properly philosophical task.

Professional Philosophy

This fourth trend is the self-designation of Odera H. Oruka, Kwasi Wiredu, Paulin J. Hountondji, and Peter O. Bodunrin. They call themselves a "school" in view of the fact that they share certain basic positions and assumptions.[52] Except for Oruka, they all share the view that a philosophical tradition in Africa is only presently—in their joint efforts—beginning to develop. They all share in the criticism of ethnophilosophy and see philosophy in Africa as the "handmaid" of science and (uncritical) modernization.

To be sure, the above enumeration of trends in African philosophy is partial and incomplete. As we noted above, Oruka himself recognizes an added hermeneutical trend in African philosophy. Furthermore, precisely because the discourse of African philosophy is still in the process of self-constitution, such categorizations cannot but be tentative. Presently, Hountondji is compiling what promises to be an exhaustive bibliographical documentation of African philosophical writings.[53] It is only after such preliminary work has been done that a definitive conceptualization of the various constitutive elements of African philosophy can be achieved.

In accordance with Mudimbe's and Gyekye's conceptions, the above enumerated trends, along with the hermeneutical perspective in African philosophy, can be seen as constituting a continuum differentiated by various ways of articulating the same fundamental concern—thus the documentation of the traditional myths and religions of Africa—ethnophilosophy; the dialogical appropriation of the wisdom of African sages—philosophic sagacity; the critical encounter and examination of the politico-philosophical texts produced by the African liberation struggle—nationalist-ideological philosophy; and the historically and hermeneutically sensitive dialogue with these texts, in and out of the context of the concrete concerns of contemporary Africa—all this and more is the legitimate task of the modern African philosopher.

IV

As we noted earlier in this paper, African philosophy—the very fact of the existence of such a discourse—threatens the stability of the philosophical prejudices that sanctioned and justified European expansion and the obliteration of African historical existence. As Outlaw puts it, in "light of the European incursion into Africa, the emergence of 'African philosophy' poses deconstructive (and reconstructive) challenges."[54] Let us conclude then by looking at the "deconstructive and reconstructive" challenges of African philosophy.

The "deconstructive challenge" of African philosophy is directed at the Eurocentric residues inherited from colonialism. Educational, political, juridical, and cultural institutions have been taken over by the independent states of Africa, but the basic parameters within which they function, the cultural codes inscribed within them, and the Eurocentric principles and attitudes that inform these institutions remain unthought and unchanged. The "deconstructive" orientation of African philosophy is thus aimed at the unmasking of these Eurocentric residues in modern Africa that still sanction—in the guise of science and enlightenment—the continued political subordination and intellectual domination of Africa. This subordination—which is concretely embedded in the institutional structures left over from colonialism and the internalized conscious self-awareness of Europeanized Africans—is ultimately grounded on the delusions of the Western metaphysical tradition.

Conversely, and in conjunction with the above, the "reconstructive challenge" of African philosophy is aimed at critically revitalizing—in the context of the modern world—the historico-cultural possibilities of the broken African heritage. It is an indigenizing theoretical-practical project. Borrowing the words of Ngũgĩ wa Thiong'o, one can describe it as an effort to "[d]ecolonize the mind,"[55], or in the words of Amilcar Cabral as an effort to "return to the source."[56]

The discourse of African philosophy is thus directly and historically linked to the demise of European hegemony (colonialism and neocolonialism) and is aimed at fulfilling/completing this demise. It is a reflective and critical effort to rethink the African situation beyond the confines of Eurocentric concepts and categories. In this indigenized context, furthermore, questions of "class struggle" (the "universal" concern of Marxist theory!) and the empowerment of the oppressed can fruitfully be posed and engaged.

It should be noted that, insofar as Marxist theory is itself a European cultural-historical product, it is only through an indigenizing appropriation that elements of this theory can be positively utilized in the African situation. In other words, as Cabral emphatically asserts, "we have our own class struggles" in Africa.[57] These "class struggles" are not replicas, nor extensions, of the "global" European "class struggle." Rather, these "class struggles" have their own politico-historical-cultural specificity, inscribed within the confines and the dynamic that structures the vitality of the diverse cultural totalities that constitute contemporary Africa.

The concrete resurrection of Africa, beyond the tutelage of Europe, requires—in all spheres of life—a rethinking of the contemporary state of affairs in terms that are conducive and congenial to the emancipation and growth of Africa and its diverse peoples. This then is the task of the African philosopher.

In the insightful words of Frantz Fanon,

culture is the whole body of efforts made by a people in the sphere of thought [philosophy!] to describe, justify, and praise the actions through which that people has created itself and keeps itself in existence.[58]

Africa has been for some time now in the process of recovering and establishing its own cultural-historical existence after almost a century of colonial rule. In order to be properly undertaken, this recovery requires a rethinking of much that we have inherited—consciously and subliminally—from the colonial past. It also requires the revitalization of the broken and suppressed indigenous African heritage. Africa, in other words, needs to rid itself of the cultural, historical, political, economic, and existential indigence created by colonialism and perpetuated by neocolonialism and *mistaken* for the true indigenousness of the formerly colonized African. In this respect, the tasks of the African philosopher acquire historical and political importance in the contemporary situation of the continent.

Seen in this light, African philosophy is a vital part of what Cabral has called the overall historical process of "re-Africanization."[59] As part of the cultural-intellectual production of a people—a continent—the efforts of the African philosopher are interior to the "efforts made by a people in the sphere of thought" to constitute and "keep itself in existence." For in the last quarter of the twentieth century, the very existence of Africa, the historicalness and concrete indigenous particularity of cultural, political, and economic life is at stake.

This then is the point in question around which the questioning of African philosophy and the questions of African philosophers revolve. As Fanon has observed: "Each generation must, out of relative obscurity, discover its mission, fulfil it, or betray it."[60] But, to discover and explore the yet to *Be*, this is the task of thinking!

Thinking, furthermore, is always interior to the lived possibilities and limits of a "generation" or a historicalness within which and out of which a "mission" can be envisioned and traced out. Thus, to "fulfil" or "betray" is to *affirm* or *deny* the inherent and lived possibilities of our own most historicalness. For "our paths, I say, the political as well as the cultural paths, aren't ready traced on any map . . . they remain to be discovered."[61]

NOTES

All emphasis throughout the text is in the original unless otherwise indicated.

1. Addis Hiwet, *Ethiopia, From Autocracy to Revolution* (Review of African Political Economy, 1975), chapter one. As Hiwet explains, modern Ethiopia (minus colonized Eritrea) came into existence at the end of the nineteenth century as the result of the expansionist developments of the Abyssinian kingdom, in collusion and contention with imperial Europe, engaged in the colonial scramble for Africa. Thus, modern Ethiopia established itself by the colonial subjugation of the Oromo and Somali territories that today constitute the southern, south-eastern and the south-western parts of its territory.

2. Basil Davidson, *Africa in Modern History* (Penguin Books, 1985), part two, section four.
3. Basil Davidson and Antonio Bronda, *Cross Roads in Africa* (Spokesman Press, 1980), p. 47, emphasis added.
4. T. S. Eliot, *A Choice of Kipling's Verse* (Anchor Books, 1962), p. 143.
5. In this regard, see the *Critical Inquiry* issue entitled, " 'Race' Writing and Difference," vol. 12, no. 1, Autumn 1985; Edward W. Said, "Representing the Colonized: Anthropology's Interlocutors," *Critical Inquiry*, vol. 15, no. 2, Winter 1989; Richard H. Popkin, "The Philosophical Basis of Eighteenth-Century Racism," in *Studies in Eighteenth-Century Culture*, vol. 3 (Case Western Reserve University Press, 1973), Harold E. Pagliano, ed.; Cornel West, *Prophesy Deliverance!* (Westminister Press, 1982), chapter 2; Dona Richards, "The Ideology of European Dominance," *Présence Africaine*, no. 111, 3rd quarterly, 1979.
6. *Kant on History*, Lewis White Beck, ed. (Bobbs-Merrill, 1963), p. 3.
7. James Schmidt, "The Question of Enlightenment," *Journal of the History of Ideas*, vol. 50, no. 2, April–June 1989.
8. Antonio Gramsci, *Quaderni Del Carcere*, vol. 2, edizione critica dell'Instituto Gramsci, a cura di Valentino Gerratana (Torino: Giulio Einaudi, 1975), p. 1484, my own translation.
9. Enrique Dussel, *Philosophy of Liberation* (Orbis Books, 1985), pp. 1–8.
10. As quoted by Richard H. Popkin, "Hume's Racism," *The Philosophical Forum*, vol. 9, nos. 2–3, Winter–Spring 1977–1978; for Hume's remark, see p. 213; for Kant's remark, see p. 218.
11. Ibid., p. 218.
12. *Kant on History*, Lewis White Beck, ed., p. 24, emphasis added.
13. Georg Wilhelm Friedrich Hegel, *The Philosophy of History*, (Dover Publications, 1956), p. 99.
14. Lucius Outlaw, "African 'Philosophy': Deconstructive and Reconstructive Challenges," *Contemporary Philosophy: A New Survey*, vol. 5, African Philosophy, Guttorm Floistad, ed. (Martinus Nijhoff Publishers, 1987), p. 18.
15. For a systematic elaboration of this point, see my paper "The Idea of Colonialism in Hegel's *Philosophy of Right*," *International Philosophical Quarterly*, vol. 29, no. 3, issue no. 115, September 1989.
16. In this regard, see my paper "Karl Marx and African Emancipatory Thought," forthcoming, *Parxis International*.
17. Karl Marx, "The Future Results of British Rule in India" (written in 1853), in Karl Marx and Frederick Engels, *On Colonialism* (International Publishers, 1972), p. 82.
18. Frederick Engels, "Letters to Joseph Bloch" (written in 1890), *The Marx-Engels Reader*, second edition, R. C. Tucker, ed. (Norton, 1978), p. 762.
19. *Hegel's Philosophy of Right*, T. M. Knox, trans. (Oxford University Press, 1973), p. 219, paragraph #351, emphasis added.

20. Edward W. Said, *The Question of Palestine* (Vintage Books, 1980), p. 78.
21. Frantz Fanon, *Black Skin, White Masks* (Grove Press, 1967), passim. For an insightful description of the dilemma created by this situation in the consciousness of the colonized and Europeanized African, see the novel by Cheikh Hamidou Kane, *Ambiguous Adventure* (Collier Books, 1969), passim and specifically p. 140. For an interesting—even if slightly Eurocentric—cinematographic rendering of this dilemma, see Pier Paolo Pasolini's *Notes for an African Orestes* (1970 production).
22. Albert Memmi, *The Colonizer and the Colonized* (Beacon Press, 1965), part two, the section entitled the "Mythical Portrait of the Colonized." In the same text, see also the discussion of the "Nero complex," p. 52.
23. Basil Davidson, *Africa in Modern History*, p. 44.
24. Aimé Césaire, *Return to My Native Land* (Penguin Books, 1969), p. 88.
25. Theophilus Okere, *African Philosophy A Historico-Hermeneutical Investigation of the Conditions of its Possibility* (University Press of America, 1983), p. xiv.
26. Placide Tempels, *Bantu Philosophy* (*Présence Africaine,* 1969), see especially chapter 7.
27. V. Y. Mudimbe, "African Gnosis: Philosophy and the Order of Knowledge," *African Studies Review*, vol. 28, no. 2–3, June–September 1985, p. 154.
28. E. Wamba-Dia-Wamba, "Philosophy in Africa: Challenges of the African Philosopher," *Mawazo*, vol. 5, no. 2, December 1983. [Also included in this volume on p. 244.]
29. Okere, *African Philosophy*, p. vii.
30. Ibid., p. 121.
31. Okonda Okolo, "Tradition et destin: Horizons d'une hermeneutique philosophique africaine," *Présence Africaine*, no. 114, 2nd quarterly 1980, p. 25. Also included in this volume, translated by Kango Lare-Lantone, p. 208.
32. Marcien Towa, "Conditions d'affirmation d'une pensee philosophique africaine moderne," *Présence Africaine*, nos. 117–18, 1st and 2nd quarterlies 1981, p. 348. Also included in this volume, translated by Aster Gashaw, pp. 194–195.
33. For a detailed discussion of this point, see my paper "Heidegger and Gadamer: Thinking as 'Meditative' and as 'Effective-Historical Consciousness,' " *Man and World*, vol. 20, no. 1, 1987. *Passim.*
34. Okolo, "Tradition et destin," p. 21, emphasis added. [Also included in this volume, p. 204.]
35. Vincent Descombes, *Modern French Philosophy* (Cambridge University Press, 1980), p. 1.
36. Paulin J. Hountondji, *African Philosophy: Myth and Reality* (Indiana University Press, 1983), p. 66. [Also included in this volume, p. 123.]
37. Okere, *African Philosophy*, p. 124.
38. Outlaw, "African 'Philosophy': Deconstructive and Reconstructive Challenges," p. 11.

39. In this respect, see Olabiyi Yai, "Theory and Practice in African Philosophy: The Poverty of Speculative Philosophy," *Second Order*, vol. 6, no. 2, July 1977.
40. Henry Odera Oruka, "Four Trends in Current African Philosophy," *Philosophy in the Present Situation of Africa*, Alwin Diemer, ed. (Franz Steiner Verlag Wiesbaden, 1981).
41. Henry Odera Oruka, "African Philosophy: A Brief Personal History and Current Debate," *Contemporary Philosophy: A New Survey*, vol. 5, African Philosophy, Guttorm Floistad, ed. (Martinus Nijhoff Publishers, 1987), pp. 72–74.
42. V. Y. Mudimbe, "African Philosophy as an Ideological Practice: The Case of French-Speaking Africa," *African Studies Review*, vol. 26, no. 3–4, September–December 1983.
43. Kwame Gyekye, *An Essay On African Philosophical Thought* (Cambridge University Press, 1987), pp. 11–12.
44. Henry Odera Oruka, "The Fundamental Principles in the Question of 'African Philosophy,'" *Second Order*, vol. 4, no. 2, 1975, p. 49.
45. John S. Mbiti, *African Religions and Philosophy* (Heinemann, 1988), p. 1.
46. Ibid.
47. K. C. Anyanwu, "Cultural Philosophy as a Philosophy of Integration and Tolerance," *International Philosophical Quarterly*, vol. 25, no. 3, issue no. 99, September 1985. See also Anyanwu and E. A. Ruch, *African Philosophy* (Catholic Book Agency, 1981), especially the introduction, entitled "Is There an African Philosophy?"
48. Outlaw, "African 'Philosophy': Deconstructive and Reconstructive Challenges," pp. 19–20; Oruka, "African Philosophy: A Brief Personal History and Current Debate," p. 46.
49. Fanon, *Black Skin, White Masks*, p. 230.
50. Henry Odera Oruka, "Sagacity in African Philosophy," *International Philosophical Quarterly*, vol. 23, no. 4, issue no. 92, December 1983. [Also included in this volume, pp. 47–62.]
51. Wamba, "Philosophy in Africa: Challenges of the African Philosopher," p. 88. Also included in this volume, p. 237.
52. Oruka, "Four Trends in Current African Philosophy," p. 7, no. 15.
53. In this regard, see Kwame Anthony Appiah's report, *Sapina*, vol. 2, no. 1, January–April 1989, p. 54.
54. Outlaw, "African 'Philosophy': Deconstructive and Reconstructive Challenges," p. 11.
55. Ngũgĩ wa Thiong'o, *Decolonising The Mind* (Heinemann, 1987).
56. Amilcar Cabral, *Return to the Source: Selected Speeches* (Monthly Review Press, 1973), p. 63.
57. Amilcar Cabral, *Revolution in Guinea: Selected Texts* (Monthly Review Press, 1969), p. 68.

58. Frantz Fanon, *The Wretched of the Earth* (Grove Press, 1963), p. 233.
59. Cabral, *Revolution in Guinea*, p. 76.
60. Fanon, *Wretched of the Earth*, p. 206.
61. Aimé Césaire, *Letter to Maurice Thorez*, English translation by *Présence Africaine* (*Présence Africaine*, 1957), pp. 6–7.

IS THERE AN AFRICAN PHILOSOPHY?

INTRODUCTION

Professor E. Possoz of Brussels, in the preface to *Bantu Philosophy* by Placide Tempels, made the following observation: "Up to the present, ethnographers have denied all abstract thought to tribal peoples. The civilized Christian European was exalted, the savage and pagan man was denigrated. Out of this concept a theory of colonisation was born which now threatens to fail." This article questions whether or not Western ethnographers were correct in denying "abstract thought to tribal peoples," that is, denying them philosophy, or whether, in the words of Possoz, "a true estimate of indigenous peoples can now take the place of the misunderstanding and fanaticism of the ethnology of the past and the former attitude of aversion entertained with regard to them."[1]

If you scan the catalogs of major universities in America and Europe, you will find that no philosophy department offers any course on African philosophy. Several universities—Columbia, Boston University, UCLA, Northwestern, and Duquesne, to mention but a few—have centers of African studies that offer courses on African history, sociology, literature, art, government, economics, and so on. But none of these schools, as far as I know, gives any courses on African philosophy. The big departments of philosophy offer courses in Asian and Indian philosophy, but there is a noticeable absence of African philosophy from their list of courses. Even a young country like the United States, a country usually regarded as Western, now has its own brand of philosophy.

I am currently using in one of my courses a book by Sheldon P. Peterfreund entitled *An Introduction to American Philosophy*.[2] And yet Africa, a continent from where man originated, if we care to pay attention to archeological discoveries, is not studied from a philosophical angle.

Among philosophers themselves, as one observes from articles read during philosophical conferences and published books, there seems to be an unwillingness to qualify philosophy with the adjective *African*. Occasional reference is made to Egypt, but one gets the impression that scholars would wish to avoid mentioning it if that were possible. This feeling is verified in the quick effort these authors make to include Egypt and her contribution in what they call Greek philosophy or Western philosophy. Any number of books on the history of philosophy will tell you that Greek philosophy was born in the Ionian city-states. We are told that Pythagoras, Thales, and the rest of the Ionian philosophers visited Egypt, but what influence their study in Egypt had on their own philosophies is normally watered down. As an example, Joseph Owens, in his *History of Ancient Western Philosophy*, said: "Contacts with other peoples stimulated and helped Ionian thinking. But whatever preparatory role such activities may have played, and whatever indirect influence Egyptian, Iranian currents of thought may have exercised, no one has yet been able to trace the origins of Greek philosophy proper to any source other than the Greeks themselves."[3]

The German philosopher Hegel, another historian who "constrained to go back in history," could not but concede that "the Greeks received the substantial beginnings of their religion, culture, their common bond of fellowship, more or less from Asia, Syria and Egypt." He immediately contradicts himself in an effort to disregard the importance of such "substantial influence" by suggesting that "the Greeks have so greatly obliterated the foreign nature of this origin, turned it around and altogether made [it] so different, that what they, as we, prize, know and love in it is essentially their own." Since Hegel in this section of his work is tracing the origin of German civilization, it is understandable why he would stress the "making so different and turning around" of the foreign (African and Asian) influence, before the Greeks passed it on to the Germans.[4]

Several other authors could be quoted to show what I would regard as a concerted effort on the part of Western scholars to deny Africa any contribution in the field of philosophy.

If we grant the allegation just made, the next question that logically comes up is, What is the reason? Why would the study of African philosophy be excluded in Asian, American, and European universities? Why this nihilistic attitude toward African philosophy by Western scholars? From my own observation, I would like to limit the reasons to two, though there are more, undoubtedly.

1. The popular Western European and American conception of Africa.

2. Western philosophy as an academic and dehumanized philosophy.

THE POPULAR WESTERN EUROPEAN AND AMERICAN CONCEPTION OF AFRICA

The Africa that is portrayed in books by Western ethnologists and historians is the Africa of the savage Africans who did nothing, developed nothing, or created nothing historical. There are the stereotyped racist conceptions about Africa—the propaganda angle of the Christian missionaries, learned historians, ethnographers, and explorers. Africa is described as a Dark Continent, as C. P. Groves, in his *The Planting of Christianity in Africa* wrote, "It is the paradox of this vast continent that while sharing in the earliest history of the human race, it was yet not opened up until the late nineteenth century."[5] The implication is that before the 1850s all Africa was in darkness—no roads, no schools, no governments, and no civilization.

There are the writings of colonial anthropologists and historians who for various reasons do not credit Africa's sons and daughters with being human, much less able to produce human culture, civil traits, and society. It is not that there was no written evidence and documentation of the greatness and achievement of Africa before colonialism. Rather there was a concerted effort to hide these facts from popular knowledge so that slavery and the economic exploitation of the African continent could be justified on the pretext that Africans were not really human beings to possess rights like the Europeans.

What could be done in the face of the glaring accounts of Africa's contribution to civilization and scholarship by Herodotus (the father of European historians) and other balanced writers? In his writings, Herodotus stated unequivocally that most of the Greek culture was copied from the Nile kingdoms of Nubia—Sudan, Ethiopia, and Egypt. Since these facts could not be doubted, the racist historians of the recent past introduced their own color and racial distinctions even among indigenous Africans, in contradiction to what Herodotus reported in his *Histories*. These people began by separating Africans into those south of the Sahara and those to the north. They did not stop at that: They even claimed to locate the existence of the caucasoid race anywhere there was a monumental achievement in Africa, for example, Sphinx of Ghizeh, the monuments in Sudan, and the stone structures of Zimbabwe (Southern Rhodesia). They claim the early human fossil found in Tanzania was caucasoid.

A quotation from M. D. W. Jeffreys's article, "The Negro Enigma," reveals what I have been trying to articulate. "The Swanscombe skull found in Great Britain is dated 250,000 years and is our stock, not African. The skeletal remains dug up by the Leakeys in East Africa are us, not African. Boskop man, found in the Cape, is dated 50,000 years and falls into our group, not that of Africa. There are no African skulls of any antiquity, the oldest known is about 6,000 B.C."[6]

This statement shows a profound disregard for documentation and is a picture of racist propaganda. He is simply telling lies. The Leakeys never entertained any doubts about the racial group of the East African skeletal fossil—it was African. The skeleton was dated over one million years old and therefore older than the Swanscombe skull found in Britain. A more recent discovery by a Harvard scientist of a fossil dated 5½ million years old in Kenya further disproves Jeffrey's claims.

Still not satisfied with his obvious state of confusion and deep racism, Jeffreys reached his climax when he wrote: "Now in Africa there is continuous evidence, unlike anywhere else on the globe, of man's uninterrupted occupation of the earth for close on a million years. Africa is thus today accepted by many scientists as the cradle of human species. Thus, in Africa from the Old Stone Age to modern time, modern man is the tool-maker. Nowhere is the African [Black] associated with any of these stone-age cultures."[7]

Such ideas and worse about Africa are what one gets from books, movies, and stories. The correct, historical, and documented views about Africa are never popularized, despite the fact that these accounts are and were given by European scholars. H. G. Wells, in his *Short History of the World*, states: "Three main regions and three main kinds of wandering and imperfectly settled people there were in those remote days of the first civilization in Sumeria and early Egypt. Away in the forests of Europe were the blonde Nordic peoples hunters and herdsmen, a lowly race. The primitive civilization saw little of this race before 1,500 B.C."[8] Again in *History of Nations* it is written, "The African continent is no recent discovery; it is not a new world like America and Australia . . . while yet Europe was the home of the wandering barbarians, one of the most wonderful civilizations on record had begun to work its destiny on the banks of the Nile."[9]

Count Constantin Volney, who visited Egypt in 1787, wrote that "what Herodotus said had solved for him the problem of why the people of Egypt were so black and wooly haired . . . and especially the Great Sphinx of Ghizeh . . . the Supreme symbol of worship and power." Reflecting on how he met the state of Egypt in its reduced image of grandeur, the count wrote: "To think that a race of black men who are today our slaves and the object of our contempt, is the same one to whom we owe our arts, sciences and even the very use of speech." Of the blacks Count Volney saw in the ruins of the colossal monuments there in upper Egypt (Nubia and Sudan) he wrote: "There a people now forgotten, discovered while others were yet barbarians, the elements of the arts and sciences. A race of men now rejected from society for the sable skin and wooly hair, founded on the study of the laws of nature those civil and religious systems which still govern the universe."[10]

Note the sable skin and wooly hair ascribed to the early Egyptians and Ethiopians, though the racist ethnologist Jeffreys, and others, tell us they are caucasoid, with the intention of appropriating their contributions made to world civilization and scholarship by Africans. It is obvious that these facts have been known to Western educators all along. Why then were they hidden from both black and white?

WESTERN PHILOSOPHY AS AN ACADEMIC AND DEHUMANIZED PHILOSOPHY

In his *Creative Fidelity*, dealing with Incarnate Being as the central datum of metaphysical reflection, Gabriel Marcel said: "I think I may say without exaggeration, that my whole philosophical career has been devoted to the production of currents whereby life can be reborn in regions of the mind which have yielded to apathy and are exposed to decomposition." He tells us that his philosophy is the philosophy of "encounter" even on the level of thought. He is not interested in systems of thought, intellectualized schema of intelligence as one finds in Cartesianism, Kantianism, and Hegelism. He is interested in what he calls concrete philosophy, the philosophy of the *pensée pensante*. "This philosophy of the pensée pensante can be developed only if it is constantly replenished in such a way that its uninterrupted communication with Being is guaranteed."[11] Karl Jaspers expresses this same idea in his treatment of "philosophy without science" in his *Way to Wisdom*. "This notion that philosophy must be accessible to all is justified. The circuitous paths travelled by specialists in philosophy have meaning only if they lead man to an awareness of being and of his place in it." Jaspers is here concerned with a criticism of Western philosophy which, following the scientific method, aspires to arrive at an objective certainty which is the same for every mind. This is what he calls systematic philosophy, which always reckons with the most advanced scientific findings of its time. "But essentially philosophy springs from a different source. It emerges before any science, wherever men achieve awareness. . . . In philosophy men generally assume that they are competent to form an opinion without preliminary study. Our own humanity, our own destiny, our own experience strikes us as a sufficient basis for philosophical opinions."[12] Going back to Marcel, he criticized any philosophy which aims at constructing a conceptual system with propositions rigorously connected by dialectical relations—evidenced in the post-

Kantian systems of philosophy. He regards as absurd any presumption that the universe could be encapsuled in a more or less related set of formulas. He criticizes the system of philosophy which considers the individual philosopher as an inventor and patent holder, as if anything could be less patentable than philosophy. He depreciates the teaching of philosophy in Europe as having a pernicious influence, simply because the attitude of teaching philosophy has become one in which the philosopher teaches *his* philosophy as if he is selling his own product, which he regards as better than others.

What Marcel is criticizing here is what I call Western philosophy as an academic and dehumanized philosophy. It was a disease that divorced thought from life. Philosophy became highly abstract, lifeless and artificial, emptied of real content to such a degree that human beings no longer knew what it meant to exist. Thinking overshadowed existence. Philosophers and their systems became important or famous in the degree to which their speculative analysis of the "cogito" reached the height of abstraction and idealism. Kierkegaard puts it this way: "Abstract speculation in the Cartesian and Hegelian manner has led to an unspeakable impoverishment of life. . . . Human existence, while partaking of the Universal Idea, is not itself an Idea or a purely ideal existence. Abstract thought is thought without a thinker. Concrete thought is thought which is related to a thinker." [13]

This is the aspect of philosophy that has become popular in European and American schools. Philosophy has come to be identified with Descartes, Spinoza, Leibniz, Locke, Hume, Kant, Hegel, Nietzsche, Heidegger, Sartre, and Whitehead. Since there are no such names associated with Africa, philosophy is denied Africa. (In conversation with professors and students in America who knew I was teaching African philosophy, the question always put to me was: Are there African philosophers and what have they written? I have not heard or read of any.) In other words, if there are no known academic philosophers in Africa, then there is no African philosophy.

Remember that I am in no way conceding that there are no academic philosophers in Africa. There are several of them, but their accounts were purposely withheld from history of philosophy books for reasons I have already mentioned. When they are mentioned they are grouped with Greco-Oriental philosophers. Little do some of us know that Plotinus, who wrote works on philosophy and opened a school in Rome, was from Lycon in Egypt. He made an attempt to travel to Persia and India to study their philosophies, but the expedition failed. Little do some of us know that the first woman philosopher, Hypatia, was from Alexandria and was murdered by Christians. Names like St. Augustine, Origen, Cyril, and Tertulian are not unfamiliar; they are black Africans. More pertinent to our subject is the fact that what today we call Greek or Western philosophy is copied from indigenous African philosophy of the "Mystery System." All the values of the mystery system were adopted by the Greeks and Ionians who came to Egypt to study; or studied elsewhere under Egyptian-trained teachers. These included Herodotus, Socrates, Hypocrates, Anaxagoras, Plato, Aristotle, and others. Are we not taught that Socrates is the first man to say "Man know thyself?" Yet, this expression was found commonly inscribed on Egyptian temple doors centuries before Socrates was born. Aristotle not only received his education in Africa, but he took over an entire library of works belonging to the Egyptian mystery system when he entered Egypt with Alexander the Great, after which we hear of the Corpus Aristotelium. Plato's alleged Theory of Ideas is borrowed from Egypt. Parmenides's references to "charioteers" and "winged steeds" were already dramatized in the *Judgement Scene* of the Egyptian *Book of the Dead*.

One would have to read *The Stolen Legacy* by George G. M. James to get some idea of the apprenticeship of the so-called Greek philosophers under Egyptian Mystery Priests. From his reading of Herodotus, Pliny, Diogenes Laertius, and early historians of philosophy, James noted about Pythagoras: "We are also further informed through Herodotus and Pliny, that after severe trials, including circumcision, had been imposed upon him by Egyptian priests, he was finally initiated into all their secrets. That he learnt the doctrine of metempsychosis, of which there was no trace before in the Greek religion; that his knowledge of medicine and strict system of diethetics rules, distinguished him as a product of Egypt . . . and that his attainment in geometry corresponded with the ascertained fact that Egypt was the birth place of that science."[14]

A contemporary African author, Willie E. Abraham, in his *Mind of Africa* gives an account of a Ghanaian philosopher by the name Amo Anton, born near Axim about the year 1700. He went to Holland, entered the University of Thalle and in 1729 publicly defended his dissertation. He moved on to Wittenberg, and while Kant was still a boy, became Master of Philosophy there. In 1734 he defended a work in which he argued that sensation was not a mental faculty. (Amo was a rationalist philosopher after Leibniz, whom as a boy he met at the Duke of Brunswick's.) His performance was greatly praised. And the chairman and faculty members described him as a most noble and renowned man from Africa, extraordinarily honest, diligent, and so erudite that he stood above his mates. In 1738 he produced his magnum opus, a book on logic, theory of knowledge and metaphysics.[15]

There were philosophers in the university towns of Timbucktu and Jene in West Africa who wrote works on the subject. Basil Davidson quotes the historian Leo Africanus, who wrote around 1520 concerning African scholars in the Mali and Songhai empires, "By the sixteenth century, West African writers were at work on historical, legal, moral and religious subjects."[16] Alexis Kagame has written on the concept of being among the Ruanda-Urundis. Adesany Adebayo has written on Yoruba metaphysical thinking. Placide Tempels sketched the world view and ethics of the Congo. Joseph B. Danquah in Ghana did extensive work on the concept of God among the Akans.

PHILOSOPHIZING: A UNIVERSAL EXPERIENCE

Be that as it may, my contention is that the philosophy of a people has little or nothing to do with the academic exponents of that philosophy. Philosophizing is a universal experience. Every culture has its own worldview. If you study the history of philosophy, you will find there is no agreement on the definition of philosophy. Some say it is the love of wisdom, others, the search for truth, and still others, the sense of wonder. What is generally agreed about philosophy is that it seeks to establish order among the various phenomena of the surrounding world, and it traces their unity by reducing them to their simplest elements. What are these various phenomena? They are things, facts, events, an intelligible world, an ethical world, and a metaphysical world.

These various phenomena of the surrounding world are the same in all cultures and societies. The themes dealt with in philosophy are universal. How each culture traces the unity of these themes, synthesizes, or organizes them into a totality is based on each culture's concept of life, namely the interrelationship between objects and persons and between persons and persons themselves. Hence it is that the order or unity the people of a culture establish is their own order relative to their own conception of life in which everything around them becomes meaningful. No culture has *the* order or *the* last word. Hence the establishment of various truths of a spontaneous, logical, ethical, aesthetical, and metaphysical nature, not one of them being of absolute or universal validity.

This is the basis for calling a philosophy European, Asian, Indian, or American. If what we have said is true, we can and should talk of African philosophy, because the African culture has its own way of establishing order. It has its own view of life. And "life" according to Dilthey, is the starting point of philosophy. Georg Misch, summarizes him thus: "Dilthey regarded 'life' as the starting-point of philosophy; life as actually lived and embodied or 'objectified' in the spiritual world we live in. Life, according to Dilthey, is a subject for scientific investigation insofar as history and moral philosophy or the human sciences deal with it; but our knowledge of life is, above all, contained in certain cultural or personal views of the world—which plays a prominent part in philosophy as well as in religion and poetry."[17]

Hegel underscored the cultural and relative aspect of philosophy when he said: "But men do not at certain epochs merely philosophize in general. For there is a definite philosophy which arises among a people and the definite character which permeates all the other historical sides of the Spirit of the people, which is most intimately related to them, and which constitutes their foundation. The particular form of a philosophy is thus contemporaneous with a particular constitution of the people amongst whom it makes its appearance, with their institutions and forms of government, their morality, their social life and their capabilities, customs and enjoyments of the same."[18] The notion of philosophy itself for Hegel, as can be deduced from his words, is a factor in the life history of the human experience of the individual mind and is subject to the conditions of race, culture, and civilization. A further support to the issue of philosophical relativity was given by Victor Uchendu in his monograph *The Igbo of Southeast Nigeria*. He said, "To know how a people view the world around them is to understand how they evaluate life, and a people's evaluation of life, both temporal and non-temporal, provides them with a 'charter' of action, a guide to Behaviour."[19]

The African has an unwritten timeless code of behavior and attitudes which have persisted for centuries. The condition for the possibility of this, its explanation, lies in the presence of a corpus of coordinated mental or intellectual concepts. Placide Tempels puts it better: "Behaviour can be neither universal nor permanent unless it is based upon a concatenation of ideas, a logical system of thought, a complete positive philosophy of the universe, of man and of the things which surround him, of existence, life, death and the life beyond."[20]

Having shown that there can be and there certainly is an African philosophy, I now expose the content of this philosophy as briefly as possible. We are going to treat the core areas of philosophy, any philosophy—namely, metaphysics or ontology, epistemology, and ethics.

AFRICAN METAPHYSICS OR ONTOLOGY

Henry Alpern in his *March of Philosophy* said: "Metaphysics by the very definition that it is a study of reality, of that which does not appear to our senses, of truth in the absolute sense, is the groundwork of any theory concerning all phases of human behavior. David Hume, whom no one can charge of shutting his eyes to experience, said that metaphysics is necessary for art, morality, religion, economics, sociology; for the abstract sciences, as well as for every branch of human endeavour considered from the practical angle. It is the foundation upon which one builds one's career consciously and unconsciously; it is the guide; the author of the human interests; upon its truth or falsity depends what type of man you may develop into."[21]

The ideas from this quotation explain adequately the singular and unique importance of African ontology in the overall treatment and understanding of African philosophy. In recent decades, studies that were made of the scientific, religious, and practical human endeavor of Africans have accepted their foundation as consisting in ancestor worship, animism, totemism, and magic. These are only vague ideas, because no well-founded definitions of animism, totemism, and magic have been laid down, and the roots of these conceptions have not been explored. The root is in the fundamental concept of African ontology. When we understand this ontology, the concepts of magic, ancestor worship, totemism, and sorcery, as ethnologists apply them to Africa, become ridiculous if not foolish.

What then is ontology? It is the science of "being as such," "the reality that is." The metaphysics of Western philosophy has generally been based upon a static conception of being. In the African philosophical thought, being is dynamic. Existence-in-relation sums up the African conception of life and reality. The African does not separate being from force as its attribute. Rather "the Africans speak, act, live, as if for them beings were forces. . . . Force, for them, is the nature of being, force is being, being is force." When you say, in terms of Western philosophy, that beings are differentiated by their essences or nature; Africans say that forces differ in their essences or nature. There is the divine force, terrestrial or celestial forces, human forces, and vegetable and even mineral forces.[22] When Western metaphysics defines "being" as "that which is" or "the thing insofar as it is," the African definition reads: "that which is force," or "an existent force." God of course is the Great Force. There is a hierarchy of forces starting from God, spirits, founding fathers, the dead, according to the order of primogeniture; then the living according to their rank in terms of seniority. After living men come animals, vegetables, and minerals, which are in turn categorized on their relative importance in their own classes.

THE INTERACTION FORCES:
ONE BEING INFLUENCES ANOTHER

The concept of separate beings, of substances, to use a scholastic term, which exist side by side, independent one of another, is foreign to African thought.[23] I might add parenthetically that I am not so sure that this concept of separate substances might not be the ontological basis for so much individualism and personal freedom in the Western world. The African thought holds that created beings preserve a bond one with another, an intimate ontological relationship. There is interaction of being with being, that is to say of force with force. This is more so among rational beings known as *Muntu*, a term which includes the living and the dead, Orishas, and God. *Muntu* is a force endowed with intelligence, a force which has control over irrational creatures known as *bintu*. Because of this ontological relationship among beings, the African knows and feels himself to be in intimate and personal relationship with other forces acting above or below him in the hierarchy of forces. "The human being, apart from the ontological hierarchy and interaction of forces, has no existence in the conception of the Bantu."[24] So much for the ontology—sketchy though it may be.

AFRICAN EPISTEMOLOGY
OR THEORY OF KNOWLEDGE

Theory of knowledge follows closely upon ontology. The view adopted by the African theory of knowledge is consonant with its metaphysics. Knowledge or wisdom for the African consists in how deeply he understands the nature of forces and their interaction. "True wisdom," Tempels tells us, "lies in ontological knowledge; it is the intelligence of forces, of their hierarchy, their cohesion and their interaction."[25] We said earlier that God is Force; God is also wisdom in that He knows all forces, their ordering, their dependence, their potential, and their mutual interaction. A person is said to know or have wisdom inasmuch as he approaches divine wisdom. One approaches divine knowledge when one's flesh becomes less fleshy, to use Leopold Senghor's expression, that is, the older a person gets, the more wisdom he has. The same note of hierarchy comes into play here. The ancestors have more wisdom, followed by the elders, dead or living.

Distinction must be made here of the two levels of human intelligence. Intelligence can be either *practical* or *habitual.* Practical intelligence is cleverness, slyness in dealing with the contingent aspects of forces. Habitual intelligence is active knowledge of the nature of forces, their relationship. And this includes how man, the being with intelligence, makes use of things and activates the forces asleep in them. This kind of wisdom is different from book knowledge, which is not regarded as wisdom in the strict traditional sense. "Study and personal search for knowledge does not give wisdom. One can learn to read, to write; but all that has nothing in common with 'wisdom.' It gives no ontological knowledge of the nature of beings. There are many talents and clever skills that remain far short of wisdom."[26] Having a college degree does not qualify an African as a wise person in the community. This in part explains why there has been confusion in Africa since the colonial era, because the colonial administrators regarded the educated as the wise people, and consequently and arbitrarily appointed them legislators and leaders in the community, contrary to African political philosophy, which took the eldest of the community, to be, by divine law, the repository of wisdom and the link between God, the ancestors, and the living. He is divine. Swailem Sidhom in his article, "The Theological Estimate of Man" lamented the state of things when he said: "Power is conceived by the African as something pertaining to the divine. Hence it cannot be placed into unexercised hands. But the hands are rarely exercised nowadays. Scheduled education has replaced experience and has toppled the accepted standards. Seniority of age does not mean much anymore, and a father may now be instructed by the child of his bowels. Nevertheless, power is dangerous and it kills. Like a live coal from upon the very altar of God, it can only be cared for by those who have been graduated into maturity."[27] This despair is understandable if you grasp the African's conception of existence and his philosophy of vital forces.

AFRICAN ETHICAL THEORY

Some foreign observers of the African scene have declared that the African has no sense of sin. An example is Edwin Smith, who said in his *African Ideas of God*: "It would seem that in general Africans are not conscious of any direct relation between their theism and their ethic of dynamism."[28] Others maintain that Africans have but a vague idea of the Supreme Being, that he always keeps his distance and does not associate himself with the daily lives of men. All these and more are mere prejudices. The Nigerian writer, E. Adeolu Adegbola, said about African morality: "Everywhere African morality is hinged on many sanctions. But the most fundamental sanction is the fact that God's all-seeing eyes scan the total area of human behaviour and personal relationships. God is spoken of as having eyes all over like a sieve."[29] Placide Tempels, who questioned Africans closely on this point, informs us that, "the influence of God in the daily life of man is recognized in many African proverbs and sayings. . . ."[30] He says that such authors, as I mentioned above, are speaking under the influence of Western moral theory, according to which the social order is mere conformity with conventionalized behavior. On the contrary, African morality and moral law are filled with fixed beliefs, unshakable principles held from conviction. They surely know the distinction between good and evil. They refer to moral evil as "stinking"; they feel it deeply in their spirit.

The norms of good and evil are objective and of universal validity; no room for subjectivism or solipsism and situation ethics. African ethical truths are not relative. Except for cases of ignorance, there are little or no mitigating circumstances.

The root of their knowledge of good and evil is bound up with their philosophy. The Africans see a relationship between morality and the ontological order. Everything is associated and coordinated under the all-embracing unity of "vital force." In his judgment of his conduct the African takes into consideration the fact that he is not alone; that he is a cog in a wheel of interacting forces. He knows that the most important thing in his action is not how it affects him personally, but how it affects the world order, the spiritual republic, outside of which he does not exist as a *Muntu*, outside of which he is a planet off its orbit, meaningless and nonexisting. His life is not his own in a selfish manner. It belongs to God. The strengthening of this life and its preservation are in the hands of his ancestors and elders. In the life of the community each person has his place and each has his right to well-being and happiness. Therefore, what to do and what to avoid in order to preserve, increase, and strengthen vital force in himself and others of his clan constitute morality. "Objective morality to the Bantu is ontological, immanent and intrinsic morality. Bantu moral standards depend essentially on things ontologically understood."[31]

It follows that an act will be accounted ethically good if it can be judged ontologically good and by deduction be assessed as juridically just. The same idea is introduced by Plato in the *Republic*. The individual Greek citizen is to interpret an action good or evil, not in reference to selfish interests, but in reference to the community of which he is a part. The African ethical theory is what I would like to call metaphysical ethics in one sense and ethical communalism in another sense—where an individual takes into consideration the community of vital forces in deciding the goodness or evil of his proper actions.

Human positive or customary laws are made in reference to the growth or preservation of *Muntu*'s vital force; otherwise they are meaningless. All customary law that is worthy of the name is inspired, animated, and justified from the African's point of view, by the philosophy of living forces, or growth, of influence, and of the vital hierarchy. The validity and strength of the customary law of indigenous peoples reside in its foundation in their philosophy. This is why we say in African ethical theory that an act which is characterized as ontologically good "will therefore be accounted *ethically good*; and at length, be assessed as *juridically just*."[32] "In contrast to the European sense of justice, which measures liability by material damage, it is according to African philosophy the loss in force, in joy of life that is evaluated, independently of material considerations."[33]

CONCLUSION

The rediscovery of African philosophy has influenced African scholars in writing about African personality or what the French-speaking Africans call Negritude. Kwame Nkrumah, Julius Nyerere, Léopold Senghor, Aimé Césaire, Nnamdi Azikiwe, and Chinua

Achebe have written prose and verse to celebrate this philosophy—a philosophy of unity and complete encounter of all things and beings, which by reason of the dynamic character of African ontology, has surfaced on the communal structure of our society based on the division of labor and rights; in which man attains growth and recognition by how well he fulfills a function for the overall well-being of the community. We Africans have not yet yielded to the subtlety (and I pray we shall never) which would allow our traditional lawmakers and judges to design customary laws divorced from our philosophy, from the nature of beings, as we understand them, and from our view of the world.

NOTES

1. Tempels, *Bantu Philosophy* (Paris, 1969), p. 14.
2. Peterfreund, *An Introduction to American Philosophy* (New York, 1959).
3. Owens, *A History of Ancient Western Philosophy* (New York, 1959), p. 5.
4. Georg W. F. Hegel, *Lectures on the History of Philosophy*, ed. E. S. Haldane (London, 1968), 1: 150.
5. Groves, *The Planting of Christianity in Africa*, 4 vols. (London, 1948–1958), p. 1, quoted in Yosef ben-Jochannan, *Black Man of the Nile* (New York, 1970), p. 32.
6. Jeffreys, "The Negro Enigma," *West African Review* (September 1951), p. 3.
7. Ibid., p. 4.
8. Wells, *A Short History of the World* (London, 1927), p. 59.
9. *History of Nations*, vol. 18 (1906), p. 1, quoted by ben-Jochannan, *Black Man of the Nile*, p. 76.
10. Volney, *Ruins of Empire*, p. 16, quoted by ben-Jochannan, *Black Man of the Nile*, p. 77.
11. Marcel, *Creative Fidelity* (New York, 1969), pp. 12 and 13.
12. Jaspers, *Way to Wisdom* (New Haven, Conn., 1966), pp. 8 and 9.
13. Quoted in Kurt F. Reinhardt, *The Existentialist Revolt* (New York, 1964), p. 19.
14. James, *The Stolen Legacy* (New York, 1954), p. 43.
15. Abraham, *The Mind of Africa* (Chicago, 1966), p. 129.
16. Davidson, *A History of West Africa* (New York, 1966), p. 166.
17. Misch, *The Dawn of Philosophy* (London, 1950), p. 47.
18. Hegel, *Lectures on the History of Philosophy* (London, 1968), 1: 53.
19. Uchendu, *The Igbo of Southeast Nigeria* (New York, 1965), p. 12.
20. Tempels, *Bantu Philosophy* (Paris: Présence Africaine, 1969), p. 19.
21. Alpern, *The March of Philosophy* (New York, 1934), p. 99.

22. Tempels, *Bantu Philosophy*, pp. 51 and 52.
23. Ibid., p. 58.
24. Ibid., p. 104.
25. Ibid., p. 73.
26. Ibid., p. 74.
27. Sidhom, "The Theological Estimate of Man," in *Biblical Revelation and African Beliefs*, ed. Kwesi Dickinson (London, 1969), p. 115.
28. Smith, *African Ideas of God* (London, 1950), p. 22.
29. Dickinson, *Biblical Revelation*, p. 116.
30. Tempels, *Bantu Philosophy*, p. 117.
31. Ibid., p. 121.
32. Ibid.
33. Janheinz Jahn, *Muntu: An Outline of the New African Culture* (New York, 1961), p. 117.

HENRY ODERA ORUKA

SAGACITY IN
AFRICAN PHILOSOPHY[1]

HISTORICAL PHASES

The issue of "African philosophy" has now gone through several significant historical phases. It first went through the myth of pre-philosophy, a stage at which the black man's culture and even mind was claimed to be extremely alien to reason, logic, and various habits of scientific inquiry. This is a situation bravely described by the anthropologists of the Lévy-Bruhl type: the description is of the "primitive" man and "primitive" mentality. This mentality, so the argument went, is pre-logical, pre-scientific, pre-literate, etc.

The term "pre-philosophy" is of course a logical consequence of the culture and life of the primitive man. It leaves the hope that this culture might one day evolve into a scientific and reason-oriented culture. Yet, Lévy-Bruhl and the anthropologists of his kind left no such hope: for them, the situation was that of unphilosophy rather than pre-philosophy. What they claimed to have established in Africa were (1) the impossibility for a philosophic dialogue and (2) an obvious nonexistence of a tradition of organized philosophical systems. The second claim is a logical consequence of the first, while the first follows as a tautology from the fact of the nature of the black man's mind, a "primitive mentality."

Beyond the phase of pre-philosophy, the issue came to a second phase embodying a second myth: the myth of a *unique* philosophy, a specialized and wholly customs-dictated philosophy. In the words of our colleague, P. Hountondji, this is "ethnophilosophy." Ethnophilosophy, as we now well know, requires a communal consensus. It identifies with the totality of customs and common beliefs of a people. It is a folk philosophy. It forms a sharp contrast with philosophy developed by reason and logic. It is also, as thought, impersonal: it is not identified with any particular individual(s). It is the philosophy of everybody; it is understood and accepted by everyone. It is at best a form of religion. But it would in other cases function perfectly like a taboo and superstition.

Although the phenomenon of ethnophilosophy still persists in various forms, we are currently in a new phase: the phase of professional philosophy. It is "professional" precisely because it is technical philosophy having professionally trained philosophers as its managers. One remarkable characteristic of this philosophy is that it employs techniques commonly associated with European or Western philosophy. Yet, contrary to the general claim, such techniques are not unique to the West.

Current African professional philosophy is predominantly a metaphilosophy. Its central theme is the question "What is philosophy?" And a corollary of this question is "What is African philosophy?" In actual practice this philosophy is a discussion of the claim to the effect that some given thoughts or beliefs qualify or do not qualify as philosophy. And so it becomes a philosophical analysis and interpretation of the general concept, "philosophy."

Purely as a philosophy, the phase of professional philosophy has some significant limitations. First, it is mostly a criticism of ethnophilosophy and as yet lacks a dominating subject matter of its own. To avoid this limitation it needs to address itself to specific philosophical issues and concepts rather than discuss the mere possibilities of a philosophy, albeit, an African philosophy.

Secondly, this philosophy lacks a history, a prolonged period of debates and available literature within which to preserve and expand itself. This is a problem that calls for the current African and black philosophers to "let one hundred flowers bloom." The future will sort out those flowers and preserve a tradition.

Thirdly, professional philosophy in Africa needs to enhance its degree of self-criticism. Those involved need to intensify the debate among themselves and with others outside themselves.

THE FOUR TRENDS

Recently I characterized four trends in current African philosophy: ethnophilosophy, philosophic sagacity, nationalist-ideological philosophy, and professional philosophy.[2] These four trends appear to characterize the crossroads of philosophy in modern Africa. There are some who feel that no approach except that of ethnophilosophy represents the right path. This claim is already well refuted by the literature emanating from professional philosophy. Yet, the latter also has an arrogant claim of its own. The claim is not representative of all those who subscribe to this school, but it nevertheless represents a significant portion of the school. It is the claim that authentic African philosophy can and must only be a scientific (i.e., systematic) and/or written philosophy. It thus rules out philosophic sagacity as a part of African philosophy, since this trend is largely unwritten and apparently "pre-scientific." Within our ranks the position of Prof. P. Bodunrin and that of Prof. P. Hountondji are representative of this claim.

In this paper I will limit my war front by sparing Prof. Hountondji for today and wage a defensive battle against Prof. Bodunrin. The battle is on the issue of *philosophic sagacity*. This is still widely unknown as a proper aspect of philosophy in Africa. Nevertheless, it is the only trend that it seems to me can give an all-acceptable decisive blow to the position of ethnophilosophy. None of the other two trends can objectively decisively play this role. And the reason is because they (i.e., professional philosophy and nationalist-ideological philosophy) are generally suspected of smuggling Western techniques into African philosophy. Those who make this charge can hardly be convinced, say, that professional philosophy in Africa is a refutation of the presuppositions of ethnophilosophy. They would maintain that it is a fallacy to use professional philosophy (in their view a "foreign" philosophy) to reject ethnophilosophy.

It should be noted that ethnophilosophy implies that traditional Africa is free from (1) philosophic, rational discourse and (2) personalized philosophical activity. Philosophy here is treated as a general communal activity in which ready-made beliefs and emotions rather than reflection decide the outcome. Philosophic sagacity stands to prove the contrary. It shows that the problem in traditional Africa is not lack of logic, reason, or scientific curiosity, since we can find many sages there with a system of thought employing a rigorous use of these mental gifts. It shows that communal consensus, a fact typical of most traditional societies, should not be seen as a hindrance for individual critical reflection. Just as religion and all kinds of dogmatic fanaticism did not kill philosophy in the West, traditional African folk wisdoms and taboos left some room for real philosophic thought.

PHILOSOPHIC SAGACITY
AND CULTURE PHILOSOPHY

In a paper titled "The Question of African Philosophy,"[3] Prof. Peter Bodunrin of Ibadan uses the four trends I had identified in current African philosophy as a starting point to present, so far, his most explicit and decisive argument on the subject. Generally, Bodunrin's paper is harmonious with "the four trends" analysis. Nevertheless, there are two or three points which he raises that are likely to block understanding the true nature of African philosophy and especially that aspect of it which we had identified as "philosophic sagacity."

It is hence important to show the distinction that exists between what, in Nairobi, we termed "philosophic sagacity" and the position of certain researchers whose findings Bodunrin and others confuse with philosophic sagacity. Bodunrin mentions at least two types of approaches besides our own which he claims leads to the exposition of philosophic sagacity: (1) that of Marcel Griaule in the famous *Conversations with Ogotemmeli* (1965), and (2) the type of research that has been carried out among the Yoruba of Nigeria by Prof. J. O. Sodipo and Dr. Barry Hallen, both of the University of Ife.[4]

Prof. Bodunrin thinks Ogotemmeli in Griaule's study "displays a great philosophic sagacity in his exposition of the secret doctrines of his group."[5] Sodipo and Hallen identify certain wise persons versed in the traditional Yoruba thought. They visit them and carry out a dialogue with them on, for example, the Yoruba concept of a person or any other concept worthy of philosophical attention.

The answers obtained are as diverse in details as the persons interviewed but contain essential similarities. These essential similarities . . . are then written up by the trained philosopher to get the Yoruba concept of a person.[6]

Before we return to the two above-mentioned approaches, let me make a distinction between "philosophic sagacity" on the one hand and "culture philosophy" (a philosophy of a culture) on the other. Philosophic sagacity is a reflection of a person who is: (1) a sage and (2) a thinker. As a sage the person is versed in the wisdoms and traditions of his people, and very often he is recognized by the people themselves as having this gift. In certain cases, however, he may not be so recognized. Being a sage, however, does not necessarily make one a philosopher. Some of the sages are simply moralists and the disciplined diehard faithfuls to a tradition. Others are merely historians and good interpreters of the history and customs of their people. In short, they are *wise* within the conventional and historical confines of their culture. But they may not be wise (rational) in understanding or solving the inconsistencies of their culture nor coping with the foreign innovations that encroach on it. In other words, they are the spokesmen of their people, but they speak what after all is known to almost every average person within the culture.

Some sages go beyond mere sagacity and attain a philosophic capacity. As sages they are versed in the beliefs and wisdoms of their people. But as thinkers, they are rationally critical and they opt for or recommend only those aspects of the beliefs and wisdoms which satisfy their rational scrutiny. In this respect they are potentially or contemporarily in clash with the diehard adherents of the prevailing common beliefs. Such sages are also capable of conceiving and rationally recommending ideas offering alternatives to the commonly accepted opinions and practices. They transcend the communal wisdom. They are lucky if the people recognize this special gift in them. Then they are treated with special respect and their suggestions peacefully and positively reform the people. Should the people fail to recognize their gift, then their safety in the community would demand that they remain silent and keep mum. Socrates is a good example of the unrecognized sage who failed to keep silent. And so he came to the expected logically predictable fate.

So much for philosophic sagacity. Now, something about culture philosophy. Every culture has ideas and beliefs which underlie and justify it. Let us for the sake of simplicity refer to these as the *mythos* of a culture. To be really conversant with a culture one must be familiar with its *mythos*. The *mythos* forms a system which in a broad and loose sense can be referred to as the people's philosophy. Its contents make up the "philosophy" as underlying the culture in question and acting as its immediate and ultimate justification. Sages and every reasonable man in society are supposed to be conversant with the philosophy of their culture (i.e., with its *mythos*). To distinguish such *mythos* from philosophy proper, let us refer to it as "a culture philosophy." To have expertise in a culture philosophy is often the mark of the sages of the culture in question. However, in a free or well-informed society every reasonable person is conversant with the prevailing culture philosophy.

Beliefs or truth-claims within a culture philosophy are generally treated as "absolutes." Anything outside or contradictory to the culture is treated with indifference and even hostility. Those sages or persons who are experts in the culture defend this philosophy and the structure of their society with the zeal of fanatical ideologists defending their political line.

Philosophic sagacity, however, is often a product and a reflective reevaluation of the culture philosophy. The few sages who possess the philosophic inclination make a critical assessment of their culture and its underlying beliefs. Using the power of *reason* rather than the celebrated beliefs of the communal consensus and explanation, the sage philosopher produces a system within a system, and order within an order.

The first order is that of the culture philosophy. It is absolute in its ideas and truth-claims and has an ideological war with anything to the contrary. Ordinary sages (the nonphilosophic sages) are specialists in explaining and maintaining this order. They may even distinguish themselves in various aspects of the system. Some may be poets, herbalists, medicine men, musicians, fortune tellers, etc., etc.

The common thing they have is that their explanations or thought do not go beyond the premises and conclusions given by the prevailing culture.

In contrast, the second order is that of philosophic sagacity. It is a critical reflection on the first order. In many other cases it is a critical rebellion against the first order conformity and anachronism.[7] While the first order glorifies the communal conformity, philosophic sagacity is skeptical of communal consensus, and it employs reason to assess it. While the first order is purely absolutist and ideological, the second order is generally open-minded and rationalistic. Its truths are given as tentative and ratiocinative, not as God-sent messages.

GRIAULE'S OGOTEMMELI

Now Marcel Griaule's Ogotemmeli, in spite of the seemingly significant ideas attributed to him, is not a sage in the second order. He is an expert in culture philosophy of the Dogon community. He says hardly anything which suggests a thought beyond the generally given and revered Dogon beliefs. And even most of what he says is known to be common knowledge to the average member of his tribe. In the preface to the book we find the following explanation concerning Ogotemmeli's thoughts:

But although the full range of this teaching is known only to the elders and to certain initiates, it is not esoteric in character since anyone who reaches old age can acquire it. Moreover, totemic priests of all ages are acquainted with those parts of the doctrine which specifically concern them, while the ritual observances are practised by the whole people.[8]

Moreover when we come to analyse what Ogotemmeli thinks about women and compare it, say, with what Mbuya[9] thinks on the same subject, we cannot fail to differentiate the two minds as regards philosophy:

Ogotemmeli: "After God made woman, he gave her bad blood, which has to flow every month."[10]

For Ogotemmeli, woman's difference from man is taken as a curse and punishment from God. And it is clear that such ideas are no more than a recitation of the communal myths of the tribe.

Mbuya, for example, knows, as Ogotemmeli does, what his community thinks about *women*. But he nevertheless makes his own rational assessment about women. He argues:

A man has the physical capacity to run faster than a woman. But on the other hand a woman has the physical capacity to undergo the pains of carrying and bearing a baby which a man lacks. So we cannot correctly say one is superior or inferior to the other. . . . In truth . . . the two sexes are naturally equal or balanced. . . .[11]

This sort of argument is independent of the communal chorus of the general Luo beliefs about women.

THE SODIPO-HALLEN APPROACH

When we turn to the approach of Sodipo and Hallen, the situation does not improve. First, they select as their informers the Yoruba "*Onisegun* (masters of medicine), herbalists, 'native' doctors" as the professional group with whom they primarily worked.[12] Secondly, although the answers and ideas of their informers are likely not to be exactly alike, the researchers are deeply concerned to unite all the similarities and systematize them as being representative of the thoughts of the ordinary Yoruba. I believe here they are very right. The outcome is *representative*. But precisely because it is so representative it ceases to be a philosophy in the second order sense. So it cannot be a philosophic sagacity. It remains at the level of the culture philosophy, which, to be exact, we can refer to as *cultural prejudices*.

It is, therefore, very interesting to note how the authors argue in reaction to Robin Horton's contention that traditional thought is explanatory but not reflective.

. . . We have outlined a system that is more reflective, more theoretically attuned, more skeptical, and more empirical than has previously been entertained.[13]

The question really is not whether what has been outlined is more reflective than what has been said before. That is something else. The question is whether a system of communal beliefs, a people's mythos about themselves and nature (a culture philosophy) can ever be "reflective" and "theoretically attuned" without some sympathetic midwife helping and causing it to be so. Such a system is really what it is, a first order system. But some person might cover it with the masks of a second order. This, however, does not yet make it really a philosophy. It only becomes a *philosophication*. I mean by "philosophication" the attempt to dress beliefs which are otherwise non-philosophical with the ornament of philosophy, and then claim that such beliefs constitute a philosophy.

Given the arguments in the foregoing paragraphs, it should follow that thoughts of Griaule's Ogotemmeli and the outcome of the Sodipo-Hallen *Onisegum* interviews fail by definition to qualify as philosophic sagacity. They may, however, still be some other form of sagacity.

BODUNRIN'S OBJECTION

In the light of what has been discussed in the previous two sections, the points raised by Prof. Bodunrin become easier to explain. Bodunrin raises two main objections: (1) that philosophic sagacity, through the way we approach it in Kenya, becomes a joint product of both the sage concerned and his interviewer, the trained philosopher, and (2) that even if this proves that there are men and women in traditional Africa "capable of a serious philosophic discourse," still he observes:

. . . it is one thing to show that there are men capable of philosophical dialogue in Africa and another to show that there are African philosophers in the sense of those who have engaged in organized systematic reflections on the thoughts, beliefs and practices of their people.[14]

And Bodunrin adds that those who deny philosophy to Africa are not denying that Africans traditionally are capable of a serious philosophical dialogue. They are denying, he claims, the existence of a "tradition of organized critical reflections such as the philosopher and the sage are trying to help create."[15]

The first objection can be answered fairly quickly. It is not a strong objection, even in Bodunrin's own words. The philosopher, of course, given his interview with the sage, would in some ways help the seer to explicate or give birth to his otherwise implicit ideas. The outcome may be termed a joint creation of the two and not a sole responsibility of the sage. This can be granted. But in granting this, we must also grant, as a matter of historical fact, that nearly all philosophers including even the professional ones such as Moore and Russell hold their philosophies as joint works with those philosophers who initially inspired or provoked them.

Most of the philosophers come to create new ideas or style of philosophy only as a result of responding to the ideas or works of some other philosophers or persons. For example, the linguistic style of philosophy which originated with G. E. Moore and B. Russell at the beginning of this century was originally a reaction by Moore and Russell to the challenges of Hegel's Metaphysics. Russell, for example, began his philosophical career as a Hegelian. It is very probable that without this encounter with Hegel, the style of philosophy that Moore and Russell initiated would have taken a significantly different turn.

Moore and Russell produced a philosophical system as a negative response to that of Hegel. Others on the other hand produced philosophical systems by reacting positively to Hegel and then attempting to improve on or transcend Hegel. The philosophy of Karl Marx, for example, is a well-known example of this reaction. And so the "dialectical materialism" and "historical materialism" of Karl Marx can, in many ways, be treated as a joint creation of both Hegel and Marx. Yet, it is never awkward to treat them simply as Marx's ideas.

There is, therefore, no legitimate philosophical objection to a philosopher helping or provoking another to give birth to a new philosophical thought or system. The same should apply to the issue of philosophic sagacity. The trained philosopher, interviewing the sage, plays the role of philosophical provocation. The outcome no less belongs to the sage than the thoughts of professional philosophers, reacting to others, belong to them. It is a fact that without philosophical debates, conferences, rivals, many philosophers including even the most prolific of them would remain unproductive. I believe that even those of us in Africa who currently claim to be on the right track on the question of African philosophy have been helped in no mean way in adopting this position by the provocation of ethnophilosophy.

Bodunrin's second objection is much more serious and has far reaching implications for the nature and development of African philosophy. On the basis of this objection, Bodunrin argues that we, in Africa, should admit that we are having "a late start in philosophy." The justification for this lies in the claim he makes that there has been hitherto no organized systematic philosophical reflections by the Africans themselves. And this, he claims, is what the European denial of philosophy in Africa amounts to.

It is not true that the European denial amounts simply to what Prof. Bodunrin proposes. Otherwise people like Senghor in his *Negritude* would not have gone to that length of asserting that *reason* is Hellenic and *emotion* is Negro. And Aimé Césaire, for example, in the *Return to My Native Land*, taking European denial for granted, rejects *reason* and embraces the "reason-free" black traditionalism.

The European denial is much more fundamental than what Prof. Bodunrin formulates. It denies to Africans not just the "existence of a tradition of organized critical reflections on the thoughts, beliefs and practices of their people"; it denies the possibility for a reflection of any kind (i.e, for any critical use of reason). In other words, the African or black man's mind is claimed to be incapable of any serious rational discourse. In a paper titled, "Reason and Tradition," Prof. Paulin Hountondji, referring to the works of Lévy-Bruhl, writes:

. . . the 'primitive,' Lévy-Bruhl says, always behaves according to tradition. . . . The author of '*Mental functions among lower societies*' terms this attitude "misoneism" (in French: Misoneisme). . . . Whatever the term used, this description implies that the so-called primitive is definitely alien to all kinds of reasoning and free judgement and makes tradition an absolute. . . .

Of course, Lévy-Bruhl is only mentioned as an example. A whole range of Western anthropologists and writers have been, like him, underestimating and devaluating non-Western traditions on behalf of reason.[16]

The devaluation of African (black) tradition on behalf of reason became very successful propaganda both in Africa and even in the Diaspora. So from Leonard Harris in "Philosophy Born of Struggle,"[17] we are informed of the examples of the African-American scholars whose works query the "existence of the philosophic mode of thinking" in the African-American experience and assign "emotively charged language" as "characteristic of the Afro-American personality."

To deny reason to a people is to deny them the possibility for a "serious philosophical dialogue" and as a consequence a tradition of organized reflections on their beliefs and society. By failing to understand that the European denial includes the denial of reason, Prof. Bodunrin misses the fundamental point of the whole debate.

I had argued in the "Four Trends" that literacy is not a precondition for philosophy. Bodunrin grants this, although he tries unsuccessfully to water it down. He writes:

Surely writing is not a prerequisite for philosophy but I doubt whether philosophy can progress adequately without writing. Had others not written down the sayings of Socrates and Buddha, we would today not regard them as philosophers, for their thoughts would have been lost in the mythological world of proverbs and pithy sayings.[18]

To exist as a philosopher it is not necessary that one's thought must progress or be available to the future generation. Sufficient for the existence of a philosopher is that one's contemporaries recognize one's philosophical ability and practice. How many of the contemporary African philosophers will have their ideas known beyond their death? Many of us shall have our works buried unrecognized within the myriad of the many kinds of literature that are being produced in the field. Yet this fact would not in itself deny the point that authors of such works existed as philosophers. Lack of knowledge about one's or a people's philosophy is not a proof of the nonexistence of such a philosophy. But let us not digress.

Besides granting literacy as a nonprecondition for philosophy, Bodunrin also grants the possibility of "a serious philosophical discourse" in traditional Africa. And with these two admissions, his acceptance of the absence of a tradition of organized philosophical reflections remains ungrounded. For with a serious philosophical discourse, a practice would be created (albeit an oral one) within which such dialogues are realized. And a culture which gives rise to such dialogues forms in fact a tradition of a philosophical reflection.

It is evident that the whole point of Prof. Bodunrin's objection amounts merely to the position that without writing there would be no tradition of a philosophical reflection. And since traditional Africa had no practice of writing the conclusion is obvious.

ON WRITING AND ORAL TRADITION

It appears the practice of writing has encouraged many people to make less and less use of their memories. The more this practice grows, the more people come to behave as if nothing is memorable unless preserved by writing. I once met a gentleman who, asked to give the number of his children, declined to comply because, he claimed, he had not kept a written record of his children. In a tradition without writing people make full use of their memories. They even improve their memories by the use of symbols of various kinds. In my own community I know of people, practically illiterate, whose memories are as good as books and, in many ways, better than bad books. My own father, the late Oruka Ranginya (1900–1979), for example, was able to recite to us and the people of the clan his genealogy up to the period when the Luo of Kenya parted with the Uganda and Sudanese Luos several hundred years ago. He would at each generation make a special mention of the few warriors and wise men of the generation and the kinds of achievement they made. Asked to explain how he came to acquire this knowledge and maintain such a superb memory, he answered that he was one of the best pupils of the elders from whom he orally received the information. During his youth, he used to claim, he spent many years in the company of the elders.

The point here is not whether my father's knowledge about his genealogy is correct or incorrect. It all could be incorrect. The important thing is that it is consistent. And the real point is that with this type of memory, there was a great deal that the traditional African could systematize and preserve in memories passed from generation to generation.

Now, to argue that Africa is having "a late start in philosophy" just because we have no written records of her past philosophical activities is wrongfully to limit the sources from which we could detect traces of such activities. However, suppose we admit this claim; there would be a possible interpretation that traditional Africa can have no positive influence in the development of philosophy in modern Africa. And thus if current African philosophers have any natural or cultural attachment to traditional Africa this would amount to a serious limitation of their own philosophical ability. The logical conclusion, then, is that to be authentically philosophical, Africans must be indifferent to traditional Africa. They must, to refine their philosophical ability and understanding, be uninfluenced or unguided by the languages and thoughts developed in traditional Africa. And this would be absurd. So Prof. Bodunrin needs to think twice about the problem.

APPENDIX: AN EXAMPLE OF "AFRICAN SAGACITY"

Theme: God

NAME: PAUL MBUYA K'AKOKO
DISTRICT: SOUTH NYANZA
TOPIC: GOD & RELIGION
BRIEF PERSONAL DATA: Former Paramount Chief, Karachwonyo Location, Member East African Legislative Assembly, "Ker" (Ultimate Moral Leader) of the Luos, a Christian and a Luo traditionalist, married to 2 wives. Had several children.
A SUMMARY OF IDEAS:

1. The Luos had no Religion (Dini) in the European sense before the whites came to Kenya.

2. In the European sense religion is an organized group way of worship.

3. The Luos did not organize worship. But the Luos knew of and worshiped God. They did so individually and in various ways. They generally did so by turning their faces towards the Sun or Moon. The Sun was the symbol (Fire) of God.

4. I believe God is one, both for the Whites and Blacks.

5. I also believe no one is capable of knowing really what God is. Those who claim to do so are wrong.

6. The Existence of God is necessary to curb the permission of everything, including *evil* in society.

7. *How come that without God everything would be permitted?* Leaders give rules to their societies, to those over whom they rule. But the Universe (as a society) has no leader except God. God gives rules to the universe as leaders make rules to their societies. Any society without rules would be in chaos, and so the Universe without God would have no rules and hence, chaos.

8. God can do anything, but he does only the good things.

9. *What makes you think contrary to the traditional Luo belief that every people (tribe) have their own God?* The Luo were mistaken in this belief. God is one for every person, tribe or race. There is one supreme God governing nature.

10. *Proof:* We have more *Kwe* (peace) and *Chanro* (uniformity) in the world than we have chaos: A goat, for example, brings forth a goat, not a hen. And a dog produces a dog, not a man. And this is a proof that there is one supermind governing nature and the world. *Chanro* (uniformity) is always the work of a mind. But chaos (*Kethruok* or *Nginjruok*) is often an accident arising from the absence of mind. At death, for example, the body rots (*Kethore*) because the mind abandons the body.

NOTES

1. This paper was first read to the Africana Philosophy Conference at Haverford College, Haverford, Pennsylvania, July 20–23, 1982.
2. A paper for the commemoration of Dr. Anthony William Amo conference, Accra, July 1978. A somewhat modified version was sent to the 16th World Congress of Philosophy, Dusseldorf, September 1978. A Swedish translation of the later by Dr. Ann-Mari Dahlquist is published in *Filosofiska Tidscrift*, Upsala, I (February 1981).

3. *Philosophy*, 56 (April 1981), 161–79.

4. A comprehensive report on the Sodipo-Hallen research is contained in *An African Epistemology: The Knowledge-Belief Distinction and Yoruba Thought*, University of Ife, 1981, presented to the Nigerian Philosophical Association Conference, Ibadan, February 1981.

5. Bodunrin, loc. cit., p. 162.

6. Ibid., p. 168.

7. In *Philosophy and An African Culture* (Cambridge Univ. Press, 1980), Professor Wiredu mentions "three evils" that can afflict a society: anachronism, authoritarianism, and supernaturalism. Although Wiredu restricts these to the modern Ghanaian (and in general African) society, these evils are characteristic of almost every established cultural system. Just as Ghanaian society is anachronistic, the same holds true of, say, British society.

8. Marcel Griaule: *Conversations with Ogotemmeli: An Introduction to Dogon Religious Ideas*, introduced by G. Dieterien (Oxford Univ. Press, 1965), pp. 2–3.

9. Paul Mbuya is one of the sage philosophers of traditional Kenya. He lived to be the *Ker* of his Luo community. *Ker* is the ultimate moral leader and guide of the Luos.

10. Griaule, op. cit., p. 146.

11. Paul Mbuya, in the "Thoughts of Kenyan Sages," Research Findings, Dept. of Philosophy, University of Nairobi.

12. Sodipo-Hallen, op. cit., p. 1.

13. Ibid., p. 62.

14. Bodunrin, loc. cit., p. 170.

15. Ibid., p. 170.

16. A paper to the 2nd Afro-Asian Philosophy Conference on Philosophy and Cultures (Nairobi, October 30–November 3, 1983), p. 4, coming out as chap. 20 in the publication of the proceedings, Bookwise Publishers, Nairobi.

17. A paper to the 2nd Afro-Asian Philosophy Conference, coming out as chap. 15 in the publication of the proceedings.

18. Bodunrin, loc. cit., p. 177.

PETER O. BODUNRIN

THE QUESTION OF AFRICAN PHILOSOPHY

Philosophy in Africa has for more than a decade now been dominated by the discussion of one compound question, namely, is there an African philosophy, and if there is, what is it? The first part of the question has generally been unhesitatingly answered in the affirmative. Dispute has been primarily over the second part of the question as various specimens of African philosophy presented do not seem to pass muster. Those of us who refuse to accept certain specimens as philosophy have generally been rather illogically said also to deny an affirmative answer to the first part of the question. In a paper presented at the International Symposium in Memory of Dr. William Amo,[1] the Ghanaian philosopher who taught in German universities in the early part of the eighteenth century, Professor Odera Oruka identified four trends, perhaps more appropriately approaches, in current African philosophy. The four trends identified by Oruka are as follows:

1. *Ethnophilosophy*. This is the term Paulin Hountondji used to refer to the works of those anthropologists, sociologists, ethnographers and philosophers who present the collective worldviews of African peoples, their myths and folk-lores and folk-wisdom, as philosophy.[2] What ethnophilosophers try to do is 'to describe a world outlook or thought system of a particular African community or the whole of Africa'. As opposed to seeing philosophy as a body of logically argued thoughts of individuals, ethnophilosophers see African philosophy as communal thought and give its emotional appeal as one of its unique features. Representative authors in this category are

Tempels, Senghor, Mbiti and Kagame.[3] Oruka says that this is strictly speaking not philosophy, but philosophy only in a 'debased' sense of the word.

2. *Philosophic sagacity.* This trend implicitly rejects a holistic approach to African philosophy. Rather than seek African philosophy by the study of general world outlooks, customs, folk-lores, etc., the attempt is made to identify men in the society who are reputed for their wisdom. The aim is to show that 'literacy is not a necessary condition for philosophical reflection and exposition', and that in Africa there are 'critical independent thinkers who guide their thought and judgments by the power of reason and inborn insight rather than by the authority of the communal consensus',[4] and that there are in Africa men uninfluenced by outside sources who are capable of critical and dialectical inquiry. In Marcel Griaule's *Conversations with Ogotemmeli: An Introduction to Dogan Religious Ideas*, published for the International African Institute by the Oxford University Press (1965), Ogotemmeli displays a great philosophic sagacity in his exposition of the secret doctrines of his group. How much is Ogotemmeli's own philosophy and how much belongs to his secret group may not be known.

3. *Nationalist-ideological philosophy.* This is represented by the works of politicians like Kwame Nkrumah, Julius Nyerere and Leopold Senghor.[5] It is an attempt to evolve a new and, if possible, unique political theory based on traditional African socialism and familyhood. It is argued that a true and meaningful freedom must be accompanied by a true mental liberation and a return, whenever possible and desirable, to genuine and authentic traditional African humanism.

4. *Professional philosophy.* This is the work of many trained philosophers. Many of them reject the assumptions of ethno-philosophy and take a universalist view of philosophy. Philosophy, many of them argue, must have the same meaning in all cultures although the subjects that receive priority, and perhaps the method of dealing with them, may be dictated by cultural biases and the existential situation in the society within which the philosophers operate. According to this school, African philosophy is the philosophy done

by African philosophers whether it be in the area of logic, metaphysics, ethics or history of philosophy. It is desirable that the works be set in some African context, but it is not necessary that they be so. Thus, if African philosophers were to engage in debates on Plato's epistemology, or on theoretical identities, their works would qualify as African philosophy. It is the view of this school that debate among African philosophers is only just beginning and that the tradition of philosophy in the strict sense of the word is just now being established. According to this school, criticism and argument are essential characteristics of anything which is to pass as philosophy. Hence mere descriptive accounts of African thought systems or the thought systems of any other society would not pass as philosophy. Oruka identifies four African philosophers—Kwasi Wiredu, Paulin Hountondji, himself and myself—whose works reflect this position.[6] I agree with Oruka that the four of us broadly belong to the same 'school'. We have met more frequently perhaps than any other group in Africa and have exchanged and discussed our published and unpublished works to the extent that I am afraid I may be doing just what Ayer did in *Language, Truth and Logic*, expounding, explaining and defending the views of a school. Nevertheless, some subtle differences, as is to be expected, remain among us. In this paper, I shall not repeat in detail our usual arguments for rejecting the works of others as not being philosophical.

Recent discussions and further reflections on the matter have convinced me that the different positions as to the nature of African philosophy held by various contemporary Africans reflect different understandings of the meanings of philosophy itself. I now think that our not wholly terminological dispute as to what is and what is not to count as African philosophy cannot be settled without answering some important questions. Some of these questions are: What exactly are African philosophers trying to do, namely, what challenges are they trying to meet? What is the proper answer to these challenges? In other words, what would constitute an appropriate answer to the problems African philosophers are trying to solve? What is the difference between a piece of philosophical discourse and discourse in some other discipline? What is it for a given idea or philosophy to be correctly definable as African philosophy? I shall attempt in this paper to answer these and related questions.

Philosophy begins in wonder. The universe itself provided men with the first source of wonder. There are the stars, the oceans, the phenomena of birth, life, death, growth and decay. Men wondered about the fate of the dead. About the living, they wondered about the purpose of life, about what is the proper way to behave. They wonder about whether there is a guiding force behind all these things, etc. All human societies have answers to these questions. The life of a society is organized according to what are accepted as the answers to these fundamental questions. These answers may in fact be grounded in error and ignorance but they are usually not questioned. Rarely do men turn around to criticize themselves without some (usually external) impetus, rarely do men feel the necessity to provide justifications for their beliefs without some challenge.

In Africa, the challenge to the traditional worldview and belief systems came chiefly from contact with Western Europeans. For although there must have been some contact through trade and other means between the different peoples of sub-Saharan Africa from time immemorial, yet because of the similarity of their environment and hence the similarity of the problems the universe posed for them, the worldviews of these peoples, their customs and social organizations were not sufficiently dissimilar to provide significant challenges to one another. The similarity which social anthropologists have found among several African cultures is not surprising for, given identical problems, it is to be expected that some solutions would be similar since human options are not infinite. But things changed upon contact with the West. Large parts of Africa were colonized, evangelization began and writing was introduced. Two different worldviews came face to face.[7] The four trends identified by Oruka are different attempts to meet the challenges created by the new situation. What are those challenges?

1. Partly out of a desire to understand the Africans better in order to make their governance or conversion to Christianity easier, or, simply out of curiosity in the presence of new and, to the Europeans, strange ways of life, European ethnographers began to study the

Africans. Their findings were unanimous in concluding that not only were the Africans radically different from Europeans in the hue of their skin, but that they were also radically different in their mode of life and in their capacity for rational thinking. They emphasized the irrational and nonlogical nature of African thought. Many of the early anthropologists and ethnographers being clergymen, their interest was in the religious and spiritistic thoughts of the African. The usual verdict was that the African mentality was primitive, irrational and illogical. With the growth of education among Africans it began to be realized that an unworthy picture of Africans was being presented and that a misinformed and false interpretation was being given to African thought and way of life. A new interpretation which would do the black man proud was called for.[8] This is what the authors described by Oruka as practitioners of ethnophilosophy are trying to do.

2. The second challenge came with the rise of African, or shall we say, black nationalism. There was struggle for political independence. It was felt that political independence must be accompanied with a total mental liberation, and if possible a total severance of all intellectual ties with the colonial masters. By this time Africans had acquired Western modes of life in many ways—we wore Western type of dress, spoke English or French, etc. The political system was modeled after the Westminster pattern or after that of some other European parliament. The traditional method of government was displaced in most places. This was not without tension. It is easier and less damaging to a people's self-pride to adopt a foreign language, a foreign mode of dress and culinary habits than it is to adopt and internalize foreign ways of social organization. The Westminster model was failing in several places. We began to think of the traditional social order and to seek salvation in the pristine values of our ancestors. Nationalist-ideological philosophy is a response to this challenge.

3. A third challenge arises from man's natural urge to look for comparisons everywhere. The way we understand the world is by putting things into categories. If you come across a strange object somewhere you think of what it is like, you compare it with other

things of the same sort you have seen elsewhere. Africans who study the intellectual history of other peoples naturally want to know the intellectual history of their own people. They are naturally curious to find out whether there are African opposite numbers to the philosophers they have studied, say, in Western intellectual history, or at least whether there are equivalent concepts to the ones they have come across in Western philosophy, and if so how the concepts are related or different in their logical behaviour from those of Western philosophy. This point has become immensely important because of the honorific way in which philosophy has come to be seen. Philosophy has become a value-laden expression such that for a people not to have philosophy is for them to be considered intellectually inferior to others who have. No one laments the lack of African physics. African mathematicians have, as far as I know, not been asked to produce African mathematics. No one has asked that our increasing number of expressways be built the African way. Yet philosophers in Africa are asked, if not directly, yet in a subtle way, to produce an autochthonous African species of their discipline.[9] It is natural for the nationalist nonphilosopher colleague on a university curriculum committee to wonder why a philosophy department in an African university is not offering courses in African philosophy while there are courses on British philosophy, American philosophy, European philosophy, etc. He would simply argue that if these other peoples have philosophies, the African too must have a philosophy. Unacquainted with what is taught in these other courses and fully acquainted with the many rich 'philosophical' and witty sayings and religious practices of his own people, the nationalist cannot understand why African philosophers do not teach African philosophy. To fail to teach African philosophy is almost tantamount to crime and an unpatriotic omission. What seems to be unclear to many is the sense in which a philosophy or an idea is described as the philosophy or idea of a people. What does an expression like 'British philosophy' really mean? I shall address myself to this question towards the end of this paper.

Philosophers might try to face the challenges by introducing ethnophilosophy or teaching the political ideologies of African politicians as philosophy. They may also adopt the method of the social anthropologists and engage in field work: have a tape recorder in hand and visit, and conduct interviews with, people who are reputed to be wise men in the society, hoping that they will discover African philosophy that way.

4. Added to the foregoing, there is a rather recent and growing challenge arising from the scarcity of resources in Africa. Philosophy, and indeed the whole of the education sector, has to compete with other social needs in the allocation of scarce resources. Roads must be built, hospitals equipped and agriculture developed. In these circumstances, that a philosopher like any one else may be required to show the relevance of his discipline is understandable. The emergence of African this and African that is a familiar phenomenon in the African academic scene. It is as if anything becomes relevant once you stick on it the prefix 'African'. It might even be argued that if historians and students of literature have succeeded in creating African history and African literature, we too ought to create African philosophy. It is against these challenges that we must now examine the different approaches mentioned earlier. We shall consider them in a rather different order, treating nationalist-ideological and philosophic sagacity first, and ethnophilosophy last. Ethnophilosophy is the one which stands in the sharpest opposition to the position we wish to urge, and it is in consideration of it that our own conception of philosophy will become clearer. We can give the other positions a fair day fairly quickly.

I sympathize with the efforts of our African political thinkers. It would be great indeed if we could evolve a new political system, a new sociopolitical order which is different from those found elsewhere and based on an autochthonous African philosophy. That indeed is a worthwhile aspiration which one must not give up without trial. But I am disturbed at certain presuppositions of attempts so far made. To begin with, I think that the past the political philosophers seek to recapture cannot be recaptured. Nkrumah seems to realize this in his *Consciencism*. That is why he advocates a new African socialism that would take into account the existential situation of Africa. Contact with the West through colonization and Christianity and the spread of Islam have had far-reaching effects on African traditional life. Any reconstruction of our social order must take these into account. Yet Nkrumah and Nyerere both think that the traditional way of life must be their *point de départ*. But the traditional African society was not as complex as the modern African societies. The crisis of conscience which we have in the modern African society was not there. In the sphere of morality there was a fairly general agreement as to what was right and what was expected of one. In a predominantly nonmoney economy where people lived and worked all their lives in the same locale and among the same close relatives African communalism was workable. Africa is becoming rapidly urbanized. The population of a typical big city neighbourhood today is heterogeneous. People come from different places, have different backgrounds, do not necessarily have blood ties and are less concerned with the affairs of one another than people used to be. The security of the traditional setting is disappearing. African traditional communalism worked because of the feelings of familyhood that sustained it. This was not a feeling of familyhood of the human race, but a feeling of closeness among those who could claim a common ancestry.[10] I do not know how to check continued urbanization with its attendant problems. We may advocate the organization of our cities into manageable units and encourage the sense of belonging among people however diverse their origins, as Wiredu suggested.[11] Still, it should be realized that this would have to be based on new premises, not on the old ones.

Political thinkers are also guilty of romanticizing the African past. Certainly not everything about our past was glorious. Anyone who has watched *Roots* (even if he has not read the book), and however melodramatic the movie version might have been, does not need to be told that.[12] The interminable land disputes between communities, sometimes within the same village, show that the communalism we talk about was between members of very closed groups. A way of life which made it possible for our ancestors to be subjugated by a handful of Europeans cannot be described as totally glorious. Any reconstruction of our past must examine features of our thought system and our society that made this possible.[13] African humanism must not be a backward-looking humanism. There is no country whose traditional ideology could cope with the demands of the modern world. Despite claims to the contrary, the works of Nkrumah, Senghor and Nyerere are not entirely divorced from foreign influence. Indeed they have studied philosophy in Western schools and the influence of this training is noticeable in their idioms. However, they do not claim to be merely describing for us the African traditional philosophy, nor do they claim that their work represents the collective view of the traditional African. What they are doing is trying to *base* a philosophy of *their own* on the traditional African past. The fact that they may have given an inaccurate picture of the past is beside the point. Divorced from their nationalistic-ideological bias and with a more critical approach, their work may be a significant contribution to political theory, and it is hairsplitting trying to make a distinction between political theory and political philosophy. What is needed in these works is more rigour and more systematization.

There appear to be two ways of approaching the investigation of philosophic sagacity. One is the procedure currently being used by Dr. Barry Hallen, an American philosopher at the University of Ife. He is investigating the Yoruba concept of a person. Certain persons who are reputed for their knowledge of Yoruba thought and religion are identified. The philosopher, tape recorder in hand, visits them and attempts to get into a real dialogue with them on the Yoruba concept of a person. The answers obtained are as diverse in their details as the persons interviewed, but contain essential similarities. These essential similarities or common features are then written up by the trained philosopher to get the Yoruba concept of a person. He may do follow-up visits to have his account checked. In the dialogue the philosopher is expected to try not to impose preestablished conceptual categories on his African colleague. Perhaps during the dialogue both parties would point out the inconsistencies[14] in each other's position, leading to abandonment of, or amendments to, positions. I see nothing in principle unphilosophical in this approach and would not object to it. One might wish to point out that that is not how we approach our study of Western philosophy. This would not be a valid objection. Philosophers still visit one another for philosophical discussions although conferences, seminars and the pages of learned journals are now the principal forums for philosophic exchanges. In a predominantly illiterate culture it is not obvious that the method described above is an unphilosophical way of approaching our subject, if one had the interest in probing folk thought. Another is the method of Dr. Oruka and his colleagues at the University of Nairobi, Kenya. It consists in recording the philosophy of an individual Kenyan (they hope to find many more such Kenyans) uninfluenced by modern education. It is not pretended that they are recording the common thought of the Kenyan Luo tribe. The purpose seems to be to find out the critical thinking of some native Kenyans, and thereby establish that there are native Africans capable of doing rigorous philosophy.

But a number of questions must be asked. First, whose philosophy does the philosopher produce as a result of such research? What does he succeed in doing *vis-à-vis* the challenges earlier discussed? I suggest that what the philosopher is doing here is helping people to give birth to philosophical ideas already in them. The product of the joint enquiry of the traditional sage and the trained philosopher is a new phenomenon. Both the traditional sage and the trained philosopher inevitably enter the dialogue with certain presuppositions. What they come out with is a new creation out of their reflections on the beliefs previously held by them. But, and this is the important point to remember, the philosopher and the sage are 'doing their own thing'. They are doing African philosophy only because the participants are Africans *or* are working in Africa, *and* are interested in a philosophical problem (howbeit universal) from an African point of view. As will be argued later, if they were merely interested in how and what Africans think about persons their work would not be philosophically interesting, not any more interesting than the works of ethnographers. Second, this 'going out quite literally into the market place . . . something we are told philosophers used to do before they became encapsulated in our academic institutions',[15] is not to be understood as being the same as what Socrates and his contemporaries did in the Athenian *agora*. Metaphors can be misleading. Socrates's interlocutors, if Plato's dialogues have any verisimilitude, are his intellectual peers. Among them were etymologists like Euthyphro (*Cratylus* 396d) after whom Plato named the *Euthyphro*, renowned orators like Gorgias (*Symposium* 198c), mathematicians like Theaetetus, etc. The Athenian *agora* was not a mere marketplace in our sense of the word; it was the speakers' corner, the conference centre and the seminar auditorium of the Athenian free and leisure class citizenry. Socrates did not leave us any written work but he was not an illiterate. There is indeed evidence that Socrates and a large section of the Athenian free adult male citizenry was not illiterate.[16] It is reasonable to assume that those who met in the *agora* for intellectual discussions were well-educated persons thoroughly familiar with the written and oral traditions of their people. Their search was not for the Athenian conception of justice, piety or what have you. In fact, Socrates insisted almost *ad nauseam* on the necessity of distinguishing between popular conceptions of notions like justice and piety and the real meaning of these concepts—what the thing is in itself. It was in this process of searching for the real meaning of concepts (mostly ethical concepts, at first) as opposed to popular beliefs about them that Greek philosophy was born. It was a criticism of traditional cultural beliefs.

Philosophy is a conscious creation. One cannot be said to have a philosophy in the strict sense of the word until one has consciously reflected on one's beliefs. It is unlikely that such conscious reflection did not take place in traditional Africa; it is however left to research to show to what extent it has. That it has cannot be denied *a priori*. However, this social-anthropologist's method of field enquiry seems to me to be an implicit admission that an African philosophical tradition is yet in the making. The philosopher and the sage are helping this creative work. Those interested in philosophic sagacity would succeed and have succeeded in showing that ability to philosophize is not necessarily tied to literacy and that there exist among Africans men and women capable of engaging in serious philosophical discourse. Still, it does not seem to me that this last point is what those who do not see the definitive establishment of African philosophy in the results of such researches are denying; none but the extremely naive person could deny all the members of a whole race philosophic abilities. What some seem to be denying is the existence of a tradition of organized critical reflection such as the philosopher and the sage are trying to help create. For, it is one thing to show that there are men capable of philosophical dialogue in Africa and another to show that there are African philosophers in the sense of those who have engaged in organized systematic reflections on the thoughts, beliefs and practices of their people. Even if writing cannot be a precondition for philosophy, nevertheless, the role of writing in the creation of a philosophical tradition cannot be underrated. More will be said about this later.

Let us now come to ethnophilosophy. The sources are African folklore, tales, myths, proverbs, religious beliefs and practices, and African culture at large. In respect of these it is necessary to make clear what we are denying. We are not denying that they are worthy of the philosopher's attention. We are not denying the existence of respectable and in many ways complex, and in some sense rational and logical conceptual systems in Africa. In one sense a system of beliefs is rational if, once you understand the system, individual beliefs within it make sense; in other words, if one could see why members of the society within the system would hold such beliefs as they do in fact hold. And a belief system is logical if, once you identify the premises or assumptions upon which the system is based, individual beliefs would follow from them and can be deduced from them alone. Such a system may also even be coherent. That there are rational (in the sense described above), logical and respectable conceptual systems among African and other peoples once thought by Europeans to be mentally primitive is no longer the point at issue. As far back (far back?) as 1962 at the First International Congress of Africanists in Accra, Ghana, a well-known anthropologist, Jean-Paul Lebeuf, had asserted (howbeit with some exaggeration) the existence in Africa of 'perfectly balanced metaphysical systems in which all the phenomena of the sensible world are bound together in harmony', adding that 'it cannot be said too often that the recording of these ontologies has rendered accessible a form of thinking which is as unimpeachable in its logic as Cartesianism, although quite separate from it'.[17] The works of Professor Evans-Pritchard and more recent studies of Professor Robin Horton have gone a long way to confirm this. But not every rational, coherent and complicated conceptual system is philosophy. Science and mathematics are eminently rational, logical and, to a large extent, consistent conceptual systems, but they are not philosophical systems. I think that many ethnophilosophers mistakenly believe that all rational, logical and complicated conceptual systems are philosophical systems. I believe that they are wrong in this.

The usual criticisms against ethnophilosophers[18] have taken the following forms: (1) That some of the things they say about African culture are false, such as when one shows that Mbiti's claim that Africans have no conception of the future beyond the immediate future to be false by drawing attention to various modes of reference to the distant future in African language and social life,[19] or that Senghor is wrong for claiming that 'Negro African reasoning is intuitive by participation' by showing the unemotional rationality of some African thinking (as in Robin Horton's works). This method by itself does not show that the works so criticized are unphilosophical works. A philosophical work does not cease to be philosophical merely because it contains false claims. (2) Since we hold that philosophy is properly studied, according to us, through the examination of the thoughts of individuals, another argument we have used against ethnophilosophers is that the collective thought of peoples upon which they concentrate is not genuine philosophy. Although any attempt to give an account of the collective thoughts of a whole people lends itself to a usual objection against holistic explanations of social phenomena (namely, that they must posit the existence of group minds), this objection is, in and of itself, not sufficient to dismiss such attempts as nonphilosophical. Philosophers like anyone else may err. At any rate, it is not clear why the thought of groups, if there is such a thing, cannot be a proper subject for philosophical study. To argue that it cannot[20] is to beg the question, for it is to assume that the question of what methods and materials belong to philosophy has been settled in advance.[21] The history of philosophy is replete with discussions of different sorts of things and various approaches to the subject. One cannot dismiss the discussion of anything and the use of any method as unphilosophical without argument. To opt for one method is to take a philosophical stance.

There is no *a priori* reason why proverbs, myths of gods and angels, social practices, etc., could not be proper subjects for philosophical inquiry.

Ethnophilosophers and ourselves and indeed all who engage in cognitive endeavours have a common object (not objective) of enquiry. What we all wish to know more about is this universe of ours; its content, the events and activities which take place within it. About these things several questions may be asked to which different answers are expected. The kind of answers expected depends both on the kind of questions posed *and* on the method of enquiry. Different disciplines approach the study of the world in different ways and seek understanding at different levels and with different goals. Thus, the discovery of the most fundamental laws governing the behaviour of matter is the goal of physics; the discovery of the general laws governing the functioning of the human mind is the goal of psychology. Disciplines are not in water-tight compartments, and areas of interest overlap. And what in one generation belongs to one discipline may in another generation belong to another discipline. Scholars in each discipline generally adopt the methods accepted by their age, and deal with the sorts of questions that are of concern to their age, and work within the background of the basic assumptions of their disciplines—at least until these assumptions 'boil over'. Wright may be right that there is no one method which is *the method* of philosophy today.[22] Still, in whatever tradition of philosophy one is working and whatever method one is applying, some assumptions seem to be generally agreed on today. Thus, when one is putting forward a philosophical thesis for our acceptance, we expect him to state his case clearly, to state the issues at stake as clearly as possible so that we know what we are being invited to accept. We expect him to argue for his case—show us why we must accept his case. He may do this by showing the weaknesses of rival theories, if any, or by showing how his theory solves the problem(s) that has (have) always worried us, or how it enlarges our understanding of something else we already knew. In arguing for his thesis and in showing how the thesis makes a difference he is carrying out a synthesis the result of which may be a new view of the world. If this new view conflicts with other views he must attempt to justify which of them he thinks we ought to opt for. We expect him to let us have a say; let us, that is, ask and raise questions about his thesis. In other words we do not expect him to be so dogmatic as to think that his position is the final word on that with which it deals. We expect him to be prepared to change his view, and are ourselves prepared to change ours, according to evidence. We do not expect him to have a theological dogmatism about his position. We expect these things even of the speculative metaphysician and the existentialist. Philosophers do not always succeed in doing and being all these things. It is only required that they try to. A mere description of the empirical world cannot satisfy these conditions. The pity is that ethnophilosophers usually fall in love so much with the thought system they seek to expound that they become dogmatic in the veneration of the culture to which the thought system belongs. They hardly see why others may refuse totally to share their esteem for the system they describe. They do not raise philosophical issues about the system (because for them no problems arise once we 'understand' the system); therefore they do not attempt to give a philosophical justification of the belief system or of issues that arise in it. It is for these reasons that we find their works philosophically unsatisfactory; it is not because we consider the material on which they have worked unworthy of the philosopher's attention, or their work unscholarly. It must be pointed out, however, that an otherwise competent professional philosopher may manifest an unexpressed reverence for traditional culture by simply leaving us with an analysis of philosophical concepts and saying nothing about his analysis—as if to say he has found a new and impeccable conceptual system.

The African philosopher cannot *deliberately* ignore the study of the traditional belief system of his people. Philosophical problems arise out of real life situations. In Africa, more than in many other parts of the modern world, traditional culture and beliefs still exercise a great influence on the thinking and actions of men. At a time when many people in the West believe that philosophy has become impoverished and needs redirection, a philosophical study of traditional societies may be the answer. The point, however, is that the philosopher's approach to this study must be one of criticism, by which one does not mean 'negative appraisal,' but rational, impartial and articulate appraisal whether positive or negative. To be "critical" of received ideas is accordingly not the same thing as rejecting them: it consists rather in seriously asking oneself whether the ideas in question should be reformed, modified or conserved, and in applying one's entire intellectual and imaginative intelligence to the search for an answer.'[23] What seems to me clear is that the philosopher cannot embark on a study of African traditional thought wholesale. He would have to proceed piecemeal. He may have to begin by an examination of philosophical issues and concepts that have loomed large in the history of world philosophy, and he must not be charged for being unoriginal or being irrelevant as an African philosopher simply because he is discussing in the African context issues that have also received attention elsewhere. If a problem is philosophical it must have a universal relevance to all men. Philosophical systems are built up by systematic examination of specific features of the world and out of the relationships that are perceived to obtain between them. Some contemporary African philosophers have begun the piecemeal study of philosophical concepts embedded in African traditional thought. I shall discuss two recent attempts.

In 'Notes on the Concept of Cause and Chance in Yorùbá Traditional Thought',[24] by a comparison of several quotations from Yorùbá proverbs, the playwright Ogunde, the Ifa corpus, Hume, Horton, etc., and obviously doing the same thing which Henri Frankfort has done with Greek prescientific prephilosophic speculative thought,[25] and reaching exactly the same conclusions, Professor Sodipo successfully established the following theses: (1) That the Yorùbás do distinguish between chance and cause. (2) That scientific causal explanations (usually done in terms of impersonal entities) cannot explain certain unique features of some occurrences. Thus while the wetness of the road, the ineffectiveness of the brakes and driver carelessness, etc., may explain why accidents generally happen, they cannot explain why it has happened to a particular person, in a particular place and at exactly the time it happened. (3) That where human personal interests are at stake, as when a coin is tossed to decide who is to reign, the Yorùbás believe that in such a case luck is not due to chance but to the action of the gods or some other personal agent.

(4) The reason for this is that the preoccupation of explanation in Yorùbá traditional thought is *religious*; because it is *religious* it must satisfy 'emotional and aesthetic needs' and because of this its explanations *must be given* in terms of persons or entities that are like persons in significant respects. For it is explanations like these that can reveal the motives that lay behind particular happenings; they alone answer the *emotional* question why the thing happened *here*, *now* and to *me* in particular.[26]

I think that we must admit that this account has enabled us to see that the Yorùbá conception of cause and chance fits very well into the Yorùbá traditional system of beliefs, especially our religious belief system. It also shows that there are reasons, and understandable reasons for that matter, why the traditional Yorùbás explain significant occurrences in personal idioms. Professor Sodipo points out that for the Yorùbás, the gods take over where the scientists would have a recourse to chance. He also points out that the Yorùbás are not unaware of the technical notion of chance. What Professor Sodipo has done is to put these concepts (cause and chance) in this specific category of events (events that are significant for human beings) in context. He has 'put himself in the place of men living [in the traditional Yorùbá culture] to understand the principle and pattern of their intentions'.[27] But something is required beyond the analysis provided by Sodipo.

Since we have now, through Sodipo's analysis, come to see that there is a difference between the traditional Yorùbá account of cause and effect and the scientific account, the important question is: Which is the truer account? Which are we to prefer? The only answer one can deduce from Sodipo is; it all depends on what you want. If you want emotional or aesthetic satisfaction you ought to prefer the Yorùbá traditional account. If you want some other thing then. . . . If two accounts are so radically different one must be nearer the truth than the other, and one of the aims of philosophy is to enable us to decide which. Surely that which is emotionally and aesthetically satisfying does not for that reason alone compel our acceptance. That feature alone cannot confer truth on a proposition.

In a more important sense of 'rational', showing why a people hold a particular belief is not sufficient to show that the belief is rational.

Given any human social practice one can always find a reason for it. In the case in point here, an explanation of an event in terms of the motives of a person or a god is rational only if evidence is given for the existence of the person or god, or sufficient reasons given why their existence must be assumed *and* arguments adduced as to why the person or god should be supposed to be implicated in the particular event. Surely, to show that a belief arises from emotional needs, if this is in fact true, can hardly be construed as having shown it to be rational. In all this one notices a reluctance to evaluate lest it be understood as condemning a particular culture. This same reluctance to pass evaluative judgments is evident in Hallen's discussion of the concept of destiny in the Yorùbá thought system.[28]

Hallen argues that the Yorùbás reject the Western radical dichotomy between the rational and emotional parts of the human personality and that this fundamentally affects the structure of their beliefs and conceptual systems generally. According to Hallen there are three elements in the human personality: the individual spirit (*èmí*) which continues to live after death but without its earthly body (*ara*) and destiny (*orí*). Like the souls in Plato's *Republic* (Book X, 617d–621b) the *èmí* can go through a number of reincarnations. Before each reincarnation, the *èmí* has to choose a new destiny (*orí*) which 'encompasses every event of significance that will take place during his lifetime, including time and manner of both birth and death. . . . The *èmí* is the conscious deciding self; what it decides is determined by the *orí*, a part of the self that is not part of self-consciousness.'[29] The *orí* must be seen as somehow external to and other than the self. Hallen argues that the *orí* must not be compared to the Freudian notion of an unconscious because this would introduce the personality dichotomy into a conceptual system where it does not occur. The *orí* has both reason and desires of his own. Here is the interesting passage from Hallen:

A Yorùbá will say that once a destiny is 'fixed' by *Olórun* it cannot be changed. It must take place. Nevertheless on other occasions the same person will say that it is possible to 'miss' the destiny one has been apportioned, in the sense of becoming confused and lost during one's lifetime and doing things for which one is not at all suited. Or an external force can interfere with one's destiny. Neither of these is entirely consistent with the belief that once a destiny is fixed, it is unalterable and must take place. Or with the fact that people will flatter and praise their destiny in hopes of improving it. Or with the aforementioned possibility that a person might be blamed for not making the most of the destiny allotted to him.[30]

Hallen rightly points out that the inconsistency implied in the Yorùbá conception of destiny (orí) must not be seen as evidence of primitive mentality. Human beings everywhere sometimes hold (usually unconsciously) inconsistent beliefs. However, Hallen argues that the inconsistency in this case is merely apparent and becomes a problem only if we judge the Yorùbá conceptual system in terms of the Western hypothetico-deductive paradigm:

Rather the various beliefs that may be called upon when an explanation or prediction is required should be compared to the various moveable partitions that are ranged along the wings of a stage and may be swung into position depending upon the demands of the next scene. Each partition corresponds to a certain belief. There are other belief panels in the wings that would be inconsistent with it if they were brought into play simultaneously. But this does not happen (except in very exceptional circumstances) because when a certain kind of problem occupies stage centre the same partition is always moved out to serve as its explanatory background.[31]

Again what we see here as in Sodipo's account of the Yorùbá concept of cause and chance is a good account of why the Yorùbás do not find it odd to live with inconsistent beliefs. Hallen's account can hardly be construed as showing that the Yorùbás hold consistent views on destiny as expressed in their concept of orí; rather his account explains why the Yorubas do not see any inconsistencies in their belief system. But this does not remove the inconsistency. It is better to recognize here the existence of genuine perennial philosophical problems—the problems of determinism and freedom, the self and consciousness—to which philosophers have not yet found a solution, than to portray the Africans as radically different from the rest of mankind in their conceptual system and in being immune to the laws of logic. In an attempt to establish the uniqueness of the African both Sodipo and Hallen have refused to cite parallel beliefs from elsewhere lest perhaps they be accused of importing alien models into their study or appear to be doing nothing new. Our culture may be dear to us, but truth must be dearer.

The discussion is already getting too long, but there are still two more points to be considered. One is the call that we produce an African philosophy even if there is yet none, as if philosophers could put up a command performance. We are told that if historians and students of literature could create the African species of their disciplines, African philosophers can do the same. Those who argue this way miss the essential differences between philosophy and these other disciplines. Peoples and nations *necessarily* have a history as long as their existence spans space and time and as long as they engage in human social activities. Unless they are simply stupid, those who are reported to have said that Africans had no history can only mean that they do not know of any significant events (by what standards significance is to be determined is another matter) that took place in African history. Our historians have proved them wrong by a close study of our oral traditions coupled with archaeological and other material evidence. African writers are doing for African literature what Aeschylus, Sophocles and Euripides did for Greek literature. They took popular myths, well-known celebrations, and popular customs, and gave them a literary twist. It is in doing this that they are helping to create African literature. However, it seems to me that what one may properly compare with philosophy is historical and literary criticism. These are, in Africa, as far as I know, a product of the modern age. The influence of writing in all these cannot be underestimated. Writing helps us to pin down ideas and to crystallize them in our minds. It makes the ideas of one day available for later use. It is by its means that the thoughts of one age are made available to succeeding generations with the least distortion. We do not always, as it were, have to begin again. How much of the present discussion would I carry in my memory ten years from now? How much of it, if I were to rely on oral transmission, would remain undistorted for the future? Surely, writing is not a prerequisite for philosophy but I doubt whether philosophy can progress adequately without writing. Had others not written down the sayings of Socrates, the pre-Socratics and Buddha, we would today not regard them as philosophers, for their thoughts would have been lost in the mythological world of proverbs and pithy sayings.

The remaining point is this: What does an expression like 'British Philosophy' mean?[32] It does not mean the philosophy of the average Englishman, nor a philosophy generally known among the British people. The average Briton is not aware of much of *Principia Mathematica* or of the contents of the *Tractatus*. British philosophy is not a monolithic tradition. At this point in time empiricism and logical analysis seem to be the predominating features of that tradition but by no means can all present philosophers in the British tradition be described as empiricists or analysts. Towards the close of the last century, the dominant figure was Bradley, a Hegelian idealist. British philosophy is not a body of thoughts that had its origins in the British Isles. Greek thought (itself informed by early Egyptian thought), continental idealism, and scientific philosophy (the philosophy of the Vienna Circle) have all had influences on British thought. Some of the most influential figures in British philosophy have not even been British by birth (e.g., Wittgenstein and Popper). Similarly, Alfred North Whitehead was born in England and began his philosophical career in England, but his later philosophical work belongs to the history of American philosophy. The thoughts of the ancient Greeks belong to the history of Western philosophy but the ancient Greeks and ancient Britons were mutually ignorant of each other. Caesar described the Britons as barbarians when he first went there. The point I am trying to make is that the philosophy of a country or region of the world is not definable in terms of the thought-content of the tradition nor in terms of the national origins of the thinkers. As Wiredu puts it, 'for a set of ideas to be a genuine possession of a people, they need not have originated them, they need only appropriate them, make use of them, develop them, if the spirit so moves them, and thrive on them. The intellectual history of mankind is a series of mutual borrowings and adaptations among races, nations, tribes, and even smaller sub-groups.'[33] And 'the work of a philosopher is part of a given tradition if and only if it is either produced within the context of that tradition or taken up and used in it'.[34] If these points are realized the philosopher should be allowed the intellectual liberties allowed his colleagues in other disciplines. He may be asked to apply his training to the study of his culture and this would be an understandable request, but it would have to be understood that his reaction will be guided by his own philosophical interests.

The view of philosophy advocated here is not narrow. It enables us to study African traditional thought, but it cautions that it be done properly. Philosophy as a discipline does, and must, have autonomy. The view that anything can pass for philosophy will hurt the development of philosophy in Africa. Not everyone is a philosopher. Philosophy requires training. Why must we lament a late start in philosophy? No one laments our late start in mathematics. I think that we must disabuse ourselves of the evaluative and honorific undertones that philosophy has come to have and regard it just as one discipline among others. That certainly is the way professional philosophers see their subject. It is just another of man's cognitive activities, not especially superior to others. A department of philosophy in a university is one among many other academic departments in the university, but in order that the foundations of the discipline be well laid it is necessary that the boundaries of it be clearly delimited. We are probably all capable of doing philosophy, but we are not all philosophers, just as we are not all historians. We must advocate rigour. Whether we like it or not we will have science and technology. We have to acquire the thought habits needed to cope with life in a technological age. It is now time to begin self-criticism in Africa. Philosophers cannot afford to expend all their energies on the often unproductive and self-stultifying we-versus-you scholarship. We as Africans must talk to one another. We are likely to have a more honest and frank debate that way. If Marx is right that the important thing is to change the world, then it seems to me that our choice is obvious. No doubt many things are worth preserving in our traditional culture—especially in the moral sphere—but we stand in danger of losing these if we do not take pains to separate these from those aspects that are undesirable. This we can do only by the method of philosophical criticism.[35]

NOTES

1. H. O. Oruka, 'Four Trends in Current African Philosophy', presented at the *William Amo Symposium* in Accra, 24–29 July 1978.
2. Paulin Hountondji, 'Le Mythe de la Philosophie Spontanee', in *Cahiers Philosophiques Africains*, no. 1 (Lumbumbashi, 1972). Although Oruka had Hountondji in mind, it must be realized that Hountondji was not the first to use this expression. Kwame Nkrumah had written a thesis on 'Ethno-philosophy' in his student days in America.
3. (i) Placide Tempels, *Bantu Philosophy* (Paris: *Présence Africaine*, 1959); (ii) Leopold S. Senghor, *On African Socialism*, trans. with introduction by Mercer Cook (New York: Frederic A. Praeger, 1964); (iii) J. S. Mbiti, *African Religions and Philosophies* (New York: Doubleday, 1970); (iv) *La Philosophie Bantu— Rwandaise de l'Etre* (Brussels: Academie des Sciences Coloniales, 1956).
4. This is from an unpublished version of the paper referred to in note 1 above.
5. Kwame Nkrumah, *Consciencism: Philosophy and Ideology* (New York: Monthly Review Press, 1970) and J. K. Nyerere, *Ujamaa: Essays on Socialism* (OUP 1968).
6. See the revised version of Oruka's paper referred to in note 4, footnote 15.
7. Just as the contact of the Greeks with the Egyptians, and that of Medieval Europe with Arabic thought had influences on the thoughts of those peoples.
8. Jean-Paul Lebeuf called attention to this in 1962. See 'The Philosopher's Interest in African Thought: A Synopsis,' *Second Order: An African Journal of Philosophy I*, no. 1 (1972), 43.
9. Some of my colleagues criticized the syllabus I drew up for the Philosophy Department, University of Ibadan, in 1974 as being not sufficiently African and too Western.
10. This is in disagreement with Professor Ntumba's universalist interpretation of African familyhood, and Nyerere's own claim in his *Ujamaa*. See note 5 above.
11. Kwasi Wiredu, 'Philosophy and Our Culture', *Proceedings of the Ghana Academy of Arts and Sciences* (forthcoming).
12. Alex Haley, *Roots* (New York: Doubleday, 1976).
13. Kwasi Wiredu, loc. cit.
14. *Inconsistencies?* This point will be discussed later.
15. Barry Hallen, 'A Philosopher's Approach to Traditional Culture', *Theoria to Theory 9*, No. 4 (1975), 259–72.
16. In defending himself against the charge of atheism brought against him by Meletus, Socrates said that the views attributed to him were in fact those of Anaxagoras whom he would not plagiarize. Anaxagoras' book, Socrates adds, was readily available at a cheap price at every corner store. Of the Athenian jury Socrates asks Meletus, 'Have you so poor an opinion of these gentlemen, and do you assume them to be so illiterate as not to know that the writings of Anax-

agoras of Clazomenae are full of theories like these?' (Plato, *Apology*, 26d).

17. Quoted by W. A. Hart, loc cit., note 8 above.

18. I do not use this term with any pejorative connotations.

19. E. G. J. A. Ayoade's 'Time in Yorùbá Thought', *African Philosophy: An Introduction*, Richard A. Wright, ed. (University Press of America, 1977), 83–106.

20. I argued this way in my 'Problems and Prescriptions for an Action Philosophy in Africa', *Proceedings of the Inter-African Council of Philosophy*, Proceedings of the 1975 Accra Conference.

21. See R. Wright's arguments in his book cited in note 19 above, pp. 21–24.

22. Ibid., 23–25.

23. H. S. Staniland, 'What is Philosophy?' *Second Order: An African Journal of Philosophy*, 7 (1978).

24. *Second Order, 2*, no. 2 (1973) 12–20.

25. Henri Frankfort, *Before Philosophy* (Penguin, 1951).

26. Sodipo, op. cit., 18.

27. W. A. Hart, op. cit. 47, quoting from Evans-Pritchard.

28. Barry Hallen, loc. cit., note 15 above, pp. 265–70.

29. Ibid., 266.

30. Ibid., 268.

31. Ibid., 270.

32. In the line of argument that follows, I am greatly indebted to Professor Kwasi Wiredu's 'What Is African Philosophy?', presented at the *William Amo International Symposium* referred to earlier.

33. Ibid., 7.

34. Ibid., 11–12.

35. An earlier version of this paper was read to the Philosophy Department, University of Notre Dame, Notre Dame, Indiana, USA, and before the Ibadan Philosophical Society. My thanks are due to the audiences in these two places. My thanks are also due to Professor Kwasi Wiredu of the Department of Philosophy, University of Ghana, Legon, for his useful criticism of a later draft.

KWASI WIREDU

ON DEFINING
AFRICAN PHILOSOPHY[1]

Philosophy as an academic discipline is relatively young in most parts of Africa south of the Sahara. This is not to say that philosophy as a habit of reflection is similarly new in that part of the world. Any group of human beings will have to have some world outlook, that is, some general conceptions about the world in which they live and about themselves both as individuals and as members of society. Implied here is a contrast between two senses of the word "philosophy," one narrow and the other broad. In the first sense, philosophy is a technical discipline in which our (i.e., the human) world outlook is subjected to systematic scrutiny by rigorous ratiocinative methods (ideally, that is). In the second sense, philosophy is that way of viewing man and the world which results in a world outlook in the first place. It might be said, then, that philosophy in the first sense is a second-order enterprise, for it is a reflection on philosophy in the second sense. If so, philosophy in the first sense is of a doubly second-order character, for that on which it reflects—namely, our world outlook—is itself a reflection on the more particularistic, more episodic, judgments of ordinary, day-to-day living.

The distinction between the two senses of "philosophy" is not to be taken as a rigid one, for they shade into one another by insensible degrees. Nevertheless, it is most important to bear this firmly in mind when approaching one of the liveliest issues in African philosophical circles today. This is the question: "What is African philosophy?" The issue is sometimes posed in a needlessly provocative form by asking whether there is anything like African philosophy. Conceiving of philosophy exclusively in the first sense promotes skepticism as to the existence of African philosophy. On the other hand, an unanalytically affirmative answer is apt to betray domination by the second sense.

Until a decade and a half or so ago, the dominant conception of African philosophy was of a piece with the unanalytical approach. The phrase "African philosophy" was held—in the words of John Mbiti in his *African Religions and Philosophy*,[2] regarded, in some places, as the classic exposition of African philosophy—to refer to "the understanding, attitude of mind, logic and perception behind the manner in which African peoples think, act or speak in different situations of life."[3] On this showing, the existence of African philosophy seemed distinctly compatible with a philosophical inarticulateness on the part of the traditional African. This did not seem to have worried Mbiti, who even remarked, "What, therefore, is 'African philosophy,' may not amount to more than simply my own process of philosophizing the items under consideration: but this cannot be helped, and in any case I am by birth an African."[4] African philosophy, then, was held to be an implicit philosophy; it was the philosophy implicit in the life, thought, and talk of the traditional African, the main sources of which were the "religion, proverbs, oral traditions, ethics and morals of the society concerned."[5]

The question that has arisen for some contemporary Africans who are interested in exploiting the logical, scientific, and methodological resources of the modern world in their own philosophizing is why their efforts should be put beyond the pale of African philosophy *by definition*. We shall return to this issue in due course, but for now it might be of interest to note that, by the terms of his own definition, his—or, indeed, any African's—"philosophizing" of relevant African data can only consist of making explicit what is implicit therein. It follows that the results of contemporary work in philosophy in Africa can never attain any status other than that of a semianthropological paraphrase of African traditional beliefs. Certainly, except for a few fortunate deviations, this seems to be the status of Mbiti's *African Religions and Philosophy*. Were this to become standard, it would be difficult to conceive of any prospect of a developing tradition of African philosophy in the modern world.

Exactly a decade before the publication of Mbiti's work, Placide Tempels, a Belgian missionary, had expounded much the same conception of African philosophy in his *Bantu Philosophy*.[6] Witness, for example: "We do not claim, of course, that the Bantu are capable of formulating a philosophical treatise, complete with an adequate vocabulary. It is our job to proceed to such systematic development. It is we who will be able to tell them, in precise terms, what their inmost concept of being is."[7] This blunt paternalism, though it apparently did not jar the sensibilities of African intellectuals when it came into print—the book was actually published by *Présence Africaine*—has come increasingly to be felt among African philosophers to be insufferable.[8]

More than this, Hountondji, perhaps the severest critic of the conception of African philosophy represented by Tempels and Mbiti, has objected to their tendency to postulate unanimity in philosophical belief among various African peoples, or even within the entire African race.[9] Hountondji's strictures are just, in my opinion. Father Tempels, for example, generalized about African philosophy with little thought of empirical warrant. If he thought that the particular Bantu people unto whom he ministered held a certain view—say, "Force is the nature of being, force is being and being is force"—he thereupon credited it to Africans in general.[10] The esteem in which Tempels's book was held for a long time, even in African intellectual circles, was, perhaps, partly responsible for the rampancy of facile generalizations about African philosophical thought in the scanty literature that, in the name of African philosophy, grew up in the peripheries of colonial and early postcolonial anthropology.

It is a major irony that Mbiti, who, in an early chapter of his *African Religions and Philosophy*, criticized Father Tempels for generalizing too boldly about African thought, himself promptly proceeded to excel in that practice in subsequent chapters.[11] The most famous example of this procedure in his book was his treatment of what he called "the African concept of time." On the basis of a study of some aspects of the vocabulary of some East African languages, Mbiti drew remarkable conclusions about the thinking of "African peoples in their traditional life." He asserted: "For them, time is simply the composition of events which have occurred, those which are taking place now and those which are immediately to occur. What has not taken place or what has no likelihood of an immediate occurrence falls in the category of 'No time.' "[12]

Not only has this claim been criticized by African philosophers from outside East Africa as inapplicable to Africans generally, but it has also been disputed by some East African thinkers. In a review of Mbiti's book, Kwame Gyekye[13] adduces various considerations relating to the language and thought of the Akans of Ghana to show that, contrary to Mbiti, at least some African people have a conception of an infinite future. He might even more simply have called attention to the fact that the Akans have a word, *afeboo*, that offers a means of referring directly to the infinite future. Alexis Kagame, who has extensively researched into the languages of East and Central Africa, maintains (albeit somewhat paradoxically) that although Mbiti's thesis might be true for Bantu individuals, it is not true for Bantu social or political groups. "It is evident that, for them, 'future' time is infinite."[14] Actually, it can be demonstrated, by a detailed analysis of Mbiti's chapter on time, that, after all, what he calls the African conception of time is as "three dimensional" and as conversant with the idea of an infinite future as what he calls "the linear concept of time in western thought." It is, indeed, unfortunate that the chapter in question was vitiated by the author's misconstrual of his own premises, for it is philosophically the most interesting chapter of the book and contains eloquent reflections, which sometimes attain poetic elegance. Nevertheless, it is important to note that the mishap arose from a tendency for hasty attributions of philosophical doctrines to Africans in general, a tendency that, though not as yet extinct in the literature, appears now to be on the wane.

It is apparent from the foregoing discussion that there are two basic schools of thought on the question of the definition of African philosophy. The first maintains that African philosophy is the traditional philosophy that has been inherited by today's Africans through their oral traditions. According to this view, the duty of a contemporary African philosopher, as far as African philosophy is concerned, is to collect, interpret, and disseminate African proverbs, folktales, myths, and other traditional material of a philosophical tendency.

The second school of thought, in opposition to this, maintains that African philosophy, in this day and age, ought to take cognizance of modern developments in knowledge and reflection. According to this line of thought, African philosophy is mainly the result of the thought of African philosophers, traditional as well as modern. Those who advocate the second approach to African philosophy do not regard merely interpreting traditional thought as an adequate fulfillment of philosophy's historic functions. They do not believe, further, that in modern times philosophy can remain a communal body of thought. Accordingly, they emphasize the importance of debate and the inevitability of pluralism. Hountondji has been particularly keen on emphasizing this aspect of the matter.[15]

Hountondji regards African philosophy as "literature produced by Africans and dealing with philosophical problems."[16] This definition seems to exclude African traditional communal thought from the bounds of African philosophy. However, it includes within these bounds writings that expound and interpret African traditional worldviews. He is not unaware of the apparent paradox; but he insists that there is a significant distinction here. These worldviews are, he says, "spontaneous, implicit, and collective," whereas philosophy must be "explicit, methodical, and rational."[17] Nevertheless, he maintains that the writings in question, which he calls ethnophilosophy, "themselves . . . evolve through a number of philosophical concepts and thus bring about a typical kind of philosophical literature."[18]

It should be noted that, on Hountondji's view, a work of this sort, which is philosophical and also about an African traditional worldview, is still not to be included in African philosophy unless it is produced by an African. Thus, while both Tempels's *Bantu Philosophy* and Mbiti's *African Religions and Philosophy* belong to the ethnophilosophical class, only the latter can be considered as forming part of African philosophy. Notice, furthermore, that according to the same definition, a philosophical work by an African need not be about a specifically African topic in order to qualify as African philosophy. This aspect of Hountondji's definition is, I think, progressive, on the whole. And this is important. No one can deny, for example, that mathematics and science ought to have an eminent place in education in contemporary Africa. If so, it is hardly sensible to suggest that research in the philosophy of mathematics or the methodology of science automatically puts a contemporary African philosopher outside African philosophy simply because such work may have no special links with Africa.

Hountondji puts the matter thus:

. . . just as the anthropological study of African societies by Western scholars belongs to Western scientific literature, likewise the philosophical studies of the Western tradition by African scholars are part and parcel of the African philosophical literature, as are all philosophical investigations made by Africans about concepts which may have no special or privileged links with African experience.[19]

Among the writings he cites to illustrate his point are a number of my articles, including my "Kant's Synthetic A Priori in Geometry and the Rise of Non-Euclidean Geometries,"[20] but I hope it is not ungracious on my part to urge a qualification. If an interest in the sort of problems in the philosophy of mathematics that I discussed in that article never develops in African thought, and no tradition emerges on our continent into which my article might naturally fit, then it would not be unjust to exclude it from African philosophy. The philosophy of a people is always a tradition; and a tradition presupposes a certain minimum of organic relationships among (at least some of) its elements. If a tradition of modern philosophy is to develop and flourish in Africa, there will have to be philosophical interaction and cross-fertilization among contemporary African workers in philosophy.

Of course, since the future is infinite, there is always the possibility that, however isolated a part (or the whole) of a person's philosophical work may currently be in the context of the thought of his own area of origin, it might eventually come to have a place in it. But if, at this particular point in time, the question is raised whether the article in question can be said to be "part and parcel" of African philosophy, the answer must be, I suggest, that, while it is certainly "part and parcel" of the existing corpus of African writings in philosophy, the question is nevertheless somewhat premature, since the African tradition of modern philosophy is still in the making.

My hope has always been that Africans will not leave the advancement of the human understanding of such things as logic and the philosophies of science and mathematics to other peoples forever. After all, all African universities teach science and mathematics, and a number of them teach logic and the philosophy of science, and other subjects cognate (if not identical) to the philosophy of mathematics. Thus, I view Hountondji's inclusion of my article in African philosophy as a well-intentioned *anticipation*, which I hope the future will substantiate.

The fact that when we talk of the philosophy of a people we are thinking of a tradition has a corollary for Hountondji's insistence that for a work to be a part of African philosophy its author has to be an African. H. Odera Oruka, who basically belongs to the same side as Hountondji in the great divide on the proper definition of African philosophy, has criticized this contention, arguing that basing a demarcation of this sort "simply on racial lines or historical relevance seems to be spurious."[21] But from our point of view, the difficulty with Hountondji's requirement is not due to its racial character as such; for, after all, what we are trying to define is the philosophy of a people or race, and it seems obvious that the larger part of any literary corpus that could appropriately be called "African philosophy" would have to have emanated from Africans. The problem, rather, is that the requirement seems to ignore the possibility that the work of an alien might come to have an organic relationship with the philosophical tradition of a given people and thus become an integral part of it.

This possibility has historical instantiations. For example, Ludwig Wittgenstein was Austrian, but his *Tractatus Logico-Philosophicus* and *Philosophical Investigations* are, famously, part and parcel of the twentieth-century British traditions of analytic and linguistic philosophy. Marx was neither Russian nor Chinese, but his thought forms a crucial part of the philosophies of contemporary Russia and China.

Hountondji's definition of African philosophy seems to imply that writing is an essential condition for the existence of a philosophy. This aspect of his definition has also been much criticized. Socrates has been a favorite counterexample: Here is a philosopher who wrote nothing but produced a historically influential philosophy. However, it is important to note the limitations of this counterexample. Socrates was himself raised on a tradition of written thought. What is more, his historical influence has been due to his philosophy having been written down by Plato, as Hountondji has pointed out. More generally, it is well nigh inconceivable that a purely oral tradition could have formed, preserved, and transmitted across generations the entire contents of such a work as Kant's *Critique of Pure Reason*. Given that when we speak of the philosophy of a people we are talking of a tradition, this is a very decisive consideration, indeed, for regarding writing as an indispensable condition for African philosophy *in the modern world.* I shall return to this point in due course.

Be that as it may, it is indisputable that the Socrates example establishes a point that can easily be established independently: A philosophical thesis is philosophical whether written or merely spoken. Moreover—and this has an obvious bearing on Hountondji's view that a philosophy has, necessarily, to be "methodical and rational"[22]—a philosophical thesis is not one whit the less philosophical for being unsupported by rational argument or for being thrown up in an unmethodical context, say, in a rhapsodic poem or a situational epigram. Certainly, it would be inconsistent to suggest that the thesis that every event that happens was bound to happen is philosophical when advanced and argued in, for instance, Richard Taylor's *Metaphysics*,[23] but not philosophical when expressed by my grandfather in an isolated proverb. Nor is a mystic's unratiocinative claim that reality is spiritual any less philosophical than the same proposition propounded in the earnestly argumentative discourses of Bishop Berkeley. Personally, I am all for rationality, rigor, objectivity, etc., in philosophy, but the point is that if we demand that a philosophy has to have all these attributes by definition, then we are debarred from pointing out what is a well-known fact—that some philosophies are unrigorous, or unsystematic, or dogmatic, or irrational or even anti-rational.

To return to the question of writing, it is obvious, at all events, that writing cannot be a precondition for philosophical *thinking*, for one must think a thought before writing it down. The absence of writing in our traditional societies of old cannot, therefore, prevent us from talking of the philosophies of our traditional communities. Neither can the fact that we do not have, from that milieu, a legacy of systems of abstract thought elaborated by specified individuals exercise a similar inhibition. There are irrational, superstitious elements in our traditional thought; but there are also rational ones. And there is a wealth of concepts, idioms, and other verbal turnings in our language that have a definite philosophical import.[24]

Oruka, in his "The Fundamental Principles of African Philosophy," brings out this latter aspect of African philosophy when he refers to the thought of a certain class of Africa's living traditional sages. These sages

(some of whom must turn out to be philosophers) have their own "elaborate" and argumentative reasons for their "doctrines" and views. And such reasons can, given the patience and dedication of a trained philosopher-inquirer, be extracted from the sages and can be written into philosophical literature.[25]

There is a recognition here that among the traditional folks of Africa uninfluenced by modern education there are genuine philosophers, people capable of fundamental reflection on man and the world.[26] Such people are able to subject the folk philosophies of their own communities to criticism and modification. Earlier students of African traditional philosophy do not seem to have noted the existence of this class of traditional thinkers; they seem to have only sought information as to the folk worldviews of various African peoples. And as far as they were concerned, all those who gave them information were simply "informants."[27] The information they gathered in this way, without further ado, was labeled "African philosophy," and this is largely responsible for the impression that African philosophy is a monolithic body of nonargumentative communal beliefs, and nothing else. This way of construing African philosophy is objectionable not only because it identifies African philosophy as such with traditional African philosophy, which has some very untoward consequences,[28] but also because, even of traditional philosophy, it perceives only one type, namely, the nonindividualized type.

However, there is an intimate relation between the thought of the individual, traditional sage-philosophers and the communal world outlook of their people. The communal philosophy provides the point of departure for the sage-philosopher. It provides, in fact, his philosophical education and must, in many ways, determine his theoretical options. On the other hand, a little reflection must show that the communal thought itself is the pooling together of these elements of the thought of the individual philosophers of the community that remain stuck in the common imagination. Because of the lack of writing in most parts of traditional Africa, any complex arguments and clarifications propounded by the philosophers are liable to be swamped in the pool of communal memory. Even so, those parts of the communal thought that relate to the fundamental aspects of the world outlook of a given people must be accounted philosophical.

In spite of his recognition of the class of sage-philosophers in traditional African communities, Oruka seems to think that to speak of traditional communal thought as philosophical (in its relevant aspects) is to operate with a "debased" concept of philosophy.[29] In fact, however, not only is it the case that it is this communal thought that provides the sage-philosopher with his philosophical nourishment, but also it is the thought of the sage-philosopher (albeit in the form of highly compressed "abstracts") that forms and enriches communal thought. It is possible that Oruka is making a somewhat different point, namely, that the concept of philosophy becomes debased if, in the contemporary world, the term "African philosophy" is used to mean just traditional African thought. In this he would, of course, be justified. It just cannot be correct in general to equate philosophy with traditional philosophy. And this is as true in Africa as anywhere else. But this reflection is without prejudice to the fact that in Africa we have traditional philosophies of long-standing ancestries.

If, instead of asking, "Is there an African philosophy?", it had been asked, "Is there an African traditional philosophy?", it would have been clearly unproblematic to answer in the affirmative. It is, however, the first question that, on occasion, has exercised the minds of contemporary Africans and others. If one should raise the question whether there are traditional philosophies in Africa and answer in the affirmative, one would have answered a simple, if odd, question correctly. But there would be a less straightforward question left over that, if anything, it is more urgent to confront. The question is: "Can we speak of African philosophy as a contemporary discipline?"

In trying to face this question, one encounters the following semantic complication. In any society in which there is a developed tradition of written philosophy, any reference to the philosophy of that area is normally taken simply as a reference to that tradition. Thus, "British philosophy" means the tradition of written philosophy that has its head and spring in the (written) philosophies of ancient Greece and Rome. Not that the British people do not have, or never have had, any traditional philosophies.[30] But the point seems to be that whatever there is of value in that body of thought is considered already to have been taken up and assimilated in the thought of the individual philosophers whose works constitute the British tradition of philosophy. Thus, for example, the British philosopher writing today does not seem to feel any need to have recourse to any traditional philosophy of his or her society.

If the phrase "African philosophy" is interpreted in the way that the phrase "British philosophy" is (quite legitimately) construed, then it might begin to seem that some skepticism is in order, for in most parts of Africa we do not have a substantial tradition of written philosophy. It is exactly in this kind of context that it is useful to distinguish between a traditional (unwritten) philosophy and a nontraditional (written) philosophy. In most parts of Africa, there is an emerging tradition of written philosophy. If this movement exploits the resources of traditional philosophy, then the time will come when the phrase "African philosophy" will refer simply to the African tradition of written philosophy, and then Hountondji's definition will come into its own. I was looking ahead to such a future when, in "On an African Orientation in Philosophy," I wrote:

From this point of view, one might suggest without being whimsical that the term "African Philosophy" should be reserved for the results of that needful enterprise. African philosophy, as distinct from African *traditional world-*

views, is the philosophy that is being produced by contemporary African philosophers. It is still in the making."[31]

This is not, of course, to say that the time is at hand in Africa when traditional philosophy can be ignored. On the contrary, this is the time when there is the maximum need to study African traditional philosophy. Because of the historical accident of colonialism, the main part of the philosophical training of contemporary African scholars has come to derive from foreign sources. Why should the African uncritically assimilate the conceptual schemes embedded in foreign languages and cultures? Philosophical truth can indeed be disentangled from cultural contingencies. But for this purpose nothing is more useful than the ability to compare different languages and cultures in relation to their philosophical prepossessions. Insofar as a study of African traditional philosophy may enable one to do just this, it can be philosophically beneficial to the African as well as the non-African.

A second reason for the usefulness of such a study is this: it seems to be a fact about human beings generally that technical progress is apt to outstrip moral insight. Accordingly, the philosophical thought of a traditional (i.e., preliterate and nonindustrialized) society may hold some lessons of moral significance for a more industrialized society.

The third reason is closely connected with this last. An obvious fact about the thought of a traditional society is that it is communalistic in orientation. By contrast, the more industrialized a society is, the more individualistic it seems to become. Now it is quite plain that some of the most unlovable aspects of life in the so-called advanced countries are connected with this individualism. It is reasonable to expect that a critical examination of individualism in the context of a study of a communally oriented philosophy might yield some useful insights for people engaged in the quest for industrialization as well as for those who are far advanced in that process. Of course, both communalism and individualism may have their strengths and weaknesses. But an objective appraisal of them is likely to be hampered if studied exclusively from the point of view of any one of these modes of life. Thus, a study of both traditional African philosophy and various systems of modern philosophy is likely to be existentially beneficial. It is, therefore, a welcome development that a number of contemporary African philosophers knowledgeable in modern Western philosophy are increasingly devoting time to research into the philosophical thought of our forebears. It is noticeable, moreover, that they have tended to eschew the facile approach of earlier studies of African philosophy noted above.

By all indications—or, at any rate, by many of the indications—the tendency at the present time in studies of African traditional philosophy is toward specialized studies of specific ethnic groups in Africa. In the English-speaking world (to which I am mostly restricting myself in this discussion), an early book-length classic of this sort of study was J. B. Danquah's *The Akan Doctrine of God.*[32] In more recent times, J. Olubi Sodipo's "Notes on the Concept of Cause and Chance in Yoruba Traditional Thought" has attracted a lot of attention.[33] This article is a painstaking analysis designed to show, contrary to earlier misapprehensions, that the traditional Yorubas have the concepts of cause and chance but that when events have a significant bearing on human fortunes, certain types of why questions, which are religious and can only be answered in a manner that satisfies emotional and aesthetic needs, come into play in their explanations. Such explanations, therefore, have to be given "in terms of persons or entities that are like persons in significant respects."[34] Sodipo's article has been one of the important stimulants of critical philosophical exchanges among contemporary African philosophers, eliciting responses from, for example, H. Odera Oruka in his "The Fundamental Principles in the Question of 'African Philosophy' "[35] and from Peter O. Bodunrin in his "The Question of African Philosophy."[36]

The latest results of Sodipo's research into Yoruba thought are embodied in an essay entitled "An African Epistemology: The Knowledge-Belief Distinction in Yoruba Thought,"[37] written jointly with his colleague Barry Hallen. The essay is based on the authors' extensive discussions with a number of Yoruba traditional practitioners of medicine reputed to be particularly well versed in the language and thought of the Yorùbá people. One striking feature of the essay is the great attention paid to language. My own essay "The Concept of Truth in the Akan Language," read at the same conference, attached similar importance to language and sought to shed some light on the theory of truth by means of a consideration of the Akan language.

By reflecting on the Akan language, my former colleague Kwame Gyekye has reached some conclusions with regard to the question of whether philosophical theses are language relative. He maintains that, in spite of the materialistic impression that the etymology of various Akan words for mental processes and dispositions do tend to communicate, the Akan conception of a person is irreducibly dualistic, postulating a material body and a spiritual soul (*okra*). Here, then, he concludes, is a philosophical doctrine that is not relative to its medium of expression. Other philosophical theses may be language relative, but this, he argues, cannot be decided *a priori*.[38] His "The Akan Concept of a Person" is also of interest in this connection.[39]

My interpretation of the Akan language is not as unqualifiedly dualistic as Gyekye's, although my results support his general conclusion on the question of the language dependency of philosophical issues. In "A Philosophical Perspective on the Concept of Human Communication,"[40] I have pointed out that the Akan conception of mind is of the nonsubstance variety and therefore cuts across the monism/dualism antithesis. I provided a relatively more ample exposition in "Body, Mind and Spirit in Traditional Akan Thought."[41] I argued that in Akan thought and language the question of the nature of mind is quite distinct from the problem of the existence of what, in the absence of a suitable word, might be called "spirit." I explained that, although it is assumed that there is some kind of entity called *okra* in us that accounts for our being alive, it is not supposed that mind is any kind of entity at all. Thus, the Akans might, perhaps, be called dualists with respect to their concepts of body and spirit, but neither dualists nor monists with respect to their conception of mind. In this, their thought differs interestingly from some of the most dominant trends in the philosophy of mind in the Western world.

Conceptual contrasts of this sort seem to me to be among the most significant results that can be expected from careful analyses of the thought and language of various African peoples.

Such contrasts, it should be added, cannot have any relativistic finality; the whole point of bringing them out must be to subject them to intercultural evaluation. The thesis of the indeterminacy of radical translation advanced by the logician and philosopher W. V. Quine in his *Word and Object*[42] is of the greatest interest in this context. As a matter of fact, Sodipo and Hallen devoted plenty of critical attention to Quine's thesis in their "An African Epistemology." The question of relativism itself is one with which African philosophers will have to come to full grips.

It is worth noting that a significant amount of the current work in philosophy in Africa today is to be found in M.A. and Ph.D. theses. A particularly interesting example is Victor Ocaya's M.A. thesis, *Logic within the Acholi Language*.[43] In this thesis, the author elicits the propositional logic embedded in the language of the Acholi of Uganda and notes interesting contrasts with the natural logic of a language like English. For example, he calls attention to "the lack of natural facilities for handling double negation words in ordinary speech" in Acholi, and points out that "the Acholi language does not explicitly use the law of double negation." In this respect, incidentally, Acholi is different from the Akan language, for double negation is very natural, indeed, in the latter, a fact that should discourage any precipitous, blanket speculations about "African logic."

Another remarkable M.A. thesis is a recent work by G. Banyuy Tangwa, *Nkrumah and Nyerere on Socialism: A Comparative Study*.[44] This is a highly perceptive philosophical appraisal of two influential conceptions of socialism in Africa. *Ideologies (With Special Reference to Africa)*, a thesis by Safro Kwame, my former student and colleague in philosophy at the University of Ghana, was a remarkably determined assault on the problem of ideology in Africa.

Philosophy is both theoretical and practical, and a recent monograph by Odera Oruka entitled *Punishment and Terrorism in Africa: Problems in the Philosophy and Practice of Punishment*,[45] has combined both aspects of the subject to good effect. After a radical critique of the theories and justifications of punishment familiar in Western philosophy, he rejects the institution of punishment as morally indefensible and proposes the setting up of "clinical boards," consisting of medical doctors, psychiatrists, lawyers, economists, philosophers, sociologists, theologians, and politicians, "to sit in judgment concerning criminal treatment." Treatment, then, is to be substituted for punishment, treatment for individual criminals, by which he means "curative and non-punitive ways in which we may help a criminal to change," and treatment for the given society itself, by which he means "the ways in which social ills, bad conditions, or the obstacles to decent existence inherent in society can be cured or removed."[46] In this work, Oruka displays a critical, but constructive, approach to African tradition that is worthy of emulation. Noting that punishment in his traditional society was both retributive and compensatory, he rejects the retributive and commends the compensatory element. But he does not just commend it, he suggests ways in which it might be modified and developed, using modern facilities to serve modern needs. That this is the right way to approach tradition seems obvious, but it is relevant to note that in postcolonial Africa we are still in a phase of cultural nationalism in which it sounds like betrayal to many people to criticize aspects of the philosophical traditions of our ancestors.

While discussing the theory of punishment in traditional Africa, we might note an interesting point made by Benjamin Eruku Oguah in his "African and Western Philosophy: A Comparative Study."[47] He states that although the Fantis of Ghana held punishment to be deterrent and restitutive, their dominant view was that punishment was a means of "purifying" the offender, which was achieved through certain ritual procedures associated with the settlement of crimes and offenses. By contrast, Oguah notes:

The western judge pronounces the offender guilty, but does not have a means for ridding the offender of the guilt-feeling, which modern psychiatry shows is responsible for many nervous conditions that psychiatrists have to treat. The ritual is not only psychologically therapeutic but also its very solemnity is often enough to reform the offender.[48]

Presumably, new ways will have to be found to transform the rituals into more modern procedures.

In Wright's *African Philosophy: An Introduction*, there is an essay by Helaine K. Minkus entitled "Causal Theory in Akwapim Akan Philosophy," which typifies an approach, still encountered in works on African philosophy by Africans and others, that seems to be motivated by a simple desire to offer information on what traditional Africans think. Helaine Minkus is an American who went to live among the Akwapim Akans of Ghana for three years or so and studied their world outlook. Her essay, which is very well written indeed, is a largely accurate descriptive account not of their theory of the nature of causation, but rather of their beliefs about the causes or effects of various things such as illness, death, fertility, misfortune, "spiritual" forces, witchcraft, and sorcery. Given her own interests—she is a professor of sociology—this is fair enough. But the problem is that some African philosophers still seem unable to resist this descriptive, theoretically unreconstructive model. (On this, see the brilliant review of Wright's *African Philosophy* by Kwame Appiah.[49])

In any account of philosophy in contemporary Africa, special mention ought to be made of recent work in the Department of Philosophy at the Addis Ababa University in Ethiopia. Claude Sumner has published five volumes under the general title *Ethiopian Philosophy*. The importance of this work is that it presents and discusses translations of the written philosophical reflections of indigenous Ethiopians dating far back in history. In a paper entitled "Ethiopian Philosophy," presented at the 1981 Ibadan conference already mentioned, Sumner gave the following as the basic texts of Ethiopian philosophy covered in the volumes: *The Book of the Philosophers* [1510–1522];[50] *The Treatise of Zar'a Ya'eqob* [1667] *and of Walda Heywat: Text and Authorship* [early eighteenth century];[51] *The Treatise of Zar' a Ya'eqob and of Walda Heywat: An Analysis*;[52] *The Life and Maxims of Skendes* [first quarter of the sixteenth century];[53] and *The Life and Maxims of Skendes the Wise: Critical Edition of the Ethiopic Text*.[54] It is interesting to note that Ya'eqob was more or less a contemporary of Descartes and, independently, emphasized Reason in an analogous fashion. In having an old tradition of written philosophy, Ethiopia is unlike most of Africa south of the Sahara and rather like the Arab parts of Africa, where there is a well-established tradition of written Islamic philosophy. It has to be noted, nevertheless, that Ethiopia also has, like Africa south of the Sahara, an oral tradition of philosophy that is currently under investigation.

There is a somewhat subtle distinction that has to be borne in mind in any mention of investigations into African oral traditions of philosophy. The old, semianthropological study of African philosophy almost completely restricted itself to the folk philosophies of the continent,[55] but, as noted earlier, it is being realized increasingly that there are individuals among our traditional folk who are genuine philosophers in that they are able to reflect rationally and critically on major aspects of human experience and on the communal philosophies of their societies.

In "Four Trends in Current African Philosophy," Oruka notes the philosophical work of contemporary African political leaders under the heading of "nationalist-ideological philosophy." The reference is to the publications of Kwame Nkrumah, Léopold Senghor, Julius Nyerere, Amilcar Cabral, Kenneth Kaunda, Sekou Touré, and, perhaps we ought to add, Frantz Fanon, who either by necessity or inclination have tried to provide philosophical underpinnings for their programs of national reconstruction in the postindependence era. W. E. Abraham's celebrated *The Mind of Africa*[56] has some affinities with these works, though it stands apart by its special professional finesse and technical sophistication.[57]

This discussion would be incomplete without mentioning the fact that contemporary African philosophers, in addition to their African preoccupations, are engaged with issues of universal philosophic interest not specifically arising from the African situation. The following are only a few samples of such work: W. E. Abraham (Ghana), "Disentangling the *Cogito*";[58] J. O. Sodipo (Nigeria), "Greek Science and Religion";[59] Kwasi Wiredu (Ghana), "Logic and Ontology," Parts I–IV;[60] Kwame Gyekye (Ghana), "An Examination of the Bundle-Theory of Substance";[61] Henry Odera Oruka (Kenya), "On Evil and the Great Fairness Universe";[62] Peter Bodunrin

(Nigeria), "The Alogicality of Immortality";[63] B. E. Oguah (Ghana), "Transcendentalism, Kant's First Analogy and Time";[64] M. S. Choabi (South Africa), "The Is-Ought Controversy";[65] M. A. Makinde (Nigeria), "Formal Logic and the Paradox of the Excluded Middle";[66] Lancinay Keita (Sierra Leone), "The Fallacy of the Arrow Paradox";[67] J. T. Bedu-Addo (Ghana), "The Role of the Hypothetical Method in the *Phaedo*";[68] and Robert W. Murungi (Kenya), "On a Non-thesis of Classical Modal Logic."[69] The general issue of the nature of truth has been intensively debated among philosophers in Africa since my "Truth as Opinion."[70]

If we now return to the question considered earlier, that is, "What is African Philosophy?", this brief survey should enable us to see that African philosophy is not just the world outlooks of traditional societies. African philosophers are active today, trying (in some cases, at any rate) to achieve a synthesis of the philosophical insights of their ancestors with whatever they can extract of philosophical worth from the intellectual resources of the modern world. In truth, this is only one of their tasks; they are also reflecting on their languages and cultures in an effort to exploit their philosophical intimations. Besides all these, they are trying to grapple with some questions in such areas as logic, epistemology, and philosophy of science, which were not raised in their traditional culture. All this they are trying to do through exchanges of views among philosophers—African and non-African—working in Africa, and also with the outside world. It is in this way, and I think only in this way, that a tradition of modern philosophy can blossom in Africa. The process is gathering momentum.

Any attempt on the part of a contemporary African philosopher to define African philosophy that does not take account of this process is out of touch with reality. But for him to take account of it is not just to take notice of it; it is for him to take a position with respect to it. For in this matter, he would not be merely trying to describe a phenomenon existing entirely independently of himself, but, rather, seeking to define the principle of his own practice. Thus, the question, "What is African philosophy?" is at this juncture of our history at bottom one to be answered not with a definition *per genus et differentia*, but, rather, with a program. This is not just because the definition of philosophy everywhere involves a program, being always normative, in part, but because in many parts of Africa we are still in the process of nursing a tradition of modern philosophy.

There are a number of ways in which this can be done, as should be apparent from the above discussion. We can adopt the option of simply collecting, interpreting, and retelling those of our traditional proverbs, maxims, conceptions, folktales, etc., that bear on the fundamental issues of human existence. I consider this to be a reactionary option in the straightforward sense that it is backward looking and will keep Africa behind; it will not enable us to achieve a fundamental understanding of the world in which we currently live in order to try to change it in desirable directions, and it will make us easy prey to those peoples who have mastered the arts and techniques of modern thinking. In other words, such an approach to African philosophy would be a hindrance to modernization in Africa.[71] Nevertheless, were we to embrace this option universally, the result would be entitled to be called "African philosophy."

Alternatively, we can forget completely about our traditional thought and just learn and disseminate, and, even, possibly make original contributions to the philosophies of our erstwhile colonizers and their ilk. Here again, I consider this to be a very unintelligent option. Philosophy is culture relative in many ways, particularly with regard to language.[72] To ignore our own culture and betake ourselves exclusively to the promptings of that of the West in our philosophical thinking would be a manifestation of nothing but a deeply ingrained colonial mentality. Still, the result of such an uncritical Westernism, if it were to seize our continent long enough, would equally qualify to be called "African philosophy." For a body of thought to be legitimately associated with a given race, people, region, or nation, it is sufficient that it should be, or should become, a living tradition therein. It is indifferent whether it is home brewed or borrowed wholly or partially from other peoples. Since we are, as has been repeatedly pointed out, still trying to develop a tradition of modern philosophy, our most important task is not to describe, but to construct and reconstruct. And the real issue regarding African philosophy is how best this may be done. The main objective of this entire discussion has been to communicate and illustrate my own prescriptions.

NOTES

1. This is a much expanded version of "Philosophy in Africa Today," delivered during the 11th Annual Conference of the Canadian Association of African Studies held at the University of Calgary, Canada, in May 1981 and published in *Into the 80's: The Proceedings of the 11th Annual Conference of the Canadian Association of African Studies*, Donald I. Ray, Peter Shinnie, and Donovan Williams, editors (Vancouver: Thantalus Research Ltd., 1981). In the present form, this essay was presented to the Association Ivoirienne des Professors de Philosophie, Abidjan, Ivory Coast, and was translated into French by Sery Bailly and Gilles Vilasco. It was to have been delivered as a lecture in 1981, but due to a ban on public meetings by the Ivorien government, it was never delivered.
2. Doubleday: New York, 1969.
3. Ibid., p. 2.
4. Ibid., pp. 1–2.
5. Ibid., p. 2.
6. The book was originally written in Dutch. It was translated into French in 1945. The English translation was made from this French edition and was published by *Présence Africaine* (Paris) in 1959. The reference is to the English edition.
7. Ibid., p. 36.
8. See, for example, Paulin Hountondji, "African Philosophy, Myth and Reality," in *African Philosophy, Myth and Reality* (Bloomington/Hutchinson, London: Indiana University Press, 1983), pp. 55–70.
9. Ibid.
10. *Bantu Philosophy*, op. cit., p. 53.
11. Mbiti's comment was "The book is primarily Tempels' personal interpretation of the Baluba, and it is ambitious to call it 'Bantu philosophy' since it only deals with one people among whom he had worked for many years as a missionary. It is open to a great deal of criticism and the theory of 'vital force' cannot be applied to other African peoples with whose life and ideas I am familiar." *African Religions and Philosophy*, op. cit., p. 10.
12. Ibid., p. 17.
13. *Second Order*, vol. 4, no. 1 (January 1975), pp. 86–94. See also the animadversions in J. O. Sodipo, "Philosophy in Africa Today," *Thought and Practice*, vol. 2, no. 2 (1975), p. 120.
14. Alexis Kagame, "The Empirical Apperception of Time and the Conception of

History in Bantu Thought," in *Cultures and Time* (The UNESCO Press, 1976), pp. 101–2.

15. See his "African Philosophy, Myth and Reality," op. cit.
16. Ibid., p. 63.
17. Ibid., p. 8.
18. Ibid.
19. Ibid., p. 11
20. *Kant-Studien*, Heft 1, Bonn, 1970.
21. See Oruka's "The Fundamental Principles in the Question of 'African Philosophy' ".
22. Oruka (cf. "Fundamental Principles," op. cit.) also insists that philosophy has to be rational, critical, rigorous, objective. Our position here relies on the fact, noted above, that philosophy is susceptible to a broad, as well as a narrow, construal. In the narrow sense, it ought, of course, to be conceded to Hountondji and Oruka that philosophy must be rational, critical, etc.
23. Englewood Cliffs, NJ: Prentice-Hall, 1974.
24. In talking of the philosophies of our traditional societies, there is a somewhat subtle distinction to be noted: Not all traditional philosophy was (or, indeed, could have been) folk philosophy. There must also have been—and there surely was—philosophy of the individualized variety.
25. Oruka, op. cit.
26. See also J. O. Sodipo, "The Teaching of Philosophy: The Pre-colonial Period," a paper delivered at the UNESCO Conference on Teaching and Research in Philosophy in Africa held in Nairobi, Kenya, in June 1980; and H. Odera Oruka, "Four Trends in Current African Philosophy," presented at a conference in Accra, Ghana, in July 1978, in commemoration of William Amo (1703–1756), a Ghanaian philosopher who taught philosophy in the German universities of Halle and Jena.
27. To a certain extent, Marcel Griaule's *Conversations with Ogotemmeli* (Oxford: Oxford University Press, 1965) might be taken as an exception. But, even in this case, the motivation of the author was predominantly ethnographic; the aim was to learn from the sage, Ogotemmeli, the esoteric traditional teachings of a particular ethnic group, namely, the Dogon people of Mali.
28. See Kwasi Wiredu, *Philosophy and an African Culture* (New York: Cambridge University Press, 1980), chapter 3.
29. Oruka, op. cit.
30. Note that here a "traditional" philosophy means an unwritten communal philosophy that has been transmitted through an oral tradition. However, when one speaks of "traditional British philosophy," the word "traditional" refers to the British tradition of written philosophy. The reason is just what we have been trying to explain.
31. Wiredu, op. cit., p. 36.

32. 2nd edition (London: Frank Cass, 1968).

33. *Second Order*, vol. 2, no. 2 (July 1973), pp. 12–20.

34. Ibid., p. 18.

35. *Second Order*, vol. 4, no. 1 (January 1975), pp. 44–55.

36. *Philosophy*, 56, 1981, pp. 161–79. [Included in this volume.]

37. Presented during an international symposium on "Philosophy in Africa," organized by the Nigerian Philosophical Association in collaboration with UNESCO, held in Ibadan, Nigeria, February 16–19, 1981. These two thinkers have since published their results at book length under the title *Knowledge, Belief and Witchcraft: Analytic Experiments in African Philosophy* (London: Ethnographica, 1986).

38. See Kwame Gyekye, "Akan Language and the Materialist Thesis," *Studies in Language*, vol. 1, no. 2 (1977), pp. 237–44. Elaborate formulations of his views are now available in his book *An Essay on African Philosophical Thought* (New York: Cambridge University Press, 1987).

39. *International Philosophical Quarterly*, vol. 18, no. 3 (September 1978), pp. 277–87.

40. *International Social Science Journal*, vol. 32, no. 2 (1980).

41. A paper read at the Philosophy Colloquium of the Department of Philosophy, University of California, Los Angeles, during my stay there as Visiting Professor (1979–80) and published in a revised and expanded form with the title, "The Akan Concept of Mind" in the *Ibadan Journal of the Humanities* (Ibadan, Nigeria), no. 3, October 1983. It is also reprinted in *Contemporary Philosophy: A New Survey, Vol. 5: African Philosophy*, edited by G. Floistad (Dordrecht: Martinus Nijhoff Publishers; Boston: Kluwer Academic, 1987).

42. Cambridge, MA: MIT Press, 1960. It should be noted, though, that the main question here is whether Quine's thesis of the indeterminacy of radical translation implies the radical indeterminacy of translation as such. As for "radical" translation, God knows that African thought has suffered enough from it.

43. Makerere University, Kampala, Uganda, 1978.

44. Department of Philosophy, University of Ife, Nigeria.

45. East Africa Literature Bureau: Nairobi, Kenya, 1976; 2nd edition 1985.

46. Ibid., p. 90.

47. *In African Philosophy: An Introduction*, 3rd edition, Richard A. Wright, ed. (Lanham, MD: University Press of America, 1984), pp. 213–25.

48. Ibid., p. 222.

49. "How Not to Do African Philosophy," in *Universitas* (University of Ghana), vol. 6, no. 2 (November 1977).

50. Addis Ababa (Ethiopia): Central Printing Press, 1974.

51. Addis Ababa: Addis Ababa University/Commercial Printing Press, 1976.

52. Addis Ababa: Addis Ababa University/Commercial Printing Press, 1978.

53. Addis Ababa: Ministry of Culture and Sports/Commercial Printing Press, 1981.

54. Addis Ababa: Ministry of Culture and Sports, 1981.

55. Marcel Griaule's *Conversations with Ogotemmeli*, op. cit., is an apparent exception.

56. Chicago: University of Chicago Press, 1962.

57. These works fall somewhat outside the period of our specific concern, but it is of interest to note that when people talk of contemporary African social and political philosophy this literature is what they usually have in mind. There is in Africa now active work on the issues treated in that literature that can be expected to surface in print in the next few years.

58. *Mind* (January 1974).

59. *Second Order*, vol. 1, no. 1 (January 1972), pp. 66–76.

60. J. E. Wiredu, "Logic and Ontology I," *Second Order*, vol. 2, no. 1 (January 1973), pp. 71–82; "Logic and Ontology II," *Second Order*, vol. 2, no. 2 (July 1973), pp. 21–38; "Logic and Ontology III: Abstract Entities and the Analysis of Designation," *Second Order*, vol. 3, no. 2 (July 1974), pp. 33–52; "Logic and Ontology IV: Meanings, Referents and Objects," *Second Order*, vol. 4, no. 1 January 1975), pp. 25–43.

61. *Philosophy and Phenomenological Research*, vol. 34 (September 1973), pp. 51–61.

62. *Hekima: Journal of the Humanities and Social Sciences* (Nairobi, Kenya), (December 1980).

63. *Second Order*, vol. 4, no. 2 (July 1975), pp. 36–44.

64. *Second Order*, vol. 6, no. 1 (January 1977), pp. 3–20.

65. *Second Order*, vol. 3, no. 1 (January 1974), pp. 66–78.

66. *International Logic Review* (June 1977).

67. *Second Order*, vol. 6, no. 2 (July 1977), pp. 75–89.

68. *Phronesis*, vol. 24 (1979), pp. 111–32.

69. *Notre Dame Journal of Formal Logic*, vol. 15 (July 1974), pp. 494–96.

70. *Universitas* (Legon, Ghana) (March 1972), included in my *Philosophy and an African Culture* (Cambridge/New York: Cambridge University Press, 1980). See, for example, Kwabena Archampong (Ghana), "Truth and Existence," *Universitas* (June 1972); H. Odera Oruka, "Truth and Belief," *Universitas* (November 1975); Gene Blocker (U.S. and Nigeria), "Wiredu's Notion of Truth" (a paper presented during the Ibadan conference, February 1981); Peter Bodunrin, "Belief, Truth and Knowledge," forthcoming in *Second Order*; J. T. Bedu-Addo, "Wiredu on Truth as Opinion and the Akan Language," presented at the 4th Biennial Conference of the Nigerian Philosophical Association, Lagos, Nigeria, 1982.

71. See also my "How Not to Compare African Traditional Thought with Western Thought," in Wiredu, op. cit.

72. See my "On an African Orientation in Philosophy," ibid.

PAULIN J. HOUNTONDJI

AFRICAN PHILOSOPHY: MYTH AND REALITY[1]

■ must emphasize that my theme is African philosophy, myth *and* reality, whereas one might have expected the conventional formula, myth *or* reality? I am not asking whether it exists, whether it is a myth *or* a reality. I observe that it does exist, by the same right and in the same mode as all the philosophies of the world: in the form of a *literature*. I shall try to account for this misunderstood reality, deliberately ignored or suppressed even by those who produce it and who, in producing it, believe that they are merely reproducing a pre-existing thought through it: through the insubstantiality of a transparent discourse, of a fluid, compliant ether whose only function is to transmit light. My working hypothesis is that such suppression cannot be innocent: this discursive self-deception serves to conceal something else, and this apparent self-obliteration of the subject aims at camouflaging its massive omnipresence, its convulsive effort to root in reality this fiction filled with itself. Tremendous censorship of a shameful text, which presents itself as impossibly transparent and almost nonexistent but which also claims for its object (African pseudo-philosophy) the privilege of having always existed, outside any explicit formulation.

I therefore invert the relation: that which exists, that which is incontrovertibly given is that literature. As for the object it claims to restore, it is at most a way of speaking, a verbal invention, a *mythos*. When I speak of African philosophy I mean that literature, and I try to understand why it has so far made such strenuous efforts to hide behind the screen, all the more opaque for being imaginary, of an implicit 'philosophy' conceived as an unthinking, spontaneous, collective system of thought, common to all Africans or at least to all members severally, past, present and future, of such-and-such an African ethnic group. I try to understand why most African authors, when trying to engage with philosophy, have so far thought it necessary to project the misunderstood reality of their own discourse on to such palpable fiction.

Let us therefore tackle the problem at a higher level. What is in question here, substantially, is the idea of *philosophy*, or rather, of *African philosophy*. More accurately, the problem is whether the word 'philosophy', when qualified by the word 'African', must retain its habitual meaning, or whether the simple addition of an adjective necessarily changes the meaning of the substantive. What is in question, then, is the universality of the word 'philosophy' throughout its possible geographical applications.

My own view is that this universality must be preserved—not because philosophy must necessarily develop the same themes or even ask the same questions from one country or continent to another, but because these differences of *content* are meaningful precisely and only as differences of *content*, which, as such, refer back to the essential unity of a single discipline, of a single style of inquiry.

I will attempt to show, first, that the phrase 'African philosophy', in the enormous literature that has been devoted to the problem, has so far been the subject only of mythological exploitation and, second, that it is nevertheless possible to retrieve it and apply it to something else: not to the fiction of a collective system of thought, but to a set of philosophical discourses and texts.

I shall try to evince the existence of such texts and to determine both the limits and essential configurations, or general orientations, of African philosophical literature.

THE POPULAR CONCEPT OF AFRICAN PHILOSOPHY

Tempels's work will serve us as a reference.[2] We will not summarize or comment upon it but will simply recall the author's idea of philosophy, the meaning of the word 'philosophy' in the phrase 'Bantu philosophy'. More than once Tempels emphasizes that this philosophy is experienced but not thought and that its practitioners are, at best, only dimly conscious of it:

Let us not expect the first Black-in-the-street (especially if he is young) to give us a systematic account of his ontological system. Nevertheless, this ontology exists; it penetrates and informs all the primitive's thinking and dominates all his behaviour. Using the methods of analysis and synthesis of our own intellectual disciplines, we can and therefore must do the 'primitive' the service of looking for, classifying and systematizing the elements of his ontological system. (p. 15)

And further on:

We do not claim that Bantus are capable of presenting us with a philosophical treatise complete with an adequate vocabulary. It is our own intellectual training that enables us to effect its systematic development. It is up to us to provide them with an accurate account of their conception of entities, in such a way that they will recognize themselves in our words and will agree, saying: 'You have understood us, you know us now completely, you "know" in the same way we "know." ' (p. 24)

It is quite clear, then: the black man is here regarded, in Eboussi Boulaga's words, as the 'Monsieur Jourdain of philosophy'.[3] Unwitting philosopher, he is the rival in silliness of Molière's famous character, who spoke in prose without knowing it. Ignorant of his own thoughts, he needs an interpreter to translate them for him, or rather an interpreter who, having formulated these thoughts with the white world in mind, will accidentally drop a few crumbs which will inspire the Bantu, when he picks them up, with boundless gratitude.

We have already mentioned Césaire's criticism. That very necessary political critique, we said, stopped short because it failed to follow up its own theoretical implications. To aim cautious criticisms, 'not at Bantu philosophy, but at the political uses to which it is being put',[4] was to avoid questioning the genealogy of the concept itself and to treat its appearance in scientific literature as an accident, as though its only function were this very political one. It was, in fact, tantamount to shying away from an exposure of the profoundly conservative nature of the ethnophilosophical project itself.

It follows that not only *Bantu Philosophy* but the whole of ethnophilosophical literature must be subjected to an expanded and more profound version of Césaire's political criticism. For if, as a result of what might be called the ethnological division of labour (a sort of scientific equivalent of the military scramble for the Third World by the great powers), Tempels can pass for the great specialist in the Bantu area, and if, too, his reconstruction of African 'philosophy' is the more sensational because of his one-to-one contrasts between this African pseudophilosophy and an equally imaginary European philosophy,[5] similar attempts have been made by other European authors for other regions of Africa. To quote only a few, Marcel Griaule has devoted to the Dogons of the present-day Republic of Mali a book currently regarded as a classic of Dogon wisdom, *Dieu d'eau*,[6] followed by another, in collaboration with Germaine Dieterlen, entitled *Le Renard pâle*.[7] Dominique Zahan has made known to the world the religion, the spirituality and what he calls the 'philosophy' of the Bambara.[8] Louis-Vincent Thomas has carried out painstaking research among the Diola of Senegal and has expatiated on their wisdom, their system of thought or, as he calls it, their 'philosophy'.[9]

As might have been expected, the example of these European authors has been widely followed at home. Many Africans have plunged into the same field of research, correcting on occasion—but without ever questioning its basic assumptions—the work of their Western models. Among them is the abbé Alexis Kagamé of Rwanda, with his *Philosophie bantou–rwandaise de l'être*,[10] already cited. Then there is Mgr. Makarakiza of Burundi, who published in 1959 a study entitled *La Dialectique des Barundi*.[11] The South African priest Antoine Mabona distinguished himself in 1960 with an article entitled 'African philosophy', then in 1963 with a text on 'The Depths of African Philosophy' and finally in 1964 with a meditation on 'La spiritualité africaine'.[12] In this concert Father A. Rahajarizafy has sounded the note of the Great Island by trying to define Malagasy 'philosophy' in an article of 1963 on 'Sagesse malgache et théologie chrétienne'.[13] In 1962, François-Marie Lufuluabo, a Franciscan from the former Belgian Congo, appeared in the firmament with a booklet,

Vers une théodicée bantoue, followed in 1963 by an article entitled 'La Conception bantoue face au christianisme', signing off in 1964 with another booklet on *La Notion luba-bantoue de l'être*.[14] Then, in 1965, his compatriot, the abbé Vincent Mulago, devoted a chapter to African 'philosophy' in his *Visage africain du christianisme*.[15] The former Protestant clergyman Jean-Calvin Bahoken, of Cameroun, was clearing his *Clairières métaphysiques africaines*[16] in 1967, and two years later the Kenyan pastor John Mbiti, probably fascinated by his own childhood, revealed to the world in a now classic work, *African Religions and Philosophy*, the fact that the African ignores the future, hardly knows the present and lives entirely turned towards the past.[17]

Before we go on with the catalogue, let us note that all the authors we have just quoted are churchmen, like Tempels himself. This explains their main preoccupation, which was to find a psychological and cultural basis for rooting the Christian message in the African's mind without betraying either. Of course, this is an eminently legitimate concern, up to a point. But it means that these authors are compelled to conceive of philosophy on the model of religion, as a permanent, stable system of beliefs, unaffected by evolution, impervious to time and history, ever identical to itself.

Let us now turn to the lay authors, with, here again, only a few examples. We cannot but mention Léopold Sédar Senghor, whose chatty disquisitions on 'negritude' are often buttressed by an analysis of what he called, as early as 1939, the black man's 'conception of the world', a phrase which he later replaced, under the influence of Tempels, with the 'black metaphysic'.[18] There are also the Nigerian Adesanya, author of an article published in 1958 on 'Yoruba metaphysical thinking';[19] the Ghanaian William Abraham, author of a book which is remarkable in many ways, *The Mind of Africa*[20] (I believe that a book can be instructive, interesting, useful, even if it is founded on erroneous assumptions); the late-lamented Kwame Nkrumah, whose famous *Consciencism* can hardly be regarded as his best publication;[21] the Senegalese Alassane N'Daw, who devoted several articles to the subject;[22] the Camerounian Basile-Juleat Fouda, author of a doctoral thesis defended at Lille in 1967 on 'La

Philosophie négro-africaine de l'existence' (unpublished);[23] the Dahomean Issiaka Prosper Laleye, also the author of a thesis, 'La Conception de la personne dans la pensée traditionnelle yorùbá',[24] presented in 1970 at the Catholic University of Fribourg, in Switzerland; the Nigerian J. O. Awolalu, author of an article entitled 'The Yorùbá philosophy of life.'[25] And there are many others.[26]

Without being motivated quite so restrictively as the church ethnophilosophers, these authors were none the less intent on locating, beneath the various manifestations of African civilization, beneath the flood of history which has swept this civilization along willy-nilly, a solid bedrock which might provide a foundation of certitudes; in other words, a system of beliefs. In this quest, we find the same preoccupation as in the negritude movement—a passionate search for the identity that was denied by the colonizer—but now there is the underlying idea that one of the elements of the cultural identity is precisely 'philosophy', the idea that every culture rests on a specific, permanent, metaphysical substratum.

Let us now ask the crucial question: Is this the usual meaning of the word 'philosophy'? Is it the way it is understood, for instance, in the phrases 'European philosophy', 'nineteenth-century philosophy', etc.? Clearly not. It seems as though the word automatically changes its meaning as soon as it ceases to be applied to Europe or to America and is applied to Africa. This is a well-known phenomenon. As our Kenyan colleague Henry Odera humorously remarks:

What may be a superstition is paraded as 'African religion', and the white world is expected to endorse that it is indeed a religion but an African religion. What in all cases is a mythology is paraded as 'African philosophy', and again the white culture is expected to endorse that it is indeed a philosophy but an African philosophy. What is in all cases a dictatorship is paraded as 'African democracy', and the white culture is again expected to endorse that it is so. And what is clearly a de-development or pseudo-development is described as 'development', and again the white world is expected to endorse that it is development—but of course 'African development'.[27]

Words do indeed change their meanings miraculously as soon as they pass from the Western to the African context, and not only in the vocabulary of European or American writers but also, through faithful imitation, in that of Africans themselves. That is what happens to the word 'philosophy': applied to Africa, it is supposed to designate no longer the specific discipline it evokes in its Western context but merely a collective worldview, an implicit, spontaneous, perhaps even unconscious system of beliefs to which all Africans are supposed to adhere. This is a vulgar usage of the word, justified presumably by the supposed vulgarity of the geographical context to which it is applied.

Behind this usage, then, there is a myth at work, the myth of primitive unanimity, with its suggestion that in 'primitive' societies—that is to say, non-Western societies—everybody always agrees with everybody else. It follows that in such societies there can never be individual beliefs or philosophies but only collective systems of belief. The word 'philosophy' is then used to designate each belief-system of this kind, and it is tacitly agreed among well-bred people that in this context it could not mean anything else.

One can easily detect in this one of the founding acts of the 'science' (or rather the pseudoscience) called ethnology, namely, the generally tacit thesis that non-Western societies are absolutely specific, the silent postulate of a difference in *nature* (and not merely in the *evolutionary stage* attained, with regard to particular types of achievement), of a difference in *quality* (not merely in quantity or *scale*) between so-called 'primitive' societies and developed ones. Cultural anthropology (another name for ethnology) owes its supposed autonomy (notably in relation to sociology) to this arbitrary division of the human community into two types of society which are taken, arbitrarily and without proof, to be fundamentally different.[28]

But let us return to the myth of unanimity. It would seem at first sight that this theoretical consensus postulated by ethnophilosophy among all members of each 'primitive' community should produce a parallel consensus, at the level of results if not of methods, among all ethnophilosophers studying the same community. But, curiously enough, instead of an ideal consensus, a fine unanimity whose transparency would have revealed the spontaneous unanimity of all those 'primitive philosophers', ethnophilosophical literature offers us a rich harvest of not only diverse but also sometimes frankly contradictory works.

We have noted elsewhere such divergences between Tempels and Kagame.[29] It would probably be easy to find similar differences among the many other works relating to the 'traditional' thought of Bantus or Africans in general, if one could overcome one's understandable boredom, read all of them one by one, examine them patiently and juxtapose all the views they contain.

But I can see the objection being raised that such differences are normal, that the diversity of works is a source of wealth and not of weakness, that the internal contradictions of ethnophilosophy can be found in any science worthy of the name—physics, chemistry, mathematics, linguistics, psychoanalysis, sociology, etc.—that they are a sign of vitality, not inconsistency, a condition of progress rather than an obstacle in the path of discovery. It may be added that, as in all sciences, a reality may exist without being immediately understood, and that consequently it is not surprising if an implicit system of thought can be reconstructed only as a result of long, collective and contradictory research.

The only thing this objection overlooks is the 'slight difference' between the sciences cited and ethnophilosophy that they do not postulate anything remotely comparable with the supposed unanimity of a human community; that in these sciences, moreover, a contradiction is never stagnant but always progressive, never final or absolute but indicative of an *error*, of the *falsity* of a hypothesis or thesis, which is bound to emerge from a rational investigation of the object itself, whereas a contradiction between two ethnophilosophical theses is necessarily circular, since it can never be resolved by experimentation or any other method of verification. The point is that an ethnophilosophical contradiction is necessarily *antinomal* in the Kantian sense; thesis and antithesis are equally demonstrable—in other words, equally gratuitous. In such a case contradiction does not generate synthesis but simply demonstrates the need to reexamine the very foundations of the discipline and to provide a critique of ethnophilosophical reason and perhaps of ethnological reason too.

Ethnophilosophy can now be seen in its true light. Because it has to account for an imaginary unanimity, to interpret a text which nowhere exists and has to be constantly reinvented, it is a science without an object, a 'crazed language'[30] accountable to nothing, a discourse that has no referent, so that its falsity can never be demonstrated. Tempels can then maintain that for the Bantu being is power, and Kagamé can beg to differ: we have no means of settling the quarrel. It is clear, therefore, that the 'Bantu philosophy' of the one is not the philosophy of the Bantu but that of Tempels, that the 'Bantu-Rwandais philosophy' of the other is not that of the Rwandais but that of Kagamé. Both of them simply make use of African traditions and oral literature and project on to them their own philosophical beliefs, hoping to enhance their credibility thereby.

That is how the functioning of this thesis of a collective African philosophy works: it is a smokescreen behind which each author is able to manipulate his own philosophical views. It has nothing beyond this ideological function: it is an indeterminate discourse with no object.

TOWARD A NEW CONCEPT OF "AFRICAN PHILOSOPHY"

Behind and beyond the ethnological pretext, philosophical views remain. The dogma of unanimism has not been completely sterile, since it has at least generated a quite distinctive philosophical literature.

Here we must note a surprising fact: while they were looking for philosophy in a place where it could never be found—in the collective unconscious of African peoples, in the silent folds of their explicit discourse—the ethnophilosophers never questioned the nature and theoretical status of their own analyses. Were these relevant to philosophy? There lay the true but undetected problem. For if we want to be scientific, we cannot apply the same word to two things as different as a spontaneous, implicit and collective worldview on the one hand and, on the other, the deliberate, explicit and individual analytic activity which takes that worldview as its object. Such an analysis should be called 'philosophology' rather than 'philosophy' or, to use a less barbarous term, 'metaphilosophy'—but a metaphilosophy of the worst kind, an inegalitarian metaphilosophy, not a dialogue and confrontation with an existing philosophy but a reduction to silence, a denial, masquerading as the revival of an earlier philosophy.

For we know that in its highly elaborated forms philosophy is always, in a sense, a metaphilosophy, that it can develop only by reflecting on its own history, that all new thinkers must feed on the doctrines of their predecessors, even of their contemporaries, extending or refuting them, so as to enrich the philosophical heritage available in their own time. But in this case metaphilosophy does not rely on an exploitation of extra-philosophical data or on the arbitrary over-interpretation of social facts which in themselves bear no relation to philosophy. Metaphilosophy signifies, rather, a philosophical reflection on discourses which are themselves overtly and consciously philosophical. Ethnophilosophy, on the other hand, claims to be the description of an implicit, unexpressed worldview, which never existed anywhere but in the anthropologist's imagination. Ethnophilosophy is a pre-philosophy mistaking itself for a metaphilosophy, a philosophy which, instead of presenting its own rational justification, shelters lazily behind the authority of a tradition and projects its own theses and beliefs on to that tradition.

If we now return to our question, namely, whether philosophy resides in the worldview described or in the description itself, we can now assert that if it resides in either, it must be the second, the description of that vision, even if this is, in fact, a self-deluding invention that hides behind its own products. African philosophy does exist therefore, but in a new sense, as a literature produced by Africans and dealing with philosophical problems.

A contradiction? Oh no! Some may be surprised that, having patiently dismantled the ethnophilosophical machine, we should now be trying to restore it. They have simply failed to understand that we are merely recognizing the existence of that literature as *philosophical literature*, whatever may be its *value* and *credibility*. What we are acknowledging is what it *is*, not what it *says*. Having laid bare the mythological assumptions on which it is founded (these having suppressed all question of its status), we can now pay greater attention to the fact of its existence as a determinate form of philosophical literature which, however mystified and mystifying it may be (mystifying because mystified), nevertheless belongs to the history of African literature in general.

Let us be accurate: the issue here is only *African* ethnophilosophy. A work like *Bantu Philosophy* does not belong to African philosophy, since its author is not African; but Kagame's work is an integral part of African philosophical literature. In other words, speaking of African philosophy in a new sense, we must draw a line, within ethnophilosophical literature in general, between African and non-African writers, not because one category is better than the other, or because both might not, in the last analysis, say the same thing, but because, the subject being *African* philosophy, we cannot exclude a geographical variable, taken here as empirical, contingent, extrinsic to the content or significance of the discourse and as quite apart from any questions of *theoretical connections*. Thus Tempels's work, although it deals with an African subject and has played a decisive role in the development of African ethnophilosophy, belongs to *European* scientific literature, in the same way as anthropology in general, although it deals with non-Western societies, is an embodiment of Western science, no more and no less.

A happy consequence of this demarcation is that it emphasizes certain subtle nuances and occasional serious divergences which might otherwise have passed unnoticed and which differentiate African authors whom we initially grouped together as ethnophilosophers. It is thus possible to see the immense distance which separates, for instance, Bahoken's *Clairières métaphysiques africaines*,[31] justifiably assessed as a perfect example of ideological twaddle designed by an apparently nationalistic African to flatter the exotic tastes of the Western public from Kwame Nkrumah's *Consciencism*, written chiefly for the African public and aimed at making it aware of its new cultural identity, even though Nkrumah's book, unfortunately, partakes of the ethnological conception that there can be such a thing as a collective philosophy.[32]

Another even more important consequence is that this African philosophical literature can now be seen to include philosophical works of those African authors who do not believe in the myth of a collective philosophy or who reject it explicitly. Let me cite a few of these. Fabien Eboussi Boulaga's fine article 'Le Bantou probléma-

tique'[33] has already been mentioned. Another Camerounian, Marcien
Towa, has given us a brilliant critique of ethnophilosophy in general,
the *Essai sur la problématique philosophique dans l'Afrique actuelle*,
followed by an incisive criticism of the Senghorian doctrine of negritude, *Léopold Sédar Senghor: négritude ou servitude?*[34] Henry Oruka
Odera of Kenya has published a fine article entitled 'Mythologies as
African philosophy'.[35] The Béninois (former Dahomeyan) Stanislas
Spero Adotevi earned fame in 1972 with his brilliant book *Négritude
et négrologues*.[36]

But more than that: African philosophical literature includes works
which make no attempt whatever to broach the problem of 'African
philosophy', either to assert or to deny its existence. In fact, we must
extend the concept to include all the research into Western philosophy
carried out by Africans. This broadening of the horizon implies no
contradiction: just as the writings of Western anthropologists on
African societies belong to Western scientific literature, so the philosophical writings of Africans on the history of Western thought are
an integral part of African philosophical literature. So, obviously,
African philosophical works concerning problems that are not spe-
cially related to African experience should also be included. In this
sense, the articles by the Ghanaian J. E. Wiredu on Kant, on material implication and the concept of truth,[37] are an integral part of
African philosophy, as are analyses of the concept of freedom or
the notion of free will[38] by the Kenyan Henry Odera or the Nigerian
D. E. Idoniboye. The same can be said of the research on French
seventeenth-century philosophy by the Zaïrois Elungu Pere Elungu,
Etendue et connaissance dans la philosophie de Malebranche,[39] of
the epistemological introduction to *Théologie positive et théologie
spéculative*[40] by his fellow countryman Tharcisse Tshibangu. The
work of the Camerounian N'joh Mouelle, particularly *Jalons* and *De
la médiocrité à l'excellence. Essai sur la signification humaine du
développement*,[41] may also be placed in this category, although their
subjects are not only universal but also linked with the present
historical situation of Africa.

By the same token we may readily claim works like those of the
Ashanti scholar Anton-Wilhelm Amo, who studied and taught in
German universities during the first half of the eighteenth century, as

belonging to African philosophical literature,[42] although this may be regarded as a borderline case, since Amo was trained almost entirely in the West. But is not this the case with almost every African intellectual even today?[43]

The essential point here is that we have produced a radically new definition of African philosophy, the criterion now being the geographical origin of the authors rather than an alleged specificity of content. The effect of this is to broaden the narrow horizon which has hitherto been imposed on African philosophy and to treat it, as now conceived, as a methodical inquiry with the same universal aims as those of any other philosophy in the world. In short, it destroys the dominant mythological conception of Africanness and restores the simple, obvious truth that Africa is above all a continent and the concept of Africa an empirical, geographical concept and not a metaphysical one. The purpose of this 'demythologizing' of the idea of Africa and African philosophy is simply to free our faculty for theorizing from all the intellectual impediments and prejudices which have so far prevented it from getting off the ground.[44]

FINAL REMARKS

There can no longer be any doubt about the existence of African philosophy, although its meaning is different from that to which the anthropologists have accustomed us. It exists as a particular form of scientific literature. But, of course, once this point is established, many questions remain. For instance, how shall we distinguish philosophical literature from other forms of scientific literature, such as mathematics, physics, biology, linguistics, sociology, etc., inasmuch as these disciplines also develop as specific forms of literature? In other words, what is the particular object and area of study of philosophy? In more general terms, what relation is there between scientific literature and nonscientific literature (for instance, artistic literature), and why must we include philosophical literature in the first rather than the second?

This is not the place to answer these questions. All that we have tried to do so far has been to clear the ground for questions of this kind, since they presuppose that philosophy is recognized simply as a theoretical discipline and nothing else, a discipline which, like any other, can develop only in the form of literature.

Moreover, such questions can never receive definite and immutable answers, for the definition of a science must be revised constantly in the light of its own progress, and the articulation of theoretical discourse in general—by which we mean the demarcation of the various sciences—is itself subject to historical change. At this point, it is true, a much harder question, or series of questions, arises: How is the object of a science determined? What conditions, economic, historical, ideological or other, contribute to fixing the frontiers of a discipline? How is a new science born? How does an old science die or cease to be considered a science?[45]

This is not the place to answer these questions either. But at least there is one thing we are in a position to affirm: no science, no branch of learning can appear except as an event in language or, more precisely, as the product of discussion. The first thing to do, then, is to organize such discussions in the midst of the society where the birth of these sciences is desired. In other words, whatever the specific object of philosophy may be, the first task of African philosophers today, if they wish to develop an authentic African philosophy, is to promote and sustain constant free discussion about all the problems concerning their discipline instead of being satisfied with a private and somewhat abstract dialogue between themselves and the Western world.[46] By reorienting their discourse in this way, they will easily overcome the permanent temptation of 'folklorism' that limits their research to so-called African subjects—a temptation which has owed most of its strength to the fact that their writings have been intended for a foreign public.

It is indeed a strange paradox that in present conditions the dialogue with the West can only encourage 'folklorism', a sort of collective cultural exhibitionism which compels the 'Third World' intellectual to 'defend and illustrate' the peculiarities of his tradition for the benefit of a Western public. This seemingly universal dialogue simply encourages the worst kind of cultural particularism, both because its supposed peculiarities are in the main purely imaginary and because the intellectual who defends them claims to speak in the name of his whole people although they have never asked him to do so and are usually unaware that such a dialogue is taking place.

On the contrary, it is to be hoped that when Africans start discussing theoretical problems among themselves, they will feel spontaneously the need to gather the broadest possible information on the scientific achievements of other continents and societies. They will take an interest in these achievements not because they will be held to be the best that can be attained but in order to assess more objectively, and if necessary improve, their own achievements in the same areas.

The paradox is therefore easily removed: interlocutors of the same origin rarely feel the need to exalt their own cultural particularities. Such a need arises only when one faces people from other countries and is forced to assert one's uniqueness by conforming to the current stereotypes of one's own society and civilization. Universality becomes accessible only when interlocutors are set free from the need to assert themselves in the face of others; and the best way to achieve this in Africa today is to organize internal discussion and exchange among all the scientists in the continent, within each discipline and—why not?—between one discipline and another, so as to create in our societies a scientific tradition worthy of the name. The difficult questions we have been asking concerning the origins, the definition, the boundaries, the evolution and the destiny of the various sciences, and more particularly the nature of philosophy and its relation to other disciplines, will then find their answers in the concrete history of our theoretical literature.

We must therefore plunge in and not be afraid of thinking new thoughts, of simply *thinking*. For every thought is new if we take the word in its active sense, even thought about past thoughts, provided we are not content simply to repeat hallowed themes, catechetically and parrot-fashion, with a pout or a purr, but on the contrary boldly rearticulate these themes, justify them, give them a new and sounder foundation. Conversely, every blustering declaration of loyalty to a so-called 'modern' doctrine will be at best mere folklore—when it does not turn out to be an objective mystification—unless it is accompanied by some intellectual effort to *know, understand* and *think out* the doctrine by going beyond the more sensational formulations to the problematic on which it is founded. We cannot go on acting a part indefinitely. The time has come for theoretical responsibility, for taking ourselves seriously.

In Africa now the individual must liberate himself from the weight of the past as well as from the allure of ideological fashions. Amid the diverse but, deep down, so strangely similar catechisms of conventional nationalism and of equally conventional pseudo-Marxism, amid so many state ideologies functioning in the Fascist mode, deceptive alibis behind which the powers that be can quietly do the opposite of what they say and say the opposite of what they do, amid this immense confusion in which the most vulgar police state pompously declares itself to be a 'dictatorship of the proletariat' and neo-Fascists mouthing pseudo-revolutionary platitudes are called 'Marxist-Leninists', reducing the enormous theoretical and political subversive power of Marxism to the dimensions of a truncheon, in which, in the name of revolution, they kill, massacre, torture the workers, the trade unionists, the executives, the students: in the midst of all this intellectual and political bedlam we must all open our eyes wide and clear our own path. Nothing less will make discussions between free and intellectually responsible individuals possible. Nothing less will make a philosophy possible.

As can be seen, then, the development of African philosophical literature presupposes the removal of a number of political obstacles. In particular, it requires that democratic liberties and especially the right of free criticism, the suppression of which seems to constitute the sole aim and *raison d'être* of the official ideologies, should be acknowledged and jealously guarded. It is impossible to philosophize in Africa today without being aware of this need and of the pricelessness of freedom of expression as a necessary condition for all science, for all theoretical development and, in the last resort, for all real political and economic progress, too.

Briefly, and in conclusion, African philosophy exists, but it is not what it is believed to be. It is developing objectively in the form of a literature rather than as implicit and collective thought, but as a literature of which the output remains captive to the unanimist fallacy. Yet, happily, it is possible to detect signs of a new spirit. The liberation of this new spirit is now the necessary precondition of any progress in this field. To achieve that we must begin at the beginning; we must restore the right to criticism and free expression which are so seriously threatened by our regimes of terror and ideological confusion.

In short, it is not enough to recognize the existence of an African philosophical literature. The most important task is to transform it from the simple collection of writings aimed at non-African readers and consequently upholding the peculiarities of a so-called African 'worldview' that it is today into the vehicle of a free and rigorous discussion among African philosophers themselves. Only then will this literature acquire universal value and enrich the common international heritage of human thought.

NOTES

1. This is a rewritten and updated version of a lecture 'stammered' at the University of Nairobi on 5 November 1973, at the invitation of the Philosophical Association of Kenya, under the title 'African Philosophy: Myth and Reality' (cf., *Thought and Practice*, vol. 1, no. 2, Nairobi, 1974, pp. 1–16). The same lecture was delivered at Cotonou on 20 December 1973 and at Porto-Novo on 10 January 1974, under the sponsorship of the National Commission for Philosophy of Dahomey.

2. P. Tempels, *La Philosophie Bantoue* (Paris: *Présence Africaine*, 1949) (AS 601). The letters AS, followed by a number, refer to the 'bibliography of African thought' published by the Rev. Father Alphonse Smet, in *Cahiers philosophiques africains*, no. 2 (July–December 1972), Lubumbashi. This 'bibliography', despite the fact that it lumps together philosophical and non-philosophical (i.e., sociological, ethnological, even literary) texts, is nevertheless a useful instrument for any research on African literature or Western literature concerning Africa. The number following the letters AS indicates the number of the text in Smet's 'Bibliography'.

3. F. Eboussi Boulaga, 'Le Bantou problématique', *Présence Africaine*, no. 66 (1968).

4. Aimé Césaire, *Discours sur le colonialisme* (Paris: Editions Réclame, 1950) (AS 95), p. 45.

5. Comparisons between the 'worldview' of Third World peoples and European philosophy involve stripping the latter also of its history, its internal diversity and its richness and reducing the multiplicity of its works and doctrines to a 'lowest common denominator'. This common stock-in-trade of European phi-

losophy is represented in Tempels by a vague system of thought made up of Aristotle, Christian theology and horse sense.
6. AS 214.
7. M. Griaule and G. Dieterlen, *Le Renard pâle* (Paris: Publications of the Institute of Ethnology, 1965) (AS 220).
8. Dominique Zahan, *Sociétés d'initiation bambara: le n'domo, le koré*, (Paris/The Hague: Mouton, 1963) (AS 718); *La Dialectique du verbe chez les Bambara* (Paris–The Hague: Mouton, 1963) (AS 713); *La Viande et la Graine, mythologie dogon* (Paris: Présence Africaine, 1968) (AS 719); *Religion, spiritualité et pensée africaines* (Paris: Payot, 1970) (AS 716). See my review of this last book in *Les Etudes philosophiques*, no. 3 (1971).
9. Louis-Vincent Thomas, *Les Diola. Essai d'analyse fonctionnelle sur une population de Basse-Casamance*, vols. I and II (Dakar: Mémoires de l'Institut Français d'Afrique Noire, 1959) (not mentioned in AS); 'Brève esquisse sur la pensée cosmologique du Diola', *African Systems of Thought*, prefaced by M. Fortes and G. Dieterlen (OUP 1965) (AS 620); 'Un Système philosophique sénégalais: la cosmologie des Diola', *Présence Africaine*, nos. 32–33 (1960) (AS 638); *Cinq Essais sur la mort africaine*, Publications de la Faculté des Lettres et Sciences humaines (Philosophie et Sciences sociales) Dakar, no. 3 (1969) (AS 621); 'La Mort et la sagesse africaine. Esquisse d'une anthropologie philosophique', *Psychopathologie Africaine*, no. 3 (1967). See also other texts by the same author, cited in AS 617–39.
10. AS 294. See also, by the same author, 'L'Ethnologie des Bantu', *Contemporary Philosophy: A Survey*, ed. Raymond Klibansky, vol. 4 (Florence, 1971) (AS 754).
11. AS 347.
12. Mongameli Antoine Mabona, 'Philosophie africaine', *Présence Africaine*, no. 30 (1960) (AS 342); 'The Depths of African Philosophy', *Personnalité africaine et Catholicisme* (Paris: Présence Africaine, 1963) (AS 343); 'La Spiritualité africaine', *Présence Africaine*, no. 52 (1964) (AS 344).
13. A. Rahajarizafy, 'Sagesse malgache et théologie chrétienne', *Personnalité africaine et Catholicisme* (Paris: Présence Africaine, 1963) (AS 504).
14. Respectively, AS 341; 'La Conception bantoue face au christianisme', *Personnalité africaine et Catholicisme* (Paris: Présence Africaine, 1963); AS 339.
15. AS 414. The chapter in question is the eighth, entitled 'Philosophical outline'; 'Dialectique existentielle des Bantous et sacramentalisme', *Aspects de la culture noire* (Paris, 1958) (AS 410).
16. Jean-Calvin Bahoken, *Clairières métaphysiques africaines* (Paris: Présence Africaine, 1967) (AS 46).
17. John Mbiti, *African Religions and Philosophy* (Heinemann 1969) (AS 372); *Concepts of God in Africa* (New York: Praeger, 1970) (AS 375); *New Testament Eschatology in an African Background: A Study of the Encounter between New Testament Theology and African Traditional Concepts* (OUP 1971).

18. See in particular the texts (written between 1937 and 1963) collected in *Liberté I. Négritude et humanisme*. As a theory of 'negritude', the Senghorian ethnology was always, above all, an ethnopsychology concerned essentially with defining the 'Negro soul', where sociology (usually idyllic descriptions of 'Negro society') and aesthetic analyses (commentaries, many of them excellent, on various works of art) are used mainly to reinforce this fantasy psychology. However, *ethnopsychology* always betrays the ambition to become an *ethnophilosophy* by accounting for the black 'conception of the world' as well as for the psychological characteristics. The project is clearly formulated in the celebrated 1939 article 'Ce que l'homme noir apporte' ('The black man's contribution') in which the black 'conception of the world', however, still appears as a psychological quality: an animism, or rather, according to Senghor, an anthropopsychism. This is no longer so in the 1956 text 'The Black African aesthetic' and the 1959 text on the 'Constitutive elements of a civilization of Black African inspiration' *Liberté I*, pp. 202–17 and 252–86: apart from a few alterations, these are reprints of Senghor's reports to the First International Congress of Black Writers and Artists, Paris, 1956, and to the Second Congress, Rome, 1959. Explicitly referring to Tempels, but still wishing to *explain* the black's 'metaphysics' in terms of black 'psychophysiology', Senghor defines it rather as a system of ideas, an 'existential ontology' (ibid., pp. 203–4, 264–68).

The reader will therefore readily understand that I should feel reluctant to situate ethnophilosophy 'in the wake of negritude' or to treat it as a '(late) aspect of the negritude movement', as Marcien Towa does in *Essai sur la problématique philosophique dans l'Afrique actuelle* (Yaoundé: Editions Clé, 1971), pp. 23, 25. If *African* ethnophilosophers are undoubtedly part of the negritude movement, they owe the philosophical pretensions of their nationalist discourse rather to the ethnophilosophy of *European* Africanists.

19. A. Adesanya, 'Yorùbá metaphysical thinking', *Odu*, no. 5 (1958) (AS 15).
20. W. Abraham, *The Mind of Africa* (Chicago: University of Chicago Press and Weidenfeld & Nicolson, 1962) (AS 5).
21. AS 436 and 438. This book will be discussed below, chapters 6 and 7.
22. Alassane N'Daw, 'Peut-on parler d'une pensée africaine?', *Présence Africaine*, no. 58 (1966) (AS 420); 'Pensée africaine et développement' *Problèmes sociaux congolais* (Kinshasa: CEP SI Publications 1966–1967) (AS 419).
23. This unpublished thesis is mentioned here mainly because it is discussed at length by Marcien Towa in his critique of ethnophilosophy (Towa, *Essai sur la problématique philosophique*, pp. 23–33) (AS 646).
24. Subtitled 'A phenomenological approach' and prefaced by Philippe Laburthe-Tolra (Berne: Herbert Lang, 1970) (AS 325).
25. The article was published in *Présence Africaine*, no. 73 (1970) (AS 39).
26. For instance, G. de Souza, *La Conception de 'Vie' chez les Fon* (Cotonou: Editions du Bénin, 1975); a doctoral thesis defended in 1972.

27. Henry Odera Oruka, 'Mythologies as African philosophy', *East Africa Journal*, vol. 9, no. 10 (October 1972) (not mentioned in AS).

28. See, on this point, Ola Balogun, 'Ethnology and its ideologies', *Consequence*, no. 1 (1974). See also my article on 'Le Mythe de la philosophie spontanée', *Cahiers Philosophiques Africains*, no. 1 (1972).

29. See my *African Philosophy, Myth, and Reality* (Indiana University Press, 1983), Chap. 2.

30. That is, 'Language gone mad'. I have borrowed this phrase from the Zaïrois V. Y. Mudimbe, whose book *L'Autre Face du royaume. Une introduction à la critique des langages en folie* (Lausanne: L'Age d'homme, 1973) ranks among the finest works written to this day *on* (not *of*) ethnology.

31. How revealing that this work was published in France 'with the help of the Centre National de la Recherche Scientifique'.

32. For an interpretation of the qualifications added to the 1970 edition of *Consciencism* and for an appreciation of the ideological limitations of the work, see P. J. Hountondji, *African Philosophy, Myth, and Reality* (Indiana University Press, Bloomington) chapters 6 & 7.

33. I have mentioned this article as the most vigorous and complete critique of Tempels to date for its rigorous analysis of the contradictions in his work. Eboussi Boulaga shows that these can ultimately be reduced to an interplay of value and counter-value . . . which characterizes the colonizer's judgements on the colonized. Bantuism is partly admirable and partly abominable. It is valuable when the colonized wish to forsake it for equality: then they are reminded that they are losing their 'souls'. But Bantuism becomes a vile hotchpotch of degenerate magical practices when the colonizer wishes to affirm his pre-eminence and legitimize his power. ('Le Bantou problématique', p. 32) However, Eboussi does not totally reject the idea of an 'ethnological philosophy', a philosophy which would abandon the search for an 'ontological substratum for social reality', would deal with the 'mythical discourse of "native theorists" ', instead of bypassing it with scorn (ibid., p. 9). On this point I believe a more radical view should be taken.

34. Towa, *Essai sur la problématique philosophique: Léopold Sédar Senghor: négritude ou servitude?* (Yaoundé: Editions Clé, 1971) (AS 647).

35. Odera, 'Mythologies as African philosophy'.

36. S. A. Adotevi, *Négritude et négrologues* (Paris: Union Générale d'Editions, Coll. 10/18 1972) (not mentioned in AS).

37. J. E. Wiredu, 'Kant's Synthetic *a priori* in Geometry and the Rise of Non-Euclidean Geometries', *Kantstudien*, Heft 1, Bonn (1970) (not in AS); 'Material Implication and "if . . . then" ', *International Logic Review*, no. 6, Bologna (1972) (not in AS); 'Truth as Opinion', *Universitas*, vol. 2, no. 3 (new series), University of Ghana (1973) (not in AS); 'On an African Orientation in Philosophy', *Second Order*, vol. 1, no. 2, University of Ife (1972) (not in AS).

38. H. Odera, 'The Meaning of Liberty', *Cahiers Philosophiques Africains*, no. 1, Lubumbashi (1972) (not in AS); D. E. Idoniboye, 'Free Will, the Linguistic Philosopher's Dilemma', *Cahiers Philosophiques Africains*, no. 2, Lubumbashi (1972) (not in AS).

39. E. P. Elungu, *Etendue et connaissance dans la philosophie de Malebranche* (Paris: Vrin, 1973) (not in AS). One may also mention the unpublished thesis defended in Paris in 1971 by the Senegalese A. R. N'Diaye, 'L'Ordre dans la philosophie de Malebranche'.

40. T. Tshibangu, *Théologie positive et théologie spéculative* (Louvain/Paris: Béatrice-Nauwelaerts, 1965) (not in AS).

41. E. N'joh Mouellé, *Jalons: recherche d'une mentalité neuve* (Yaoundé: Editions Clé, 1970) (AS 775); *De la médiocrité à l'excellence. Essai sur la signification humaine du développement* (Yaoundé: Editions Clé, 1970) (AS 432).

42. On Amo, see Hountondji, *African Philosophy*, chapter 5.

43. More generally, this new definition of African philosophy opens up the possibility of a history of African philosophy, whereas the very notion of such a history was unthinkable in the ideological context of ethnophilosophy. If African philosophy is seen not as an implicit world-view but as the set of philosophical writings produced by Africans, we can at last undertake to reconstruct their chequered history, including those of African-Arab authors like Ibn Khaldun, Al Ghazali, etc., whatever may be the historical and theoretical distance between these texts.

44. On the gross simplification of 'primitive' societies by Western anthropologists and the need to recognize the internal diversity of African culture by 'demythologizing' the concept of Africa itself, see Hountondji, *African Philosophy*, chapter 8.

45. For a consideration of these questions and some representative answers, see: L. Althusser, *For Marx* (1965), trans. B. Brewster (Allen Lane, 1969); L. Althusser, *et al.*, *Reading Capital* (New Left Books, 1970); G. Bachelard, *La Formation de l'esprit scientifique* (1947) (Paris: Vrin, 1969); *Le Nouvel Esprit scientifique* (1934), 9th ed. (Paris: P.U.F., 1966); G. Canguilhem, *Etudes d'histoire et de philosophie des sciences* (Paris: Vrin, 1968); M. Foucault, *The Birth of the Clinic* (1972), trans. A. M. Sheridan Smith (Tavistock, 1973); *The Order of Things* (1966), (Tavistock, 1970); *The Archaeology of Knowledge* (1969), trans. A. M. Sheridan Smith (Tavistock, 1972).

46. It is worth mentioning here the part that can be played in promoting this new type of dialogue by the departments of philosophy in African universities and the philosophical associations (e.g., the Inter-African Council for Philosophy) and their respective journals.

LANSANA KEITA

CONTEMPORARY AFRICAN PHILOSOPHY: THE SEARCH FOR A METHOD

The purpose of this paper is to present a commentary on the current state of contemporary African philosophy and to offer some criticisms and recommendations. The question concerning African philosophy has been debated for some years now and one has witnessed a number of interesting works on this topic.

I shall begin with the points made and questions raised in H. Odera Oruka's recent article, "Sagacity in African Philosophy."[1] In this essay, Oruka first states what he considers to be the four main trends in contemporary African philosophy: (1) ethnophilosophy; (2) philosophic sagacity; (3) nationalist-ideological philosophy; and (4) professional philosophy. Oruka then takes issue with the claims made by professional philosophers like Bodunrin and Hountondji that literacy ought to be a recommended requirement for philosophical discourse, and that although it is possible for a nonwritten philosophical system to satisfy the criteria for "S is a philosophical system," there must be some means of recording this system so that there is evidence of systematic discourse.

In reply to Bodunrin's statement that:

Had others not written down the sayings of Socrates and Buddha, we would today not regard them as philosophers, for their thoughts would have been lost in the mythological world of proverbs and pithy sayings.[2]

Oruka argues in reply that:

To exist as a philosopher it is not necessary that one's thoughts must progress or be available to the future generation. Sufficient for the existence of a philosopher is that one's contemporaries recognize one's philosophical ability and practice.[3]

Oruka may be correct here, but in order to satisfy skeptics it must be demonstrated that there was a general recognition that philosophical work was being done when it was, in fact, being done.

Oruka's aim is to defend the idea of philosophical sagacity, granted the strong criticism leveled against ethnophilosophy. In this connection, one might note the work of Hountondji.[4] But it appears that one of the problems facing contemporary African thought is the fact that the term "philosophy," though debated, has not been much examined as a term deriving its meaning from the historical context in which it is used. It is instructive to note that the term "philosophy" itself has witnessed important shifts in meaning throughout its existence. Consider the fact that "philosophy" in the sense of Aristotle is not "philosophy" in the sense of Quine. Newton was regarded as a natural philosopher, whereas Einstein was seen as a natural scientist. Yet even if one grants that there is a general agreement among those who embrace the European philosophical tradition on what philosophy is, there is no consensus as to what methods of investigation are proper to philosophy and what topics should be of special research interest. For example, philosophical research in the Anglo-American world does not share much in common with the methods of research in Continental philosophy. In fact, there is the general feeling in the Anglo-American world that Continental philosophy is not genuine philosophy, and those whose main interests are in that area of philosophy hold a similar disregard for Anglo-American analytic philosophy.

The questions concerning the definition of philosophy are even more problematic when the subject of African philosophy is raised. Some contemporary African philosophers argue that it is possible to express philosophical ideas without recourse to writing. But do African physicists, chemists or economists argue that it is possible to do research in their particular disciplines without recourse to writing? If not, should they? The following question is immediately pertinent:

what are the peculiar characteristics of philosophy in this context that set it off from other disciplines?

On the question concerning African philosophical thought, it seems that the structure of this thought has been determined to a great extent by the ideological systems of belief imposed on Africa by European scholarship of the precolonial and postcolonial eras. This ideology described African achievements as minimal, in the sense that the African had not developed any important civilization, African technological achievements were rudimentary, and African social structures were of questionable durability. These apparent shortcomings were explained in some quarters as due to biological deficiencies in those mental capacities necessary for creating organized and civilized society. The comments of European philosophers like Kant, Hegel and Hume on African culture are well known. It would therefore be instructive to consider some of the more important philosophical movements in Africa generated as a result of the historical confrontation of African and European ideologies.

Negritude: Recall the first responses of Negritude (a philosophical theory) which attempted to transform the supposed negative characteristics of African culture into virtues. Senghor, a key theorist of negritude, writes:

Ce qui caractérise le mieux le cosmos negro-africain, outre cette primauté donnée au réel existentiellement vécu, c'est son anthropocentrisme et, partant, son *humanisme*.[5] [See endnotes for translation.]

Senghor also writes approvingly of the Eurocentric thesis that the European mode of thinking is diametrically opposed to that of the African. Consider the following:

En effet, j'ai, souvent, pensé que l'Indo-Européen et le Negro-Africain étaient situés aux antipodes, c'est à dire aux extrèmes de l'objectivité et de la subjectivité, de la raison discursive et de la raison intuitive, du concept et de l'image, du calcul et de la passion.[6] [See endnotes for translation.]

Senghor even endorses the notion that African thought cannot distinguish between the rational, the irrational or the prerational.[7] What

Senghor probably implies here is that in traditional African cosmologies there is a fusion of language which refers to empirical objects and language which refers to metaphysical entities. But this is also the case in modern European thought which makes reservations not only for terms which have empirical reference but for purely metaphysical terms which refer to objects that enjoy a special kind of existence. For to assert that "S exists" in a concrete sense and at the same time to assert that S's existence is nonempirical is to risk, from a modern European conceptual standpoint, a conflation of the rational and the irrational. Reference is made here to terms like "spirit," "soul," "mind," etc. Senghor's error is to assume, like the colonial ethnologist, that the existence of metaphysical concepts in societies less technologically advanced than those of Europe implies that linguistic discourse in these societies does not recognize notions of rationality and irrationality.

But in the same vein, consider too the idea expressed by Aimé Césaire, one of the founders of the Negritude movement, that there was virtue in technological innocence, in response to the claims made by many European intellectuals that African technology was most rudimentary and was of little significance in human history. Aimé Césaire writes: "Hooray for those who have never invented anything. For those who have never explored anything. For those who have never tamed anything."[8] And Frantz Fanon made points about the moral guidance that the oppressed black could offer to a morally sterile Europe.[9] But the ideology of Negritude has been seriously questioned by theorists like C. A. Diop,[10] who sought to respond to the then current European ideology by arguing that civilization began in Africa (ancient Egypt), and that the ancient Egyptians (as opposed to the present hybrid population of African, Arab and others) were of African racial stock. From this point, Diop then went on to argue that the classical foundations of modern African civilization should be located in ancient Egypt, not in Greece, France or Britain. Diop's approach to the theory of African civilization is analogous in this regard to the way in which European scholars have structured the career of European civilization: modern European civilization is assumed to have its technical and intellectual roots in ancient Greek civilization; likewise, for Diop, modern African civilization should assume an intellectual and cultural legacy in the civilization of ancient Egypt.

The ideology of Negritude has also been critically examined by Paulin Hountondji who argues that the popular idea of a specific African essence and personality embracing a peculiar epistemology and sensibility is erroneous. Hountondji argues for a dynamic African culture subject to change according to the dictates of changing political and technological realities.[11]

Ethnophilosophy: European ideology claimed that African thought and belief systems could not be truly considered as containing anything of genuine intellectual merit. Lévy-Bruhl et al. argued that rationality and reflective thought are not synonymous with African thought. The terms which were coined to demonstrate the supposed qualitative gap that existed between European and African modes of thought and expression were "primitive" and "civilized." And it was implicitly understood that the term "civilized" was synonymous with the term "European." Thus the dualistic opposition of terms like "European art" and "primitive art," "European architecture" and "primitive architecture" in ordinary discourse succinctly summed up the relationship between Europe and Africa. Furthermore, humanity's most impressive intellectual achievements were supposed to have been either initiated in the European world or to have attained their most advanced expression there, even when not of European origin.

Thus European scholars generally believe that Greek philosophy, mathematics and science represent the first intellectual efforts of a rational humanity. According to this thesis, reason took its first step toward maturity in the works of the Greek scholars. But even when it is recognized that the pre-Greek civilizations should not be discounted in terms of their intellectual and technical contributions to world civilization, it is generally argued that these contributions were refined and developed by European scholars. Hence philosophy, mathematics and empirical science in their modern expression are regarded as the genuine products of the best minds of Europe.

But the ideological response to this thesis on the part of some African philosophers was to claim that traditional African thought should be judged on its own terms. Such a view of African philosophy has also been argued for by some European scholars. One witnesses here a shift from a general mood of condescension to one of empathy. Consider the following:

For in spite of our progressively close contact with African cultures over the past century, the West has chosen to see sorcery, savagery and obscenity—in short a caricature of man precisely in those moments of life when the African sets in motion his most genuine values. As strange as it may seem, no one in the West is astonished at the nuances and subtleties of Japanese or Chinese thought; but let an investigator document certain African ideas and he is considered a rash if not completely reckless "interpreter." It is almost as if the refinement of the mind were the heritage of one part of mankind and not another, unless one wants to assert by this strange value judgement that thought and reflection are necessarily expressed by a single category of signifiers.[12]

It is in the context of this postcolonial intellectual climate of thought that ethnophilosophy is nurtured. One witnesses, for example, Leo Apostel's comprehensive defense of the idea of African philosophy founded on principles of African thought as formulated by Tempels and Kagame.[13] As defined both by African and European scholars, ethnophilosophy serves the function of the subjective valorization of traditional African thought in contradistinction to colonial anthropological thought which engaged in a purportedly objective devalorization of the African's intellectual efforts. Genuine African philosophy consists, therefore, of descriptive comments on ethnological concepts of time, ethics, personhood and general cosmology. Yet questions persist as to whether the belief systems discussed may be regarded as genuinely philosophical. The contemporary debate on African philosophy is just about this.

To answer this criticism, H. Odera Oruka argues that a genuine African philosophy could be founded on the idea of "philosophical sagacity." According to Oruka, there is adequate evidence that in traditional African culture there were sages or thinkers who were original in their inquiries on diverse topics. Oruka argues that such thinkers go beyond mere sagacity and attain a philosophic capacity. As sages they are versed in the beliefs and wisdoms of their people. But as thinkers, they are rationally critical and they opt for or recommend only those aspects of the beliefs and wisdoms which satisfy their rational scrutiny. In this respect they are potentially or contemporarily in clash with the die-hard adherents of the prevailing common beliefs.[14]

In this connection, Oruka makes a distinction between two areas of traditional African thought: culture philosophy, and philosophical sagacity. The former, a synonym for ethnophilosophy, has been criticized on the grounds that it has not satisfied the appropriate criteria for philosophical literature: ethnophilosophy was not traditionally expressed in writing, nor is there any evidence that it contains thoughts of individual thinkers expressed in rational discourse. Oruka attempts to answer these queries by arguing that literate discourse may not be a necessary condition for philosophical discourse, the only necessary condition being that critical, evaluative and coherent thought be engaged in by individual thinkers. This intellectual activity Oruka defines as "philosophic sagacity."

It appears from an analysis of Oruka's ideas that his aim is to salvage the thesis that the foundations of a genuine African philosophy should be grounded in the belief systems of precolonial Africa. But it is the personal critical thought of individuals within the context of those belief systems that Oruka perceives as being sufficient for philosophical discourse. To argue, on the other hand, that a necessary condition for philosophical discourse be ideas expressed in writing would, according to Oruka, lead to the unacceptable conclusion that "to be authentically philosophical, Africans must be indifferent to traditional Africa."[15]

Oruka is correct, it seems to me, in arguing that a genuine African philosophy should not be indifferent to the traditional African belief systems and languages.[16] This caveat is directed against the ideas expressed by members of the African professional school of philosophy. Yet there may be some misunderstanding here. For those theorists toward whom Oruka directs his criticisms do argue that African philosophers should neither ignore the traditional belief systems of

Africa, nor overlook the possibilities of doing intellectual work in African languages.[17] For example, Bodunrin states the following:

The African philosopher cannot *deliberately* ignore the study of the traditional belief systems of his people. Philosophical problems arise out real life situations.[18]

Hountondji also argues that

there exists a considerable body of oral literature, esoteric or exoteric, the importance of which we are only beginning to suspect. We must have the patience to study it, analyse it, investigate its logic, its function and its merits.[19]

It also appears that Oruka's claim that philosophic sagacity is the movement in African philosophy best equipped to "give an all-acceptable decisive blow to the position of ethnophilosophy,"[20] is not fully defensible since it can be shown that philosophic sagacity as defined by Oruka himself would seem to be an attempt at mere revision of the principles of ethnophilosophy.

The thesis put forward by Oruka that philosophic sagacity differs from ethnophilosophy (culture philosophy) on the grounds that philosophic sagacity entails critical and personal thought, while ethnophilosophy does not, again cannot be sustained. Clearly, any belief system must have been first initiated by an individual thinker or a restricted group of thinkers before becoming a generally accepted belief system. And the novelty of such belief systems would certainly derive its characterization from the fact that they must have been founded on critical analyses of existing belief systems.[21]

Again, Oruka's thesis that philosophic sagacity has a stronger claim than professional philosophy or nationalist-ideological philosophy to helping in the development of a genuine African philosophy, on the basis that the latter are "generally suspected of smuggling Western techniques into African philosophy,"[22] is surely open to criticism. In the first place, it is unclear what Oruka implies by "Western techniques." It could be assumed that these techniques would include the practice of formulating ideas by means of writing, for Oruka argues himself that philosophic sagacity differs from the general western conception of philosophy only in that philosophic sagacity is not expressed in writing, but still demonstrates critical analyses and personal ideas—two main criteria of western philosophy. Yet it is difficult to see how any claim in favor of philosophic sagacity could be generally accepted unless there is proof available that it does exist. And what better method of proving the case for philosophic sagacity than committing its representative ideas to writing or some form of recording that could be made easily available to the general philosophic community? Recall one of Oruka's key points:

> To exist as a philosopher it is not necessary that one's thoughts must progress or be available to the future generation. . . . Lack of knowledge of one's or a people's philosophy is not proof of the non-existence of such a philosophy.[23]

This is true, but lack of knowledge of some phenomenon cannot also be regarded as proof of the existence of that phenomenon. The burden of proof rests with Oruka, for he must present proof of the existence of philosophic sagacity to interested parties. In fact, Oruka attempts to do so but begs the question in so doing when he demonstrates, *in writing*, that his own father was able to recall and transmit information purely by oral methods. There is no doubt that there were critical thinkers in precolonial Africa, but if the question of the viability of philosophic sagacity depends on their existence, then proof of their existence would be most readily achieved by employing the most effective modern techniques for so doing (i.e., by writing and electronic tape recording). The only way in which Oruka could answer this query, it seems, is to invite the skeptic to witness firsthand instances of philosophic sagacity (i.e., critical discussions of general philosophical concepts within an ethnic setting). Oruka could not consistently prove his claims by appeal to a modern philosophy journal: such a proof would be automatically a disproof.

I believe that Oruka's point is that a genuine modern African philosophy cannot subscribe to the professional philosophy model and remain "African philosophy." However, because of the inexorable advance of modern technology and the kinds of culture that accompany it, it is difficult to see how the question concerning the definition and direction of African philosophy could be answered without regard to modern ideas not necessarily generated within the context of traditional African society.[24] Yet there are grounds for concern on the part of those who believe that intellectual work in general and philosophy in particular in an African context should seek an African orientation. In order to examine this thesis, it is necessary to evaluate the role of professional philosophy as it is practiced in the African university environment.

Professional Philosophy: Professional philosophy as practiced in African universities is generally based on the Euro-American model. On these grounds it is understandable why some Western-trained African philosophers argue that written discourse and debate should be requirements for dialogue between members of the philosophical community. The point is also made that philosophical discourse within the African context should be carried on by means of discussions in journals, conferences, books, etc. On this basis, it is also argued that African philosophy is of recent origin. The situation is compounded by the fact that the modern universities in Africa are built on the model of the colonizers. Thus apart from a small number of modifications, the content of university curricula and the methodology of instruction are essentially the same for both ex-metropolis and ex-colony. In this context, the discipline of philosophy means European philosophy from Plato to Sartre or Wittgenstein. Bodunrin's response to criticisms of this approach is that there are no requirements that African university departments of mathematics, physics, etc., teach African physics, African mathematics. Thus there are no compelling reasons why philosophy in an African context should be specifically African.[25]

It would be useful, however, to argue that it is possible for the practice of physics in African universities to be carried out with an orientation different from that of, say, physics in English universities. Proof of the tenor of this point of view is had from the fact that the historical orientation of physics in France was somewhat different from that in the Anglo-Saxon world.[26] The reason for this is that each of the above-mentioned societies evolved its own particular program in physics to meet the goals of that society. The point is not that the laws of physics (or science) are different for different societies, but that the interpretation and application of these laws may be different. For example, a society that is seeking to establish a firm modern technological base may place more emphasis on the practical applications or modifications of well-tried scientific theories than on purely theoretical research. It is in this context that one may justifiably speak of an African mathematics, physics, philosophy or otherwise.

But it would be an error to assume that the official professional philosophy of the African university is without redeeming value. In fact, it is a properly re-directed professional philosophy that affords the best mechanism whereby the future path of African society could be adequately analyzed. Hountondji, for example, recognizes the possible illusions engendered by an excessive orientation of African philosophy toward the study of traditional belief systems. The same author makes the point of the stark contrast between the postcolonial political realities of Africa and the emphasis on the "ideological folklore" of ethnophilosophy.[27]

Perhaps one way of resolving the issue concerning the foundations of contemporary African philosophy would be to locate the historical roots of African thought in the literate ideas of ancient Egyptian thought and medieval Africa[28] in conjunction with philosophical analyses of traditional ethnic belief systems. It is somewhat surprising how some African philosophers accept the notion that the recording of ideas by writing is alien to African traditions. Wiredu, for example, states that "the African philosopher writing today has no long-standing tradition of written philosophy in his continent to draw upon."[29] Hountondji also makes the claim that African philosophy is in its developmental stages.[30] The reason for this attitude, it seems to me, is that the mental geography of contemporary people in Africa is determined not only by their ethnic ethos but also by the particular accidents and whims of European colonization. Thus while it is difficult for the colonized African intellectual to experience much psychological empathy with the scholarship of medieval African or classical Egypt, he or she is much at ease with Christian theology and Greek philosophy. Consider too the case of the contemporary Christianized African (Catholic or Protestant according to the dictates of colonial caprice), who identifies strongly with Hebrew folktales and mythology transcribed over two thousand years ago, but may have little interest in the ethos of a neighboring African ethnic group.

On the matter of literate tradition, one may add that literacy, even in the industrialized societies, is a recent phenomenon. Just a few hundred years ago, the intelligentsia in Europe was forced to communicate in Latin. Yet Hobbes, Descartes and others believed that the writings of the ancients were of particular importance to them, despite the fact that Greek and Latin were alien languages. And it should be recognized too that the writings of the ancient Greeks were first translated from Arabic, the language into which these writings were translated and debated during the heyday of Moorish scholarship. The point is that a history of ideas in Africa cannot ignore its literate ideas.

But these ideas belong to another era, and the African problematic is one of the here and now. The best compromise is for the contemporary African philosopher to be cognizant of the literate and non-literate traditions of Africa and to evaluate them in terms of their significance to the problems now being discussed by the contemporary African natural scientist, social scientist and writer. It seems to me that African philosophy would make much more useful contributions to modern Africa if it sought to help resolve questions raised by the African political scientists, economists, historians, technologists et al. The African philosopher is admirably placed to bridge the gap between the ideologies that justified the traditional social orders and those that accompany modern society in its various forms. The point is an important one since neither the contemporary African political scientist nor economist, for example, has really resolved the issues concerning the nature of the modern African state or economy. The ideas of the contemporary African researcher are usually identifiable as those of a metropolitan mentor.

Thus it is evident that the political and economic realities of contemporary Africa make it incumbent on professional philosophy to confront these realities, thereby assuming a direction different from that of orthodox professional philosophy. And its mode of confronting reality would be by means of the special empirical disciplines still not weaned from their metropolitan paradigms.

II

In this section, I want to elaborate on the last point made above. I begin by asking the pragmatic question about philosophy—what function can philosophy serve? In fact, there are good grounds for arguing that the ontological question about philosophy—what is philosophy?—does not fully explain philosophy, since it presupposes the belief that philosophical ideas should be examined only from the standpoint of their intellectual content. According to this viewpoint, philosophy is to be regarded as the embodiment of thought for its own sake.

But I am inclined to believe that it is the pragmatic question about philosophy that would lead to a fuller understanding of philosophy in general. If philosophy is understood as a human product with its particular historical emphases, then it will be possible to understand more fully the potential historical role of philosophy in Africa.

In orthodox Western philosophical circles, there is the general belief that philosophical writings should be regarded first as examples of the exercise of reason for its own sake, and that philosophy is properly concerned to examine eternal questions like: "what is truth?" "what is existence?" "what is the good?" etc. One often hears that philosophy begins in wonder, which is a kind of mystification of philosophy. To fully comprehend "philosophy" as an intellectual product, a *meta-analysis* of the activity of philosophy is necessary. Why, for example, is Plato generally regarded as a distinguished and famous philosopher and Protagoras not, or Kant (a rather obscure thinker), representative of the European mind at its best, rather than Wolfe? The reason for this, it seems to me, is that the societies in which these thinkers lived derived some pragmatic value (psychological or material) from accepting the ideas expressed by Plato rather than Protagoras, Kant rather than Wolfe. Philosophical thought, like any human product, derives its value according to its perceived usefulness. In this regard, one can map the career of philosophy in the West.

Can we define philosophy, therefore, as any set of ideas which seeks to construct an ontology appropriate for a given age or era? A received philosophy may be defined, in the main, as any set of ideas that seeks to explain the world in terms coherent, understandable and empathetic to interested parties, groups or classes in society. Skepticism, criticism, probing epistemological questions, the hallmarks of philosophy, are merely tools employed by those interested in replacing one ontology or worldview with another, or defending a received ontology from the criticisms of others. In Western thought, for example, Hume's strictures against orthodox metaphysics were not without motive. And Marx is still quite unpopular in the West since his writings are not perceived as being in the interests of the intellectually and economically dominant classes there.

When a received philosophy loses its appeal it should be regarded in the history of thought as the truth of an age—an ideology. Of course, this is not to deny that individual philosophers may be genuinely and personally concerned to explain the world as it appears to them. But individual versions of truth are rejected or gain in popularity in terms of their being truths for or against a given worldview. Witness, therefore, the construction of European philosophy from Plato to Quine, with negative ratings for thinkers generally regarded as controversial like Marx. It would appear, then, that Western philosophy as a whole is in reality a construction, a device which served and serves practical social needs. Philosophy in the West first sought to offer a general intellectual support for societies greatly influenced both by Greek thought and Christian doctrine. A happy conciliation between economic interests and technological pursuits led to the final validation of the usefulness of organized empirical knowledge. The result of this was the supersession of philosophy by empirical science as a means of understanding and exploiting nature. It is in this regard that two dominant postmedieval schools of thought, rationalism and empiricism, prepared the ground for the theoretical foundations of modern science. And the theory of modern scientific methodology was increasingly applied to all modes of human experience. Thus all facets of human behavior were subjected to scientific analysis.

The significance of the above for the career of professional philosophy in Africa is as follows: the function of philosophy in the West can be viewed as being instrumental in shaping the ideological and technological outlook of that particular civilization. The construction of European philosophy was indeed a self-conscious effort on the part of European thinkers to utilize the most complex products of human thought to fashion a self-interested civilization. Thus those African thinkers who are concerned to formulate an African philosophy might want to reflect on the fact that the shapers of articulate European thought sought little inspiration from the genuinely traditional European thought systems: those of the Gauls, the Vandals, the Celts, the Normans, the Visigoths, the Vikings, etc. Articulate European thought was founded rather on the sophisticated literate thought of ancient Greek thinkers whose ideas were borrowed, then analyzed for the needs of that civilization. But despite the fact that there is some doubt as to whether classical Greek thought could be properly recognized as European thought,[31] it nevertheless served as the foundations of medieval European thought. I assume too that the same kinds of claims could be made for the historical careers of the thought systems of Asian civilization.

Given the above analysis of the career of European philosophy, the question as to the specific causes of the particular development of contemporary European philosophy necessarily arises.

Three trends are noticeable in contemporary European thought: (1) orthodox philosophical analysis concerned with the analysis of concepts and their meanings. Philosophical analysis is not generally expected to add to the existing fund of knowledge, or to offer prescriptions as to ethical conduct. This evolutionary end result of philosophy is found more in the Anglo-American universities than elsewhere. It is less so on the continent of Europe where philosophical movements like phenomenology and existentialism, with their more human concerns, are quite popular. (2) Marx's attempts to present human thought not as an end in itself, but as heuristic, aiding humanity in the struggle against nature, may be regarded as another evolutionary result of European thought. Thus one witnesses, from the Marxist viewpoint, all the special disciplines being influenced by Marx's philosophy. (3) One witnesses too the phenomenon of the special research disciplines, having broken away from philosophy, but inheriting at the same time theoretical assumptions derived from philosophical inquiry. How else could one explain the different schools of thought and paradigms in the special disciplines?

III

In light of the above, the theoreticians of philosophy in an African context must attempt to construct a modern African philosophy with the notion that its formulation would be geared toward helping in the development of a modern African civilization. Any analysis of the contemporary world demonstrates that the more successful civilizations are those which are the most technologically advanced.[32] Recall that humanity's confrontation with nature is mediated by the knowledge of the workings of nature, including itself, and by the level of sophistication of the tools employed in the exploitation of nature. It is also clear that a knowledge of the workings of nature determines the kinds of technology which human beings fashion for their own usage. Since knowledge about the natural world is not acquired instinctually, societies, in general, provide training centers in which instruction on the knowledge of the world is passed on to their members, so that this instruction is eventually employed in the maintenance of the social order.

It is instructive to point out that this educational instruction may be divided into two parts: firstly, knowledge of the natural world and of the applications of different forms of technology to this world, and secondly, instruction in the relevant value judgements and cultural assumptions necessary for the maintenance of the society in question. Again, historical research shows that a society's value judgements are ultimately determined by knowledge of the natural world and the application of this knowledge to forms of technology.

Thus philosophy in the African context must pay attention to the above observation. Its function should be to help in the imparting of knowledge of the natural and social world and to assist in the constant discussion of the optimal set of value judgements and cultural assumptions that social individuals must make to take the fullest advantage of the sum of scientific knowledge available.

An examination of the thought systems of the technologically advanced societies demonstrates that the educational instruction of those members of society necessary for its functioning has been taken over by disciplines that may be regarded as the intellectual descendants of philosophy: the natural sciences and the social sciences. Philosophy proper is relegated, for the most part, to the history of ideas, mainly in the form of textual analyses of the original writings of philosophers, to studies in the methodology of the special sciences, to the analysis of concepts and terms and to subjective reflections on the human condition. Yet the important point to recognize is that modern Western society does not look to philosophy for solutions to technological and social problems. Philosophical debates, if they are of any importance at all, are carried on within the special disciplines themselves, but for purposes and orientations peculiar to given social and political contexts.

It would be an error, therefore, for the philosopher in the African context to assume that philosophy as it is practiced in the Western world should serve as a model for the practice of philosophy. A useful approach, it seems, would be to regard philosophical activity as engaging in theoretical analysis of issues and ideas of practical concern. But in modern society it is the social and natural sciences that discuss ideas and issues relevant to practical concerns. Thus the practice of philosophy in the African context should be concerned first with the analysis of the methodology and content of the social sciences (i.e., history, economics, anthropology, political science, etc.), for it is the methodology of research of a given discipline that determines the orientation of research in that discipline and the kinds of solutions to problems ultimately proposed. Furthermore, analysis of the methodology of the sciences of human behavior would be constantly alert to the notion that the modes and objects of human thought are potentially value-laden. And this is indeed the case with the existent research programs in African universities, inherited as they are from the colonial period.

In this connection, it would also be incumbent on the African philosophers to raise questions concerning the epistemological basis for the analysis of human behavior in terms of the special disciplines.

In other words, is it possible, for example, to fully understand people as economic beings without paying attention to the total sociological person? Or can one fully understand political institutions without regard for the study of history, etc? These theoretical questions are of practical concern in matters relating to the formulation of university curricula, and critically important for the training of an adequate work force. In these critical times, the African philosopher's contributions to African development in the areas of economic theory, political theory, historiography, anthropology, and the other sciences of human behavior should be of significance. For by the very nature of the enterprise, most of which consists of critical analysis, the philosopher is less paradigm-bound than colleagues in the social sciences, more inclined to see how the particular fits into the universal—to see the whole picture. As an historical note, it is no accident that Marx, one of the great theoreticians of the social sciences, was trained in philosophy.

Again, the practice of philosophy in the African context should be strongly concerned with the study of the methodology and applications of the natural sciences and their relationships to the social sciences. And the point to be recognized is that despite the evident universality of the methodology of the natural sciences, it is still instructive to recognize that the pursuit of empirical science is not just simply a matter of performing experiments: the methodology of scientific research is founded on a number of important theoretical assumptions which, if recognized by the researcher, could lead to investigative approaches that are more creative, hence potentially more fruitful. In this regard, it is instructive to consider the importance of the theoretical analysis of the foundations of empirical science as a possible encouragement for research. The role of theoretical analysis in this context, as a possible aid to the development of scientific research in Africa, is evident. Economic development and technological development usually proceed simultaneously.

Yet the above discussion and proposals require some comment about the modes whereby such ideas may be implemented. It has been argued above that the history of ideas in Europe may be understood as being partially determined by the material and psychological needs of that society. It follows, therefore, that there are no commanding reasons why the structure and orientation of knowledge in African society should correspond exactly to those of ex-metropolitan Europe. In this connection, and in the light of what has been discussed, a review of the academic status of philosophy in African universities is in order.

It would be useful, for example, if the methodological issue concerning the different disciplines was discussed from within the context of the disciplines themselves. Thus the philosophy of the social sciences would be pursued from within the confines of the various social sciences. The same requirement holds for theoretical discussions on the natural sciences. One might also consider the hypothesis that discussions of the methodological issues in the special areas of knowledge could be more competently carried out by those who have had extensive training in the relevant disciplines. Given the above, I recommend that further research in theoretical and methodological issues beyond the most advanced degree hitherto granted in African universities should be required in order to generate adequate competence in the area of philosophical analysis.[33] Thus the researcher concerned to examine theoretical issues in, say, applied physics would be trained to the level of physicists practicing in that area and beyond. Philosophers concerned to examine the theory and content of traditional African thought would have had training in linguistics and cognate disciplines. I assume that the results of this remodeling of the received systems of instruction in the African context would do much to shape modern modes of inquiry to fit African realities and to encourage creativity in research.

IV

Although a number of issues have been discussed above, this essay's main purpose is to discuss a possible methodology for a modern African philosophy. It is generally agreed that there is some sensed intellectual discomfort at the idea of philosophy in contemporary Africa being a replica of philosophy as practiced in the ex-metropolis. The genesis of the concepts of "traditional African philosophy" and "philosophic sagacity" derives from this issue. But I argued above that there are questions as to how traditional African philosophy and philosophic sagacity fit into the new scheme of things in contemporary Africa. I believe that intellectual effort in the African context should be strongly geared to the training of personnel in modern techniques of natural and social scientific inquiry, appropriate for application in the ongoing transformation of society. Clearly, those beliefs and theoretical ideas characterizing traditional African thought systems which are proven vital for contemporary development should be nurtured and incorporated into the social philosophies and technological orientation of modern Africa. In this context research into traditional African thought systems has an important role to play.

But if the pursuit of research in traditional African thought is to serve the narrow purpose of proving to others that "Africans knew how to think consistently before colonial times," and that "African world-views were not inherently irrational," then it is difficult to see how this debate could be of any great moment in the current transformations taking place in African society. Purely academic debates among minorities of university scholars can perhaps be afforded in the universities of the Euro-American world, but there is some doubt as to the viability of similar kinds of debates in African universities.

A cursory study of any African language demonstrates that consistency and coherence of expression should be taken for granted. How else could there be intralinguistic communication within a given society, unless consistency and coherence were assumed on the part of its members?[34] It seems to me that the old colonial ideology that dichotomized the worlds of Europe and Africa as those of reason and unreason is obsolete. The problem of Africa today is that of adapting modern techniques and modes of knowing to societies being transformed from those in which the most important factors of production were human beings themselves, to those in which the machine constitutes the major factor of production. Of course, the traditional beliefs concomitant with the traditional society are giving way to new beliefs. And the important question arises as to what should be the nature of the new beliefs.

A study of the historical development of European and Asian societies demonstrates that important ideological debates and subsequent transformations of social orders and accompanying modes of thought were witnessed in Europe and those parts of Asia now in the age of modern technology. Research will also show that a similar function is demanded of those who, in the African context, engage in intellectual pursuits.

V

The discussion in this paper was engendered by the question raised by Oruka concerning the status of African philosophy. Oruka's thesis that philosophic sagacity should replace ethnophilosophy as a legitimate representative of the foundations of African thought was criticized on the grounds that the assumed distinction between ethnophilosophy and philosophic sagacity was not supportable. It was also argued that if the definition of philosophy as proposed by Oruka were accepted (i.e., philosophy as consistent and coherent), though unwritten thought, then there may be some problem in demonstrating this claim without recourse to some publicly recognized medium of recording, like writing. But then this would contradict the thesis that philosophical ideas need not be expressed in writing to be regarded as philosophy. It was also mentioned that if the orthodox definition of philosophy as critical, written thought were accepted, then there was an evident philosophical tradition in Africa: the recorded philosophical ideas of the ancient Egyptians and scholars of medieval Africa.

Oruka was concerned to show that contemporary African philosophers would be ill-advised to ignore the belief systems of traditional Africa in their quests to establish a viable African philosophy. His paper also gives the impression that Oruka regards philosophy as a discipline which ought to be pursued for its own sake.[35] Curiously enough, Oruka does not recognize that this definition of philosophy is the modern Euro-American definition of philosophy, especially in Anglo-American circles. It was pointed out above that philosophy has often served in an ideological capacity in the course of history. Given the fact that in recent times, the ideological function of philosophy has been usurped by the special disciplines, philosophy, in the West, is not regarded as a discipline of much practical importance. It has become essentially an intellectual ode to Western civilization.

In this paper, a different path and function was proposed for philosophy in an African context. It was argued above that philosophy in contemporary Africa should be concerned not only with theoretical analysis, but also with its practical application. Thus philosophy has an important role to play in the debate concerning solutions to the social and technical problems faced by societies undergoing social transformation. It was also pointed out that the question of the role of traditional African thought systems in contemporary African philosophy is meaningful mainly in this context. This paper attempts to promote, therefore, the following conception of philosophy in the African context: a dynamic philosophy in the vanguard of each of the research disciplines, committed to the formulation of new or modified concepts and modes of knowing appropriate for social and technological development.

NOTES

1. H. Odera Oruka, "Sagacity in African Philosophy," *International Philosophical Quarterly* (Winter, 1983), pp. 383–93. [Also included in this volume.]
2. Ibid.
3. Ibid.
4. Paulin Hountondji, *African Philosophy* (Bloomington: Indiana University Press, 1983).
5. Leopold Senghor, "Preface," in Alassane N'daw, *La Pensée Africaine* (Dakar: Nouvelles Editions Africaines, 1983), p. 27.

    "What characterizes best the universe of the Negro African, besides the primacy granted to the subjective experience of the real is his anthropocentrism and consequently his *humanism*." (Author's translation.)

6. Leopold Senghor, *Liberté 3* (Paris: Editions du Seuil, 1977), p. 148.

    "In fact, I have often thought that the Indo-European and Negro-African were situated at the extremes of objectivity and subjectivity, of discursive reason and intuitive reason, of thinking in concepts and thinking in images, of reflective thought and emotional thought." (Author's translation.)

7. Ibid., p. 68.
8. Aimé Césaire, *Cahier d'un Retour au Pays Natal* (Paris: *Présence Africaine*, 1956), pp. 71–72.
9. Frantz Fanon, *Wretched of the Earth* (New York: Grove Press, 1963), pp. 311–16.
10. C. A. Diop, *Nations négres et culture* (Paris: *Présence Africaine*, 1954).
11. Hountondji, *African Philosophy*, pp. 160–64.

12. Dominique Zahan, *The Religion, Spirituality and Thought of Traditional Africa* (Chicago: University of Chicago Press, 1970), p. 3.
13. L. Apostel, *African Philosophy: Myth or Reality* (Belgium: E. Story-Scientia, 1981).
14. Oruka, "Sagacity in African Philosophy," p. 386.
15. Ibid. p. 392.
16. Ibid.
17. Hountondji, *African Philosophy*, p. 168.
18. P. O. Bodunrin, "The Question of African Philosophy," *Philosophy* 56 (1981), p. 173. [Also included in this volume.]
19. Hountondji, *African Philosophy*, p. 178.
20. Oruka, "Sagacity in African Philosophy," p. 384.
21. The belief systems of the majority of precolonial African societies were formulated for societies that were predominantly agricultural, i.e., societies that were essentially two steps away from industrial society. Thus their initial formulations must have raised questions about previous belief systems.
22. Oruka, "Sagacity in African Philosophy," p. 384.
23. Ibid., p. 391.
24. The case discussed here is analogous to the progress made in the field of medicine as practiced in contemporary Africa; modern techniques are used, but traditional methods are also examined for their effectiveness or noneffectiveness from the standpoint of modern science.
25. Bodunrin, "The Question of African Philosophy," p. 165.
26. Consider the following observations: "The concept of a 'French genius' distinct from an 'English genius' was presented by the distinguished French historian of science Pierre Duhem, who argued the case for national styles in physics. Duhem observed British physicists continually having recourse to mechanical models and wondered whether these had been inspired by the mills and factories of Victorian Britain. Duhem writes, 'We thought we were entering the tranquil and neatly-ordered abode of reason but we found ourselves in a factory.' If the model was not normally a crude one of cogwheels and pulleys, it might be marbles or billiard balls to represent atoms or pieces of elastic to represent lines of force. However, the French or German physicist (and Duhem put them together) would see a field of force in terms of a mathematical equation. The basic difference of approach was most strikingly illustrated in physics." In Maurice Crosland, *The Emergence of Science in Western Europe* (New York: Science History Publications, 1976), p. 9.
27. Hountondji, *African Philosophy*, p. 53.
28. Available references for the philosophical thought of the ancient Egyptians are as follows: Walter Scott, *Hermetica* (Oxford: Clarendon Press, 1924); G. R. S. Mead, *Thrice Greatest Hermes* (London: John Watkins, 1949); A. J. Festugiere and A. D. Nock, eds., *Corpus Hermeticum*, 4 vols. (Paris, 1945–

54). Students of literate medieval African thought could consider the following: Sadi, *Tarikh es Soudan*; Kati, *el Fettach*; Ahmed Baba, *Tekmilet ed dibadje*.

29. Kwasi Wiredu, *Philosophy and an African Culture*, (Cambridge: Cambridge University Press, 1980), p. 46.

30. Hountondji, *African Philosophy*, p. 170 et seq.

31. Recall that the Greeks had no notion of Greece being a part of Europe. Furthermore, a sober anthropological analysis of the Greek physical type and Greek culture both ancient and modern would favor describing Greek civilization as not really European. An African visitor to Greece would immediately recognize that Greek cuisine, music, racial type and general culture are not what one would expect of Europeans. If Greek culture (ancient and modern) is not truly European, then what is it? Middle Eastern? Asiatic? Afro-Asiatic? If any of these, then what should one make of the received doctrine that Western thought began with the Greeks?

32. The idea expressed here has been vigorously defended by Marcien Towa in *Essai sur la problématique philosophique dans L'Afrique actuelle* (Yaoundé: Editions Clé, 1971). Towa argues that it is only by assimilating and acquiring the scientific techniques of the European world that African society could make material progress, a necessity for the gaining of true independence.

33. The mode of implementation of this new program is subject to discussion. But the idea is a useful one. One might consider as a working model the practice in Western medical schools of requiring that further research of two years beyond training in medical school be engaged in before competence in psychiatry be achieved. Consider too the practice in some European countries of offering more than one type of the most advanced degree. French universities, for example, offer three kinds of doctorates each requiring different amounts of research.

34. It would seem to me that any language that contains terms for conjunctions, negation and disjunction, equality and inequality, and prepositions denoting spatial positions already contains the essentials for consistent logical thought. Soussou is one of the urban languages of West Africa and a cursory examination of its basic structure reveals a language equipped to formulate consistent propositions and to pose questions and answers, a necessary requirement for scientific inquiry. For example, the term "mufera" suggests an explanatory "why," while "nba" introduces an explanation. Furthermore "xa . . . nba" corresponds to "if . . . then," or "either . . . or," constructions that are crucial for scientific and logical explanation. The answer to the Lévy-Bruhls is not to demonstrate that traditional African thought contains cosmological concepts, but to show that the spoken language in question is founded on a set of syntactical rules that can support complex empirical analysis. The appropriate methodology should proceed along the lines of the above.

35. Oruka, "Sagacity in African Philosophy," p. 391.

OYEKA OWOMOYELA

AFRICA AND THE IMPERATIVE OF PHILOSOPHY: A SKEPTICAL CONSIDERATION

The African Studies Association in 1984 gave Paulin Hountondji a share in the Melville Herskovits award for the most
significant Africanist publication for the previous year. The selection
of Hountondji's book, *African Philosophy: Myth and Reality* (1983),
suggests, logically, that the association believes the book to be a
significant contribution to African Studies. One might go even a step
further and conclude that it indicates the association's concurrence
with the main premises and the general philosophical orientation of
the author's arguments. This paper outlines some serious questions
Hountondji and his fellow philosophers raise about what one's attitude
to the African past should be and what criteria should dictate the
course of development on the African continent.

Hountondji is perhaps the best known of the "professional philosophers." [1] As one would expect, each of the philosophers perceives the
issues that will be raised in this discussion from a different perspective, even when they agree broadly on the critique of ethnophilosophy; [2] Hountondji has nevertheless emerged as the most articulate and
representative in this regard, to the extent that his book has earned the
title, "the 'bible' of anti-ethnophilosophers" (Mudimbe, 1985: 199).
The focus of this essay will accordingly be on this important work,
with occasional references, of course, to those of others, in particular
the Ghanaian Kwasi Wiredu. This strategy has the attraction of
straddling the divide between Anglophone and Francophone manifestations of the new philosophical attitudes.

To best understand what grounds there might be for objections to certain of the philosophers' positions, it is expedient that one isolate the several targets of their disparagement. Chief of these is ethnophilosophy, which Hountondji (1983: 34) defines as "an ethnological work with philosophical pretensions." This includes the works of all those who like Placide Tempels, Alexis Kagame, John Mbiti, and other ethnologists have attempted to articulate African philosophies or systems of thought. Another target is African cultures or traditions themselves, as distinct from whatever the ethnophilosophers or ethnologists might correctly or mistakenly have made of them. A third is what the philosophers see as the recidivism inherent in the attraction of some Africans to certain essential or residual traditional habits and a corresponding refusal on their part to Europeanize. The last is the discipline of African Studies, including its practitioners, which the philosophers represent as an unfortunate (to say the least) refusal to join, as Wiredu (1984: 153–54) puts it, in the general march toward development.

THE CASE AGAINST ETHNOPHILOSOPHY

Hountondji and other opponents of ethnophilosophy place the responsibility for its propagation on Placide Tempels. It was the Belgian cleric who, in his book *Bantu Philosophy* (1969), blazed the trail for Kagame, Mbiti, and others toward the synthesizing of coherent philosophies from African traditions. For Hountondji and company what those scholars proffer as African philosophy is flawed in the mode of its supposed existence and in the manner of its articulation. Hountondji (1983: 56) complains: "More than once Tempels emphasizes that this philosophy is experienced but not thought and that its practitioners are, at best, only dimly conscious of it." The implication, Hountondji remarks, is that because the African is unaware of his philosophy he cannot very well express it and hence must look to the interpretive mediation of foreigners like Tempels (and their African followers, of course). He adds (1983: 57) that the image of the African as the unconscious, intuitive subscriber to a philosophy of which he is unaware makes him, in Eboussi Boulaga's words, the "Monsieur Jourdain of philosophy."

Another objection of the philosophers to ethnophilosophy derives from its formulators' suggestion (inherent in the description of its various examples) that it is collectively held, or unanimist. Such formulations as "Bantu Philosophy," "African Philosophy," "*La philosophie bantou-rwandaise*," and so forth suggest that all Bantu, all Africans, and all Rwandans espouse the respective philosophies attributed to them. The suggestion, says Hountondji (1983: 151), is an illusion consistent with the vision of anthropologists and ethnologists alike of "African village unanimity" and with their hankering for the "unique spectacle of a society without conflict, division or dissonance." True philosophy, Hountondji (1983: 179) asserts, results from individual intellectual engagement with the universe of experience, is pluralistic, and is subject to an "irreducible polysemy of discourse."

THE CASE AGAINST AFRICAN CULTURES

Quite apart from the disciplinary dispute about what is and what is not philosophy and what its proper mode of existence and the proper manner of its elaboration are or should be, Hountondji and the philosophers raise much larger questions. One concerns the adequacy of traditional African cultures. Whereas the case against ethnophilosophy could be construed as being against the misguided concoctions of foreigners and their African cohorts, the philosophers' pronouncements leave one with the certainty that the real object of their displeasure is African tradition and not what ethnophilosophers make of it.[3]

The philosophers' critique of African ways derives from a comparative evaluation of them, with modern European (or Western) ways as the norm. This is clearly evident in Wiredu's (1980: 1) description of the African way of life. He suggests two types of anachronism—the existence of "habits of thought and practice [that are] anachronistic within the development of a given society," and the anachronism of an entire society within the context of the whole world, resulting from the prevalence in the society of outmoded practices. Every society, he allows, is anachronistic to some degree. As far as Africa is concerned, however, he states: "the implications of calling a society 'underdeveloped', or in the suppositious synonym 'developing', is that it suffers from this malady in both ways." The same conviction explains Marcien Towa's sentiment, which Hountondji (1983: 172) echoes, that Africans must engage in " 'revolutionary iconoclasm', a 'destruction of traditional idols' which will enable us to 'welcome and assimilate the spirit of Europe. . . .' "

The first defect of traditional African ways, as the philosophers perceive them, is the trait they have in common with ethnophilosophy. That trait is authoritarianism. In contrasting ethnophilosophy with genuine philosophy, Hountondji (1983: 83–84) explains that while true philosophy is a debate, a "pluralistic discourse, in which different interlocutors question one another within a generation or from one generation to another," the false discipline of ethnophilosophy, in this case as revealed by Ogotemmeli through Griaule[4] (but certainly also by Tempels and company), "aspires to confer a wisdom that is eternal, intangible, a closed system sprung from the depths of time and admitting of no discussion."

While the philosopher in this instance directs his barb at ethnophilosophy, further statements of his and by his colleagues reveal that their criticism applies as well to traditional African approaches to an understanding of the universe. For example, Wiredu (1980: 4) comments as follows on the "authoritarian odour" that suffuses African cultures: "Our social arrangements are shot through and through with the principle of unquestioning obedience to our superiors, which often meant elders. Hardly any premium was placed on curiosity in those of tender age, or independence of thought in those of more considerable years." For illustration he cites the abundance of proverbs in traditional African cultures which serve as immutable authority and the lack of other proverbs that encourage "originality and independence of thought." Elsewhere (Wiredu, 1984: 157), while conceding that certain African (specifically Akan) concepts of being are "more imaginative than those of some Western philosophers," he posits an essential difference between African and Western attitudes to their ontologies. That difference, he says, "is that the Western philosopher tries to argue for his thesis, clarifying his meaning and answering objections, known or anticipated; whereas the transmitter of folk conceptions merely says: 'This is what our ancestors said.' " The statement echoes Hountondji's (1983: 170) derision of the "official ideologue" who despite the confusion on the continent contents himself with the congratulatory declaration, "Alleluia, our ancestors have thought!"[5]

Another failing the philosophers impute to traditional African cultures is their innocence of the scientific spirit, a liability that forms the nucleus of a universe of ills. As they explain, closely tied to the lack of science is the lack of literacy, one explaining the other. Hountondji (1983: 99) describes the relationship as follows:

The first precondition for a history of philosophy, the first precondition for philosophy as history, is . . . the existence of science as an organized material practice reflected in discourse. But one must go even further: the chief requirement of science itself is writing. It is difficult to imagine a scientific civilization that is not based on writing, difficult to imagine a scientific tradition in a society in which knowledge can be transmitted orally.

Similarly, Wiredu (1984: 151) says, "If a culture is both non-scientific and non-literate, then in some important respects it may be said to be backward in a rather deep sense."

Hountondji (1983: 103–4) offers some justification for valorizing writing at the expense of orality: "Oral tradition favors consolidation of knowledge into dogmatic, intangible systems, whereas archival transmission promotes better possibility of a critique of knowledge between individuals and from one generation to another." He goes on to argue that because those who must transmit knowledge orally are always fearful of forgetting, they are forced to "hoard their memories jealously, to recall them constantly, to repeat them continually, accumulating and heaping them up in a global wisdom, simultaneously present, always ready to be applied, perpetually available." A mind preoccupied with preserving knowledge is incapable of criticizing it, he continues; on the other hand, the memory that is liberated by archival storage can forget its acquisitions, provisionally question or reject them, knowing that it can always retrieve them whenever necessary. "By guaranteeing a permanent record, archives make actual memory superfluous and give full rein to the boldness of the mind," he concludes.

Pursuing the case for science, Wiredu (1980: 12–13) attributes certain unfortunate consequences to the persistence in African societies of "culturally ingrained attitudes" and a refusal to adopt logical, mathematical, analytical, experimental, or in other words, scientific, procedures where necessary. The retrograde attitudes, he suggests, explain "the weaknesses of traditional technology, warfare, architecture, medicine," and other ills that bedevil traditional life. Specifically, he cites automobile mechanics who would shun available precision instruments and rely on their intuition when tuning modern engines. In the realm of medicine he points to the influence of Africans' illogical, spiritistic conception of the universe, whereby the African abandons sober inquiry into the causes of diseases of mind and body and pursues instead "stories of malevolent witchcraft and necromancy." Moreover, he continues, many people, especially children, die from supposedly curative prescriptions that, however, have no scientific recommendation. For these reasons, he remarks, "any inclination to glorify the unanalytical cast of mind is not just retrograde; it is tragic."

Another example of irrational Africanism, according to Wiredu (1984: 154), is the prevalent practice (even among the educated) of pouring libations to spirits "in the belief that in this kind of way they can achieve development without losing their Africanness." His opprobrium, however, embraces more than the pouring of libations; it encompasses funerary rites in general, as witness his (1984: 155–56) characterization of funerals in Ghana:

When a person dies there has first to be a burial ceremony on the third day; then on the eighth day there is a funeral celebration at which customary rites are performed; then forty days afterwards there is a fortieth day celebration (*adaduanan*). Strictly that is not the end. There are such occasions as the eightieth day and first anniversary celebrations. All these involve large alcohol-quaffing gatherings.

THE CASE AGAINST RECIDIVISM

Already evident is the philosophers' conviction that Africans must discard their traditional ways in favor of modern European (or Western) ways in the name of development. Indeed, development is the powerful end that orients all their arguments, the end they believe that continued adherence to traditional ways will render unattainable. Thus, the case for the development of a valid African philosophy (in place of the impostor ethnophilosophy) is that philosophy makes science possible (Hountondji, 1983: 68), and science in turn makes development possible. As Wiredu (1980: 32) notes: "for my part, I take science to be the crucial factor in the transition from the traditional to the modern world." In another context Wiredu (1984: 153–54) writes:

Modernization is the application of the results of modern science for the improvement of the conditions of human life. It is only the more visible side of development; it is the side that is more associated with the use of advanced technology and novel techniques in various areas of life such as agriculture, health, education and recreation.

Observing that "the quest for development, then, should be viewed as a continuing world-historical process in which all peoples, Western and non-Western alike, are engaged," he advises Africans not to view modernization as a foreign invasion but as a general march toward development that involves all humankind but has hitherto left them behind.

The mere fact that Europeans were able to colonize Africa, according to the philosophers, is evidence enough of the superiority of Europeanism over Africanism. Towa's recommendation that Africans welcome and assimilate the spirit of Europe, we might recall, is that in doing so they might absorb "the secret of her power and of her victory over us." Quoting Towa, Hountondji (1983: 172) further counsels Africans about the attitude they must adopt toward their past: "regard it cooly, critically, without complacency or self-satisfaction . . . [and] try to discover not our unrecognized greatness or nobility but the secret of our defeat by the West." Along the same lines Wiredu (1980: 61) asserts that "the African, who asks himself why it came about that everywhere on his continent other peoples were able so easily to put his people in bondage, is bound to realize that the trouble lies not in our biology but in certain aspects of our culture . . . : the lack of a developed scientific method, broadly speaking."

Another philosopher, the Nigerian Peter Bodunrin (1984: 7), criticizes those he describes as "political thinkers" for romanticizing the African past: "certainly not everything about our past was glorious. . . . A way of life which made it possible for our ancestors to be subjugated by a handful of Europeans cannot be described as totally glorious."

THE CASE AGAINST AFRICAN STUDIES AND STUDENTS OF AFRICA

The philosopher's opinion of the quality of African traditional thought inevitably colors his opinion of studies and students of that subject. In this regard one should emphasize a significant difference between Hountondji and some of his colleagues. Peter Bodunrin (1984: 14), for example, believes that the African philosopher should acquaint himself with traditional beliefs as a possible quarry for ideas to improve impoverished Western philosophy. Also, Wiredu (1980: 16) interprets the venality rampant on the continent as evidence of the confusion of cultural influences that plague the modern African. He suggests that the cure might be a better familiarity with the traditional part of the cultural mix such that "clarity could begin at home." Similarly, Lancinay Keita (1984: 72) refers to the "cultural amnesia of the contemporary African whose knowledge of history and philosophy is limited to European thought systems." He blames the unfortunate situation on long centuries of the slave trade, colonialism, and the concomitant indoctrination of Africans. For Hountondji, however, the study of what he describes (1983: 67) as "so-called African subjects," rather than the universal "problematic" of philosophy, amounts to "folklorism," and, "a sort of collective cultural exhibitionism which compels the 'Third World' intellectual to 'defend and illustrate' the peculiarities of his tradition for the benefit of the Western public." The deceptive appearance of universal dialogue, he continues, only "encourages the worst kind of cultural particularism," because the particularities are only a delusion, and because the intellectuals who propagate them are impostors claiming to speak for their people, whereas the people are not even aware of the intellectuals' activities.

While Hountondji expresses opposition to the study of African traditional thought, he (Hountondji, 1983: 52) at the same time insists on the philosopher's freedom to study non-African ideas and complains about criticisms that might limit that freedom:

Each and every African philosopher now feels duty-bound to reconstruct the thought of his forefathers, the collective *Weltanschauung* of his people. To do so, he feels obliged to make himself an ethnological expert on African customs. Anything he may produce in another vein, say on Plato or Marx, Confucius or Mao Tse-tung, or in any general philosophical area unconnected with Africa, he regards as a sort of parenthesis in his thought, of which he must feel ashamed.

If he does not show shame, Hountondji adds, the critics pounce on him and drag him back "to the straight and narrow path . . . of Africanism."

Hountondji (1983: 80) moreover attributes some devious (even sinister) motives to Africanists, both native and foreign. To the extent that these ethnophilosophers define African habits of the heart and mind as distinct from the European (and, therefore, in the philosophers' opinion as inferior), their goal, he says, is actually the perpetuation of the African's status as "the 'absolute other' of the 'civilized' man." Criticizing Aimé Césaire's paean to African nontechnicality, Hountondji (1983: 159) further alleges "a complicity between Third World nationalists and 'progressive' Western anthropologists. For years they will assist each other, the former using the latter in support of their cultural claims, the latter using the former to buttress their pluralistic thesis." Bronislaw Malinowski and Melville Herskovits are his prime example of " 'progressive' Western anthropologists," while Césaire and Senghor exemplify "Third World nationalists." He seemingly approves of Césaire's brand of nationalism because it aims at political liberation. He (Hountondji, 1983: 159) lambastes Senghor's cultural nationalism, on the other hand: "This garrulous negrism . . . works as an alibi for evading the political problem of national liberation. Hypertrophy of cultural nationalism generally serves to compensate for the hypotrophy of political commitment."

Hountondji's low opinion of African Studies as a discipline has already surfaced in his description of African students of the African past as cultural exhibitionists playing to the European gallery. He charges (1983: 52) that what Europe expects of Africans is that "we should offer her our civilization as showpieces and alienate ourselves in a fictitious dialogue with her, over the heads of our people." That, he asserts, is the ulterior motive behind invitations that we establish African Studies and preserve our cultural authenticity. "We forget too easily," he chides, "that African Studies were invented by Europe and that the ethnographic sciences are an integral part of the heritage of Europe, amounting to no more than a passing episode in the theoretical tradition of the Western peoples."

By now it should be clear that the philosophers' strictures, certainly Hountondji's, apply not only to ethnophilosophy as a false discipline, but really to significant (perhaps even essential) aspects of African cultures, aspects the philosophers would have Africans abandon in order to "welcome and assimilate the spirit of Europe." Thus, not only ethnophilosophy but also African Studies and the recidivism it supposedly encourages are included in the pejorative description (Hountondji, 1983: 171) as "a powerful means of mystification in the hands of all who have a vested interest in discouraging intellectual initiative because it prompts not living thought in our peoples but simple pious ruminations on the past."

Finally, Hountondji (1983: 164) dismisses the notion of cultural pluralism as "a pretext for a conservative cultural practice." He notes also that "exotic" cultures are giving way to "the irreversible advent of a world civilization," and that cultural nationalists, instead of grasping the phenomenon, "simplify and trivialize it, emptying it of all real content by calling it 'acculturation'."

ETHNOPHILOSOPHY: INTUITIVENESS, UNANIMISM AND ANONYMITY

Philosophers are certainly entitled to debate the methodologies and parameters of their discipline. From that standpoint Hountondji is welcome to his views about the status and validity of ethnophiloso-phy.[6] Having granted the foregoing, however, one might take issue with his presentation of Placide Tempels's opinion regarding the degree of the African's conscious awareness of a philosophy, collec-tive or otherwise, or of a system of thought. The cleric (Tempels, 1969: 21) thus states his case:

We need not expect the first African who comes along, especially the young ones, to be able to give us a systematic exposition of his ontological system. None the less, this ontology exists; and it penetrates and informs all the thought of these primitives; it dominates and orientates all their behavior.

Further, in refuting Diertelen's contention that the "Ba Souto . . . do not indulge in reflective thought," Tempels (1969: 21, 23) adds, "Anyone who claims that primitive peoples possess no system of thought, excludes them thereby from the category of men. . . . I venture to think that the Bantu . . . live more than we do by Ideas and by following their own ideas."

There are grounds to object to Tempels's views and activities. He was undoubtedly a symbol of "the arrogance of Christianity" (Mud-imbe, 1985: 157) that fueled the missionary efforts, and also a participant in the European scheme to subjugate and exploit the Africans. Besides, his objective in synthesizing Bantu philosophy was to arrive at a more effective way of civilizing the savage. There is, on the other hand, some validity to his statement that not all Africans walk around with fully developed articulations of the beliefs that underlie their actions and choices readily available for presenta-tion to inquirers. Besides, one could say the same of any people anywhere, as Robin Horton (1970: 171) indeed does with regard to "the modern Western layman." Furthermore, when Barry Halen and Harold Sodipo (1986) wanted to synthesize certain Yorùbá epis-temological concepts they took great pains to identify the most reli-able informants, the onísègùn, medicine men and custodians of ethnic mysteries, because not just any layman would do.

As for the contention that the ethnophilosophers present their readers with supposedly collective or unanimist pseudo-philosophies, one wonders if there could not be some body of shared conceptions of a philosophical nature that united cohesive groups. Whatever the case might be, however, John Ayoade (1984: 96) usefully observes that ideas of necessity originate from individual minds, a basic fact that cannot be lost on any thinker. Thus even when one attributes ideas or beliefs to whole communities one says no more thereby than that the ideas or beliefs have undergone the necessary communal proofing to be judged consistent with the group's ethos. The expression "Bantu Philosophy" no more means that all "Bantu" people necessarily subscribe to it any more than "Contemporary European Philosophy" suggests the adherence of all contemporary Europeans to the philosophy so described.[7]

The *apparent* trait of unanimism moreover is consistent with African usage. Students of traditional African societies are conversant with many instances of the de-emphasis of the cult of the individual. The reason is not necessarily that Africans do not believe in individualism. Any society that encourages heroism and worships it, as Africans certainly do, evidently encourages individual excellence. Traditionally, nevertheless, the individual composer of a song would not think of copyrighting or attaching his or her name to it, nor would the carver carve his name on his product. Whatever smacks of assertive possessiveness, even over one's undisputed possessions, runs counter to the traditional spirit. One finds expressions of the underlying principles of cooperation, communalism and self-effacement in such Yorùbá sayings as *Adase ní hunni; ájose kì í hunni* (Going it alone brings disaster; cooperating never brings disaster); *Kò mù towóo rè wá kò gba towó eni* (A person who does not contribute what he/she has has no claim to what one has); *Enìkan kì í jé àwá dé* (No single person may say "here we are"); and *Asiwèrè èèyan ní nso pé irú òun kò si; irúu rèé pò o ju egbàágbèje lo* (Only an idiot claims that there is no one like himself/herself; the world is full of people like him/her). To attach one's name to an object or an idea is to assert exclusive claim and proprietorship to it, whereas traditional society frowns on the implied possessiveness and ostentatious self-importance.[8] The Yorùbá user of proverbs resorts to them in order, among other reasons, to disclaim proprietorship of the wisdom they carry, and to attribute it instead to the elders. It would seem that the ethnophilosophers are in this regard closer in their expression to the African spirit than are the professional philosophers.

For the African, one might argue (to the extent that the generalization would permit), Truth has an independent existence and is not necessarily dependent for its validity on who voices it. If philosophers argue that their discipline has no absolutes but depends on personalities they limit its attractiveness to the African mind. The traditional manner of pursuing eternal verities, by detaching them from individual agents and liberating them from whatever sentiments one might harbor of their purveyors, is more attractive.

TRADITIONAL AFRICAN CULTURES

Before commenting on the various deficiencies the new philosophers charge to traditional African cultures one should remark on the use of language (by Wiredu for example) suggesting that certain traits are common to traditional Africans. The suggestion weakens their case against the unanimist implications of ethnophilosophy. Moreover, their arguments against traditional habits have a familiar ring to them. European commentators have long held that certain hereditary, cultural, and social traits explain Africa's backwardness in comparison with Europe and the West. For example, P. T. Bauer (1976: 78–79) criticizes the refusal of certain observers to apply the same explanations to unequal economic achievements (among societies and individuals) as they would to unequal athletic, political, artistic, and intellectual accomplishments—differences in personal qualities and motivations. He argues that relatively more authoritarian traditions of Africa, in comparison with those of the West, were probably responsible for the persistence in Africa of "attitudes and mores damaging to material advance." He goes on to list examples of the attitude (Bauer, 1976: 78–79):

lack of interest in material advance, combined with resignation in the face of poverty; lack of initiative, self-reliance, and a sense of personal responsibility for the economic fortune of oneself and one's family; high leisure preference, together with a lassitude often found in tropical climates; preordained, unchanging and unchangeable universe; emphasis on performance of duties and acceptance of obligations, rather than on achievement or results, or assertion or even a recognition of personal rights; lack of sustained curiosity, experimentation and interest in change; belief in the efficacy of supernatural and occult forces and their influence over one's destiny. . . .

Needless to say, other scholars (see Baran, 1957: 142–44, 163) see the source of the economic problems of the Third World differently.[9] Bauer's argument is familiar; to the extent that our philosophers share his opinions, one might legitimately wonder if they are not themselves guilty of setting up the African as "the 'absolute other' of the 'civilized' man."

One of Wiredu's examples of traditional ills is the authoritarianism evident in the abundance of proverbs which stifle youthful initiative and the absence of balancing ones that encourage it. Another supposed manifestation of authoritarianism is the African's refusal to seek new and original explanations for beliefs and phenomena, preferring instead to say that the ancestors had spoken and leaving matters at that. If Wiredu was sufficiently clear about African traditions he would be aware of a commonplace of proverb scholarship that is as true in Africa as elsewhere—within the same culture one is liable to find proverbs that will serve both sides in a contentious issue. John Messenger is perhaps the authority most cited for the unquestioned fiat of proverbs in Africa. In a celebrated article he claims (Messenger, 1965: 303–4) that in a certain Nigerian community skillful application of proverbs often decides issues in litigation. Fortunately he offers (Messenger, 1965: 302) the best refutation for that claim in the same article by noting that the judges take great pains to ascertain the facts, to the extent even of employing mediums, because in theory at least their verdict might have life-and-death implications.

Incidentally, Wiredu himself (1980: 20–21) provides an argument to undercut his assertion about the authoritarianism of traditional cultures. Seeking to justify his criticism of African ways he pleads that his action is consistent with the openness of African systems to question:

> Those who seem to think that the criticism of traditional African philosophy is something akin to betrayal are actually more conservative than those among our elders who are real thinkers as distinct from mere repositories of traditional ideas. If you talk to some of them you soon discover that they are not afraid to criticize, reject, modify or add to traditional philosophical ideas.

If one considers, furthermore, that rather than the abject submissiveness and will-less servitude that characterizes Christian and Muslim approaches to their respective gods Africans adopt an almost brash assertiveness in their approach to theirs, one would conclude that people averse to authoritarianism in their gods would hardly tolerate it in mortals or their systems.

Africans might attribute opinions to ancestors, thereby implying that the opinions are ageless or immutable; common sense indicates, however, that "ancestors" cannot be taken in a literal sense. If we so took it we would need to determine who the ancestors were, when they lived, and, by implication, when original thinking ceased among Africans and why. New ideas surface all the time in Africa as elsewhere, and proverbs of very recent coinage exist. Attributing ideas to ancestors, therefore, only indicates a preference for *formal* self-effacement.

ILLITERACY

Hountondji argues that literacy is the precondition for philosophy, which is the precondition for science, which in turn is the precondition for technological advancement. It is not difficult to grant the point that things that are not somehow fixed may be impossible to define or measure precisely or difficult to manipulate. With regard to ideas, however, one cannot sustain an argument that unless they are fixed in writing they are not available to philosophy or reflection. If ideas are capable of transmission from one mind to another without the intermediary of documentation, then the receptive mind can be a reflective mind. Peter Bodunrin (1984: 10) concedes that "writing cannot be a precondition for philosophy," but he hedges by saying that writing is nevertheless important for the creation of a philosophical tradition. He thus aligns himself with Hountondji's assertion (1983: 106) that there might have been philosophers in traditional Africa, but not philosophy, because as far as philosophy is concerned "everything begins at the precise moment of transcription."

Hountondji further makes the interesting argument that Socrates gave birth to Greek philosophy only because his disciples committed his discourses to writing. One would conclude from it that Hountondji does not recognize the Pre-Socratics as philosophers, inasmuch as no one is sure that Thales wrote anything (Freeman, 1966: 50), nor Heraclitus, or Pythagoras for that matter (Wilbur and Allen, 1979: 60, 82). It appears that in this regard Hountondji is not in tune with the European philosophers he holds as his models.

One difficulty inherent in Hountondji's concession that Africans might very well have reflected seriously on the universe and their place in it, in other words philosophized, but yet produced no philosophy (because they did not record their thoughts)[10] is the complete subordination of the material to its medium. The proposition that Truth cannot exist except in a written mode seems to be an extreme form of materialism.

Without going into an elaborate discussion of the probable reasons for the preference in traditional Africa for nonliteracy, since there is no doubt that some sort of writing was known and practiced in various parts of the continent before contact with Europe or even with the Arabs,[11] one might suggest the unattractiveness of a medium that smacked of a secret code to communities that believed in universal participation in public life.[12] Furthermore, the Yorùbá proverbs, *Oyìnbó tó se léèdi ló sèrésà* (The white man who made the pencil also made the eraser), and *Bí òní ti rí òla ò rí béè ní babàláwoó fi ndlfá lóroorún* (Today is not necessarily a reliable preview for tomorrow, hence the diviner consults his oracle every fifth day), point to the preference for a medium that does not fix one in positions but permits a cleansing of the slate when and as necessary. The African perception of the fixity writing represents comes across quite clearly in the words of a fictional character infatuated with the European way, and, to some extent, alienated from the African. In Chinua Achebe's *No Longer at Ease* (1960: 120–21) the apostatic Isaak tells his son Obi:

> Our women make black patterns on their bodies with the juice of the *uli* tree. It was beautiful but it soon faded. If it lasted two market weeks it lasted a long time. But sometimes our elders spoke about *uli* that never faded, although no one had ever seen it. We see it today in the writing of the white man.

He goes on to explain that in the court records nothing ever changes or is alterable, because " 'What is written is written'. It is *uli* that never fades." If philosophers argue, therefore, that traditional proverbs indicate the authoritarianism of traditional systems, one could very well riposte that documents, *uli* that never fades, exude their own sort of authoritarian and restrictive odor.[13]

Ruth Finnegan's observation (1970: 18–19) about the "detachment and relatively impersonal mode of transmission" that writing and printing represent is also worth noting. These qualities are consistent with the West's vending-machine culture, wherein human interactions, in official capacities especially (but not exclusively), reek strongly of automatism. African cultures tend in the opposite direction. Horton notes (1970: 137) that Africans adopt a "personal medium" as the basis of their worldview. That personal emphasis has strong implications in their social arrangements. Which of the two tendencies one considers better depends on one's values.

Hountondji's dissertation on the debilitating effects of nonliteracy contains other weaknesses. While one would grant that certain traditional bodies of knowledge or codifications, especially those connected with rituals, are so important as to require constant recall and repetition to obviate their loss through lapses of memory, one needs to stress the fact that those functions involve specialists and not the whole community. Indeed the materials concerned are very often secrets restricted to certain rather exclusive cultic fraternities. If all members of the community spent all their time frantically recalling and repeating essential bodies of knowledge there would be no point in establishing special occasions for festivals and performances for communal reacquaintance with the mores of the group. The fact is, of course, that not only do the occasions exist, but they are so important that even group members who have wandered far and wide return home for them.[14]

Even more importantly, one could argue that contrary to Hountondji's scenario, people who inscribe the laws on parchments (or commit them to data banks) rather than on their hearts are more in danger of permanently losing them through forgetfulness or some sort of corruption. The complacency resulting from the certainty that the document is in safe storage somewhere does free the mind for other pursuits; but in time the disburdened mind might soon forget what the laws are, where they are stored, or even that they exist at all. Such is the genesis of "cultural amnesia."

SCIENCE

The philosophers' conception of science and technology as the panacea for what ails Africa deserves serious attention. Sober and reputable thinkers have convincingly discredited the usual opposition of the nonscientific, magical and superstitious traditional man and the scientific, pragmatic and rational Westerner. Bronislaw Malinowski (in Wilbur and Allen, 1979: 17) suggests that if science were defined after J. G. Crowther as "the system of behavior by which man acquires mastery over his environment," or even if it were represented as a theoretical enterprise, no people may be said to be entirely without science any more than it is without religion. On the other hand, if we took intuition to mean the absence of logical support for convictions or beliefs, and the substitution of "mythological thinking" for rationality, then one could argue, as Leo Apostel (1981: 17–18) does, that since even "mythological thinking" makes an attempt at proof, although proof of a different sort, Africans cannot be said to live by intuition alone.

Malinowski (1954: 17ff.) demonstrates, with particular reference to the Trobriand Islanders of Melanesia, that traditional peoples combine scientific and mystical approaches in dealing with their universe. In dealing with the known they rely on empirical knowledge whereas when confronted with the unknown they resort to magic. He (Malinowski, 1954: 28) points out that if one were to suggest to the Trobriander that he make his garden by magic alone he would smile at one's simplicity. He (Malinowski, 1954: 29–30) adds, "in canoe building empirical knowledge of material, of technology, and of certain principles of stability and hydrodynamics, function in company and close association with magic, each yet uncontaminated by the other." He (1954: 32) concludes that the traditional person "never relies on magic alone, while, on the contrary, he sometimes dispenses with it completely, as in fire-making and in a number of crafts and pursuits."

Robin Horton has also demonstrated the striking similarities between African traditional thought and modern science.[15] According to him (Horton, 1970: 131) the Westerner is often unable to recognize the similarities, firstly because he is unfamiliar with the theoretical thinking of his own culture, and secondly because its African counterpart is expressed in a different idiom. Like Malinowski, Horton (1970: 135) argues that in dealing with the world of "common sense" the traditional African behaves according to the principles of causality. But when he is confronted by "gross incommensurability" he resorts to theory. His behavior is thus no different from that of the Western scientist, whereas his idiom is different.

The recent experiments of Barry Halen and Harold Sodipo (1986) on Yorùbá thought deserve some mention. They set out to bridge the gap between anthropologists and theoretical philosophers skeptical of anthropological reconstructions of traditional thought systems. In particular, they conducted an experiment in Yorùbá epistemology in order to arrive at its differences from or similarities to its English counterpart. They found (1986: 80–81), much to their surprise, that the Yorùbá insist on a more rigorous standard of proof than the English before they would classify any information as knowledge. They go on to comment (Halen and Sodipo, 1986: 81), "How ironic then, that the model of African thought systems produced by English-language culture should typify them as systems that treat second-hand information (oral tradition, 'book' knowledge, etc.) as though it were true, as though it were knowledge!" Hountondji (1983: 99) concedes that precolonial Africa "had undoubtedly amassed a wealth of true knowledge, of effective techniques which have been transmitted orally from generation to generation and continue to this day to ensure the livelihood of a large part of the population of our countryside and cities." Wiredu (1984: 153) also grants the existence of "the principle of rational evidence" in Africa, pointing to the application of knowledge of soils and seeds and meteorology to farming, and the preservation of communal harmony through the determination of conflicting claims on the basis of objective investigation. Despite these concessions, however, the philosophers argue that Africans must, in effect, develop science and technology that duplicate European models. That being the case, they seem open to the charge C. E. Ayres (1927: 13) makes against scientists, that they have substituted one form of folklore for another, inasmuch as their pursuit of science amounts to nothing short of "inviolable faith."

Ayres (1927: 19) further warns that "the prime mover in our recent developments is not that galaxy of noble truths which we call science, but the thoroughly mundane and immensely potent driving force of mechanical technology. Science is the handsome Doctor Jekyll; machinery is Mr. Hyde—powerful and rather sinister." To the extent that our philosophers are infatuated with applicatory science, they seem, in comparison to Ayres, to be unphilosophical about science and technology; they have not seriously considered the ramifications of such products and by-products of science and technology as the neutron bomb, robotics and the marginalization of the working person, Kesterson, and Love Canal,[16] in order to determine whether or not science, in the final analysis, is a boon to humankind.

Before leaving the subject of science and the scientific spirit one should give some attention to Wiredu's criticism of the African habit of protracted funerals attended by the quaffing of liquor. The habit illustrates, in his view, the spiritistic manner in which the African approaches the understanding and solution of problems. Here again, unfortunately, Wiredu adopts the perspective of an outsider who lacks the insight Horton (for example) has demonstrated in this regard. Even Western medicine recognizes the need to attend to non-physiological disorders, the sort that bereavement might induce. In the West people at risk visit their analysts; in Africa the process of separation is protracted and cushioned with such festive socialization as would envelop the bereaved in the warm embrace of their extended kin. Ivan Karp's study of beer drinking among the Iteso makes valuable points that will help non-Africans and Africans suffering from "cultural amnesia" to understand the value of such social strategies. Karp (1980: 84) sees in them "mutual commensality," and argues that "beer is a symbol of diffuse solidarity and unencumbered sociability which expresses the ideal form of relations among men that Iteso would like to achieve." Having said that, one must, in fairness to Wiredu, acknowledge the unfortunate practice known in Nigeria as "spraying," meaning the mindless expenditure of (usually ill-gotten) wealth on social occasions. But one can blame even that on "cultural amnesia" and the undermining of traditional principles of accountability by colonialism and imperialism.

What Wiredu describes negatively as spiritism is not very different from what the Frankforts (1946: 5) describe rather positively as the traditional "I-Thou" relationship with the universe, in contrast with the modern "I-It" attitude. Each type has significant implications for its adherents' regard for human life and for nature. According to Francis Cornford (1957: vi), in contrast to the traditional reverential, reciprocative approach to nature, the scientific tendency seeks to master the world. In so doing it does away with what others consider most meaningful in nature; the gods and life itself are accordingly drummed out of Nature.

Finally, we must allow that despite their supposed irrationality and spiritism, traditional societies did manage to develop impressive pharmaceutics and psychiatry, for example,[17] and were by no means stagnant, despite their lack of "science and technology."

AFRICANIST AND AFRICAN STUDIES

One should not need to defend African Studies and Africanists against the imputations philosophers make about their motives. Given the experiences of the last few centuries that have resulted in the "cultural amnesia" prevalent on the continent, the most urgent need for Africans would seem to be self-rediscovery. Thus, even if Europeans had not invented African Studies, Africans would have had to invent it. Mudimbe (1985: 208) properly places the African Studies movement in the process of African renascence, noting that its inception was part of the antithethical response to the earlier thesis: "all that is African is barbarous." He mentions also that the movement was highly influenced by Sheik Anta Diop, and has more recently earned the endorsement of such philosophers as Mabika Kalanda and Eboussi Boulaga. For them, a thorough and dispassionate understanding of the African past is indispensable for effectively confronting the future.

Hountondji's suggestion that African Studies as a discipline is suspect because it was invented by Europeans and is, therefore, part of the European tradition, is strange. It is strange because it comes from someone whose central belief is that the only sort of philosophy fit for African attention is European style philosophy, and one who advocates the dissolution of African particularities (real or imaginary) in the emergent world civilization, meaning, of course, a cultural pax Europeana.

The philosophers' belief that the conquest of Africa by a handful of Europeans is the most persuasive argument for the abandonment of African ways strongly indicates their need for cultural rehabilitation. Apart from the cynicism of a might-makes-right, nothing-succeeds-like-success argument, it also shows evidence of alienation from the African spirit. Tradition tells us, for example, that when in the distant past Oduduwa invaded and conquered Ile-Ife, the ancestral home of the Yorùbá the indigenes formed the Ogbóni secret society whose function, according to Idowu (1963: 23–24), was "in all probability, to protect the indigenous institutions of the land from annihilation under the influence of the new regime." The result is that although today the Yorùbá accept Oduduwa as their ancestor, a measure of the success of the invader, the Ogbóni society remains one of the most powerful institutions of the land, a measure of the survival of indigenous mysteries and traditions. To represent what happened in Africa in the wake of European intervention as conquest by a handful of Europeans is, in any case, simplistic.

Long before Africans were colonized the Hebrews suffered a similar fate. They always relied, however, on the survival of a faithful remnant that would in more auspicious times reconstruct the essentials of Hebrewness. Even in the more recent era of colonization, Africans have not been the only peoples overrun by rampaging Europeans, but Africans are unique in their belief that their future lies in becoming, in thought, speech and habit, like their erstwhile colonizers. A true African philosophy would aim at reconciling Africans to Africaness, not at advocating dissolution in a European cultural mélange.

THE VALIDITY OF DISPARATE "FORMS"

"Suppose now," Wiredu (1980: 36) remarks, "that a critic should attribute what I have written to my particular educational background; I am bound to concede as much. In a certain obvious sense we are all children of our circumstances." His words are admirable and true. In this regard Wiredu and the philosophers are no different from other Africans raised in the era of colonialism, an era that continues in no small measure until the present day, nominal independence notwithstanding. Unfortunately, awareness of the mental conditioning does not always imply recognition of a need for deprogramming.

The philosophers sometimes betray unabashed Europhilia and an embarrassing insensitivity to racist nuances. Wiredu (1984: 157), for example, contrasts Africa with "other, better placed, parts of the world, [where] if you want to know the philosophy of the given people, you do not go to aged peasants or fetish priests or court personalities; you go to individual thinkers, in flesh, if possible, and in print." He (Wiredu, 1984: 152) gives examples of the "backward aspects of our culture" such as "assiduously participating in the pouring of libation to the spirits of our ancestors on ceremonial occasions, or frantically applauding imitation of the frenzied dancing of 'possessed' fetish priests. . . ." The disparaging references to "fetish priests" and their antics parallel Henry Odera's observation (in Hountondji, 1983: 60):

What may be a superstition is paraded as "African religion", and the white world is expected to endorse that it is indeed a religion but an African religion. What in all cases is a mythology is paraded as "African philosophy", and again the white culture is expected to endorse that it is indeed a philosophy but an African philosophy.

They also parallel Hountondji's lament (1983: 74): "What a mockery it is to compare such ambitious philosophies [as produced by Plato, Spinoza, and Hegel] and their scholarly surveys of the history of philosophy . . . with what anthropologists are today presenting as 'African systems of thought.' "

People so solicitous of the sensibilities of the white world and the white culture are in a poor position to accuse others, namely students of African traditions, of playing to the European gallery. They also cut a pathetic figure as worshippers of people who might have little use for them. Wiredu (1984: 159) correctly and wistfully observes that the African philosopher cannot take the same sort of pride in European philosophical achievements as a Western student of philosophy might. Indeed, he continues, "an African needs a certain level-headedness to touch some of these thinkers at all. Hume, for example, had absolutely no respect for black men. Nor was Marx, for another instance, particularly progressive in this respect." Yet the mentality that sees superstition and fetish priests in Africa while it sees religion and thinkers in Europe, that sees mythology and systems of thought in Africa while it sees philosophy in Europe, is kin to that which sees natives, savages and tribes in Africa while it sees citizens, civilized peoples and nations in Europe, even when the tribes are far more numerous than the nations.

The cause of the problem is miseducation (Wiredu's diagnosis is absolutely correct), and it will take a different sort of education to cure the new African of the hypnotic impulsion toward Westernism and the almost pathological conviction that African ways are important only as illustrations of things from which to distance oneself.

The basic monism of the African professional philosophers' position is obviously at variance with the pluralistic nature of the universe, which we observe in the divergencies all around us, in peoples, in fauna, in flora, and in planetary physical features. Many people would be dismayed if confronted with the possibility that in each of these classes of phenomena, one type might be selected for survival, because it has proved more acceptable in one respect than the others in that class, and all others consigned to extermination. The horse is a marvelous animal for its purposes, but one would neither wish the zebra a horse, nor wish all animals to become like horses.

More importantly, we should be mindful of the ultimate implications of the thought that one way of being and only that is desirable for all peoples. Many of the atrocities that have plagued human history have sprung from such thoughts, and Africans of all peoples forget that fact at their peril. We may allow ourselves to be impressed by the temporary success of European predation on the continent and elsewhere, but we would be perverse to see it as vindicating one and only one course of human development.

Henri Frankfort (1956: 3–18) in his discussion of the ancient civilizations of the Near East makes a persuasive case for cultural pluralism. Each civilization, he says, has an individuality, a recognizable character, an identity which it maintains throughout its development. He calls it (Frankfort, 1956: 63) the form of the civilization, which is evident in "a certain coherence among its various manifestations, a certain consistency in its orientation, a certain cultural 'style' which shapes its political and its judicial institutions, its art as well as its literature, its religion as well as its morals." Although the form changes, partly as a result of inherent developmental imperatives and partly due to external influences, it is never destroyed. He takes issue with Toynbee's and Spengler's scientific view of civilization which proposes a uniform pattern of societal development from birth to death. In this view, "an imperialistic and socialistic order follows a traditional and hierarchical society; expanding technique and trade follow greatness in art, music, and literature as certainly as dispersal of the seeds follows the maturing of a plant which will never flower again" (Frankfort: 1956: 6).

Frankfort (1956: 14) further quotes Toynbee's comparison of civilizations to motor cars traveling along a one-way street, and his distinction between so-called primitive societies and civilizations: "Primitive societies . . . may be likened to people lying torpid upon a ledge on a mountainside, with a precipice below and a precipice above; civilizations may be likened to companions of these 'sleepers of Ephesus' who have just risen to their feet and have started to climb up the face of the cliff." Both images, Frankfort comments, suggest a "predetermined orientation and limitation of cultural endeavour." Toynbee, he continues (Frankfort, 1956: 14), believes there is a cliff to climb and a street to follow, whereas in truth,

we see figures at rest or on the move in a cloudy space but know nothing about their relative position: we do not know which ledge is above or below which other ledge. Or again: we see motor cars moving, halting, or out of order. But we do not know whether they move in an alley, or on a four-drive highway, on an open plain, or within a circle—we do not even know whether there is an entrance or exit at all.

The perceptions and arguments of the professional philosophers inevitably show the consequences of what Mudimbe (1985: 150) describes as "silently depending on a Western episteme," and share the weaknesses of inauthenticity that are often associated with Négritude (Mudimbe, 1985: 170–71). Because our philosophers begin from the European model as a norm and criticize African cultures and habits accordingly, they need to take Frankfort's words (1956: 15) to heart to the effect that two divergent ways of life are not necessarily two attempts at doing the same thing, one attempt better than the other. "Bach was not trying to write like Beethoven and failing; Athens was not a relatively unsuccessful attempt to produce Rome."

Wiredu is correct to urge that clarity should begin at home. Accordingly, we must attend to a study and understanding of the form or forms of African civilizations, not simply so that we might make them serve as quarries to enrich European philosophical traditions but so that we might rediscover and resume our proper selves. Further, in order to rehabilitate our professional philosophers, African universities might need to absorb the discipline of philosophy into their institutes of African Studies. The philosophers would then have strong inducements to shed their present disdain for African Studies, and might even discover, as Frankfort (1956: 18) remarks, that "the values found in different civilizations are incommensurate."

CONCLUSION

The professional philosophers in Africa have raised many issues that one cannot adequately address in a short paper. The foregoing discussion has touched only glancingly on some of them. Certain points need stressing, however. The many references to the philosophers *en bloc* are not a suggestion that they form a monolithic group. Among those critical of ethnophilosophy, typically from Francophone countries, one finds notable differences of approach and opinion (see Mudimbe, 1985: 195–206); even individual philosophers do not remain fixed in stone in defense of their opinions, as Hountondji's modifications attest. Moreover, Anglophone philosophers tend to be more receptive to the philosophical possibilities of African traditions (Irele, 1983: 28–29) than are their Francophone colleagues. This greater receptiveness finds expression on the covers of their journal, *Second Order*, where they undertake to "regard inter-disciplinary boundaries as made for man, not man for them, and to watch out for growing points in their subject as it applies itself to new problems." Such an attitude avoids the paradox of making philosophy a closed discipline, and opens the way for the possibility of an equal dialogue between African thought and Western thought. Such a dialogue will undoubtedly be beneficial for both sides.

NOTES

1. I use the term "professional philosophers" as Irele (1983: 8) does in his introduction to Hountondji's book to refer to the faculty of the departments of philosophy in some African universities.
2. Mudimbe's (1985) article is a most authoritative and comprehensive survey of the major developments to date on African thought. For a discussion of the various approaches to ethnophilosophy, see pages 179–202.
3. Wiredu (1984: 150–51) notes that "traditional thought," in its nonscientific characteristics, is inferior to "modern science-oriented thought" and is not an African peculiarity. Yet, he notes further, some people confuse African thought

with traditional African thought, and fallaciously use that characteristic as one that distinguishes Africans from Westerners.

4. In Griaule's *Conversations With Ogotemmeli* (1965).

5. This misperception that Africans who live according to the old ways are disinclined to think for themselves seems widespread. In a generally perceptive discussion of the similarities and difference between traditional African societies and Western societies, Robin Horton (1974: 167) makes very much the same comment as do Wiredu and Hountondji, although for him the trait has another significance. In his view, "the standard justification of so much thought and action: 'That is what the old-time people told us,' " is an indication of traditional African preference for the past and corresponding dread of the future. See notes 13 and 14 below.

6. Abiola Irele (1983: 21) speaks of the anxiety of the "academic philosophers" to "remove their discipline from the shadow of the ideological preoccupations of African nationalism in order to affirm its independent, scientific character." It is fair at this point to note, as Irele (1983: 29–30) and V. Y. Mudimbe (1985: 202) have pointed out, that since the original publication of his views in French in 1976, Hountondji has responded to intense criticism of his positions by offering some clarifications. In two articles he (1981: 1982) moderates his total rejection of African thought as philosophical material (without abandoning his dismissal of the notion of a unanimist philosophy), and argues the political relevance of his case for contemporary Africa.

7. I refer here to I. M. Bochenski (1961), but there are several others that refute the notion that this sort of usage implies unanimism.

8. The suggested hubris is so alien to Yorùbá sensibilities that superstitions exist to discourage it. Accordingly, a person who shows such a trait invites envious agencies, human or nonhuman, to destroy the endowments he/she makes so much of. On the other hand astute manipulation of this cultural preference can be rewarding. A doctor who lived in Ibadan from the 1950s to the 1970s furthered his political ambitions by naming his luxurious car "Boys' Car" and handing the keys to any young man who wanted to drive it around. This is only one example of the ideal of possession in common.

9. Although Western intervention in other parts of the world could have been beneficial for them, Baran (1957: 141–42) writes, the manner of European exploitation made matters turn out differently: "that Western Europe left the rest of the world behind was . . . by no means a matter of fortuitous accident or of some racial peculiarities of different peoples. It was actually determined by the nature of Western European . . . capitalist penetration of the outside world. . . . Western European visitors rapidly determined to extract the largest possible gains from the host countries, and to take their loot home. Thus they engaged in outright plunder thinly veiled as trade, seizing and removing tremendous wealth from the places of their penetration."

10. There is a clear difference between arguing that *Weltanschauung* is not philosophy, and saying that whatever is not written is not philosophy.

11. See Janheinz Jahn (1961: 185), and Owomoyela (1985: 4–5) for a discussion of this issue.

12. The professionals apparently wish to restrict the quest for Truth to a certified fraternity. That attempt is preposterous, because Africans would consider the notion that wisdom or the quest for it should be restricted to a class preposterous. Indeed, Africans would very likely see philosophizing as a profession ludicrous.

13. The points I have made in this section highlight the African's mindfulness of the inevitability of change, and even his making allowances for the necessity of change. These run counter to Robin Horton's (1970: 166–70) aforementioned image of the African as so petrified by the possibility of change that he cannot bear any thought of the future. See note 14 below.

14. Horton (1970: 168) erroneously interprets such recreative and commemorative occasions as expressions of Africans hankering for a golden age in the past, in contrast to Westerners' looking to the future for Utopia. He believes that for Africans the passage of time means the accumulation of pollution and declining fortune. That belief contradicts the obvious reverence they have for age, and flies in the face of direct expressions of the expectation that the norm is for people to increase in fortune, not the opposite. For example, the Yorùbá say, *Iwájú iwájú lòpá èbìtì nré si* (The staff of a snare ever springs forward), and *Olánrewájú là ngbó a kì f gbó Olánrehìn* (One hears only "Fortune surges ahead," never "Fortune fades away"). My view on the role of the traditional ceremonies in question are in line with those Victor Turner (1984) expressed in his article, "Liminality and the Performative Genres."

15. In the second part of his essay he details the dissimilarities between the two, making some valid and some controversial suggestions. The essay is important, however, at least in casting doubt on "most of the well-worn dichotomies used to conceptualize the difference between scientific and traditional religious thought" (Horton, 1970: 152).

16. The Kesterson Wild Life Refuge in northern California is a classic case of the scientific dilemma. The "refuge" has become so deadly for plant and animal life that rangers now have to find ways to keep wild life out of it. It became a deathtrap ironically because of the application of scientific advances to agriculture. Love Canal and the dead lakes and streams of New England and elsewhere are also legacies of technology to humankind, as are, of course, the tons of nuclear waste that no one knows how to dispose of.

17. On January 6, 1981 the NOVA program broadcast by PBS was on "The Doctors of Nigeria"; it documented the impressive achievements of Yorùbá "native doctors" in the treatment of mental disorders, and also the ongoing cooperative research in that area by traditional healers and modern psychiatrists.

REFERENCES

Achebe, Chinua, 1960. *No Longer at Ease.* Conn.: Fawcett.
Apostel, Leo. 1981. *African Philosophy: Myth or Reality?* Gent, Belgium: Scientific Publishers, E Story-Scientia.
Ayoade, John A. A. 1984. "Time in Yorùbá Thought," pp. 93–112 in Richard A. Wright (ed.) *African Philosophy: An Introduction.* Lanham: University Press of America.
Ayres, C. E. 1927. *Science: The False Messiah.* Indianapolis: The Bobbs-Merrill Company.
Baran, Paul A. 1957. *The Political Economy of Growth.* New York: Monthly Review Press.
Baurer, P. T. 1976. *Dissent on Development: Studies and Debates in Development.* Cambridge, Mass.: Harvard University Press.
Bochenski, I. M. 1961. *Contemporary European Philosophy.* Berkeley: University of California Press.
Bodunrin, P. O. 1984. "The Question of African Philosophy," pp. 1–24 in Richard A. Wright (ed.) *African Philosophy: An Introduction.* Lanham: University Press of America.
Cornford, Francis Macdonald. 1957. *From Religion to Philosophy.* New York: Harper & Row.
————. 1978. *Before and After Socrates.* Cambridge: The University Press.
Finnegan, Ruth. 1970. *Oral Literature in Africa.* Oxford: The Clarendon Press.
Frankfort, Henri et al. 1946. *The Intellectual Adventure of Ancient Man: An Essay on Speculative Thought in the Ancient Near East.* Chicago: The University of Chicago Press.
————. 1956. *The Birth of Civilization in the Near East.* Garden City: Doubleday Anchor.
Freeman, Kathleen. 1966. *The Pre-Socratic Philosophers.* Cambridge, Mass.: Harvard University Press.
Griaule, M. 1965. *Conversations with Ogotemmeli: An Introduction to Dogon Religious Ideas.* London: Oxford University Press.
Hallen, Barry and J. O. Sodipo. 1986. *Knowledge, Belief & Witchcraft: Analytic Experiments in African Philosophy.* London: Ethnographica.
Horton, Robin. 1970. "African Traditional Thought and Western Science," pp. 131–71 in Bryan R. Wilson (ed.) *Rationality.* Oxford: Basil Blackwell.
Hountondji, Paulin. 1980. "Distances," *Recherche, Pédagogie et Culture* 49, IX: 27–33.
————. 1981. "Que peut la Philosophie?" *Présence Africaine* 119: 47–71.
————. 1983. *African Philosophy: Myth and Reality.* Bloomington: Indiana University Press.
Idowu, E. Bolaji. 1963. *Olodumare: God in Yorùbá Belief.* New York: Praeger.

Irele, Abiola. 1983. "Introduction," in Paulin Hountondji. *African Philosophy: Myth and Reality*. Bloomington: Indiana University Press.

Jahn, Janheinz. 1961. *Muntu: An Outline of Neo-African Culture*. New York: Grove Press.

Kagame, Alexis. 1956. *La Philosophie Bantou-Rwandaise de l'Etre*. Brussels: Arsom.

Karp, Ivan. 1980. "Beer Drinking and Social Experience in an African Society: An Essay in Formal Sociology," pp. 83–119 in Ivan Karp and Charles S. Bird (eds.) *Explorations in African Systems of Thought*. Bloomington: Indiana University Press.

Keita, Lancinay. 1984. "The African Philosophical Tradition," pp. 57–76 in Richard A. Wright (ed.) *African Philosophy: An Introduction*. Lanham: University Press of America.

Malinowski, Bronislaw. 1954. *Magic, Science and Religion and Other Essays*. Garden City: Doubleday Anchor.

Mbiti, John S. 1969. *African Religion and Philosophy*. New York: Praeger.

Messenger, John C., Jr. 1965. "The Role of Proverbs in a Nigerian Judicial System," pp. 299–307 in Alan Dundes (ed.) *The Study of Folklore*. Englewood Cliffs, N.J.: Prentice Hall, Inc.

Mudimbe, V. Y. 1985. "African Gnosis," *The African Studies Review* 28, 2/3: 149–233.

Owomoyela, Oyekan. 1985. "Proverbs: Exploration of an African Philosophy of Social Communication," *Ba Shiru: A Journal of African Language and Literature* 12/1: 3–16.

Tempels, Placide. 1969. *Bantu Philosophy*. Paris: *Présence Africaine*.

Turner, Victor. 1984. "Liminality and the Performative Genres," pp. 19–41 in John J. MacAloon (ed.) *Rite, Drama, Festival, Spectacle: Rehearsals Toward a Theory of Cultural Performance*. Philadelphia: ISHI.

Wilbur, J. B. and H. J. Allen (eds.). 1979. *The World of the Early Greek Philosophers*. Buffalo: Prometheus Books.

Wiredu, Kwasi. 1980. *Philosophy and an African Culture*. Cambridge: The University Press.

————. 1984. "How Not to Compare African Thought with Western Thought," pp. 149–62 in Richard A. Wright (ed.) *African Philosophy: An Introduction*. Lanham: University Press of America.

MARCIEN TOWA (Translated from the French original for this collection by Aster Gashaw)

CONDITIONS FOR THE AFFIRMATION OF A MODERN AFRICAN PHILOSOPHICAL THOUGHT

INTRODUCTION

For several years now, African philosophy has been arousing profound interest in intellectual circles. This does not hide the evident tardiness of African philosophy as compared with, for example, African history, African literature, and African theology. The advance of these other disciplines can be gauged by the number of Africans engaged in cultivating them, the importance of published works, the existence of structured associations of scholars, the frequency of colloquiums, and the proper maintenance of publications that serve as organs of expression. The present situation of African philosophy is characterized, on the contrary, by the limited number of people engaged in it, the absence of great works, and a lack of appropriate organs of expression. Professor Hountondji is deploying praiseworthy efforts to revive the African Council of Philosophy. Unfortunately, the results are not convincing.

Nevertheless, we can easily admit that modern Africa will not really attain its cultural maturity as long as it does not elevate itself resolutely to a profound thinking of its essential problems, that is to say, to philosophical reflection.

How will Africa go about doing this? We will successively focus our attention on the following:

- the obstacles to be overcome;
- the methodological conditions;
- the institutional and material conditions that need to be fulfilled in order to insure the affirmation of a living African philosophy.

THE OBSTACLES

African philosophy is confronting different kinds of obstacles: the enrollment issue, methodological obstacles, etc.

The Enrollment Issue

Modern Africa will hardly produce great philosophers as long as there are not a significant number of Africans who are devoting themselves to philosophical studies and reflection. At the present moment, few Africans work in the domain of philosophy. The reason for this is that philosophical studies offer very few sure employment outlets other than teaching. But even in this sector, the number of jobs reserved for philosophy are very limited. It is known that in Francophone countries philosophy is only taught in the last years of high school and in college. In Anglophone countries, one can expect only "religious studies" at the secondary level of education. In a number of Muslim countries, Islamic studies are the only ones which are organized; philosophy is thus practically ignored. At the International Conference of Philosophy held in Khartoum in 1976, we had another revelation. In a large number of African countries, education in philosophy is still the work of clergymen and especially of missionaries. Naturally, the preoccupations of clergymen are religious and not properly philosophical.

The Ethnophilosophic Obstacle

One should not therefore be surprised to note that most of the so-called works of African philosophy depend in fact on ethnophilosophy. This is the case with the works of the Reverend P. Tempels, Father Kagame, V. Mulago, Pastor J. Mbiti, and J. Bahoken. This is also the case with the writings of A. N'daw, B. Fonda, and Assane Sylla. I agree with P. Hountondji when he observes that these authors who claim to be simply presenting the philosophy of traditional Africa are only expressing their own conceptions. But I do not follow him when he denies all possibility of philosophy in the traditional culture and when he claims that African philosophy is nothing but the work of the ethnophilosophers. On the one hand, I am of the opinion that traditional Africa has produced philosophical texts. On the other hand, that which hides itself behind the so-called African philosophy of the ethnophilosophers does not belong properly speaking to philosophy, but rather to theology. The ethnophilosophers retroject into the African tradition Christian or Muslim dogmas so that these religions lose all foreign characteristics in the eyes of African nationalists who desire to realize a return to their roots and to reassume with pride their cultural identity. It is, notably for the Christian ethnophilosophers, a question of finding a strategy for better inculcating Africans with the evangelical message. One can see this clearly in the work of P. Tempels, whose *Bantu Philosophy* is nothing but a propaedeutic for Bantu catechism. But one can say as much about the other ethnophilosophers. In general, the list of ethnophilosophers coincides more or less with the list of African theologians.

The methodological weaknesses of ethnophilosophy from a philosophical point of view derives precisely from the fact that its real purpose is not philosophical but theological. Seen from the methodological angle, the principal characteristic of ethnophilosophy resides in its dilation of the concept of philosophy to such a point that this concept becomes coextensive with the concept of culture.[1] A real philosopher would not tolerate this dilution of his discipline, because such a dilution would be equivalent to its disappearance. For the ethnophilosopher, on the contrary, this enlargement offers the invaluable advantage of giving him the unrestricted freedom in the interpretation of the African tradition in any direction at all. A theologian is by definition an expert in the equivocal art of interpretation. No matter what his ideological options, the most lowly theologian will always manage to find in the holy writings proper texts on which to ground them. The Bible is effectively highly complex and contains all sorts of conceptions, some of which even contradict themselves.

For those who are involved in exploring the biblical writings, which cover, it is true, close to a thousand years of Hebrew literature, it is child's play to interpret the many thousands of years of culture of a whole continent in the sense of the metaphysical credo of the interpreters. The dilution of the concept of philosophy into that of culture is aimed at obtaining this facility of manipulation and sparing the effort that would be necessary if the basis of interpretation were narrower.

Even if Tempels, Mulago, and Mbiti give themselves the maximum liberty in utilizing whatever cultural element comes their way to support their prejudices, Kagame however compels himself to the more precise study of linguistic structures to uncover in them the fundamental categories of the Bantu philosophy. A large number of researchers, especially in Zaire, have been engulfed in the path opened up by Kagame. In spite of the apparent rigor of this method, it should be said that it also opens wide the door to arbitrary interpretation.

Can one extricate European philosophy from the structure of European languages? It is sufficient to transpose the question to realize immediately its absurdity. First of all, there is not one European philosophy, but a great number of European philosophies, some of which are diametrically opposed. And none of these multiple philosophies can be extricated from structures which are properly linguistic. Not only the most different and the most opposed philosophies are expressed in French, for example, but poets and magicians utilize the same tool. As a matter of fact, everything can be expressed in French. One can say as much for any other language, and therefore also for the Bantu languages. Just as the contemporary Bantu do not think the same thing, there is no reason to imagine that our ancestors who forged our languages had a singular conception of the world. A language, in principle, does not have a determined philosophic content. It is a container without contents and it is because it is empty of all content that it can receive any content. If one accepts this view, one will also agree that what Father Kagame has done at best is semantics, not philosophy.

Our opinion is that ethnophilosophy is essentially sterile. It is not animated by a true spirit of research, because ethnophilosophy is already in possession of its credo. It is easy to recognize in the pretended anchoring stones that ethnophilosophy "discovers" in the African tradition the principal dogmas of the so-called "revealed" religions: exclusivist monotheism, providence, etc. Ethnophilosophy is as stiff as the dogmas it propagates. While pretending to rehabilitate African culture, ethnophilosophy works not at revealing veracious African thought but at concealing it.

The Scientific and Epistemological Obstacles

The current of thought represented by P. Hountondji does not occlude African thought, it openly excludes it, in the name of scientificity, as not in the least pertinent. For this author, there is no African philosophy in the traditional culture and there could not be one. Hountondji conceives philosophy as the theory of theory, as epistemology. To be sure, reflection on science, epistemology, constitutes an important domain in philosophy. But this is hardly philosophy as a whole. The reduction of philosophy to epistemology ends in epistemologism.

One can see, with the reduction of philosophy to epistemology, that there cannot be philosophy where there is no science. But Hountondji supports the idea that there is no African science and as a consequence there cannot be an African philosophy. Science itself is rigorously conditioned by writing. And because our cultures are not based on writing, argues Hountondji, they could not therefore produce science. Philosophy, notes Hountondji, is a "particular theoretical discipline, with the same status as algebra or physics, or any other science; a discipline embodied consequently in a written literature, the only conceivable form of its historical existence, the condition of its development in any society."[2] He specifies his ideas thus: "[T]he chief requirement of science itself is writing. It is difficult to imagine . . . a scientific tradition in a society in which knowledge can be transmitted only orally. Therefore African civilizations could not give birth to any science, in the strict sense of the word. . . ."[3] These peremptory affirmations clash against some serious objections. C. A. Diop, T. Obenga and also others have demonstrated that Africa was not unaware of writing (assuming it does condition science to this extent), that Africa itself invented it, that Egypt also invented, according to Plato and Aristotle, geometry, arithmetic, astronomy, and many other sciences? Hountondji does not disarm but promotes quibbles: Was the use of writing widespread? Is there really a biological and a historical continuity between Egypt and ourselves? What then do we say of Meroe?

Hountondji, it seems to us, as A. Franklin had already said speaking of negritude, is a prisoner of the prejudice that views Africa as primitive and with a purely mythical mentality. He denies *a priori* the possibility of a precolonial African philosophy. The traditional culture offers only myths and art literature. Such a position amounts to turning our backs on our ancestors without even hearkening to them, to discouraging research pertinent to traditional thought and to condemning ourselves to amnesia in that which concerns the principal domain of the thinking of the essential. Hountondji affirms nevertheless the existence of a certain African philosophy, notably that of the ethnophilosophers. In the end, ethnophilosophy, as we have already seen, depends less on philosophy than on theology, and as Hountondji and other African epistemologists have not yet produced anything of significance, at least so far as we know, in the domain of epistemology, we have to admit that we should not yet speak of African philosophy in any accepted sense.

On the other hand, Hountondji's idea, according to which modern African philosophy should have as its task to "liberate in our continent, a genuine scientific tradition"[4] is incoherent, since, for Hountondji, it is always science that precedes and unilaterally determines philosophy, which only echoes the deferred counterblows [*contre-coups*] of the evolution of science.[5] Logically, we should wait for science, for the scientific theory to first establish itself in Africa so that we can then devote ourselves to the theory of this theory. It is obvious that Hountondji engages African philosophy in an impasse. In the end, his position is not very different from that of Mbargane Guisse, for whom philosophy is a speculative genre specific to certain European countries, which was born in Greece and died out in Germany with Marx. He writes summarily: "Not more than in India, in China, or Indian America, and in Europe, with the exception of ancient Greece and of Germany at the end of the eighteenth and the beginning of the nineteenth century, it does not seem to us, that in Africa, one has reached that which is technically specified as philosophical speculation. In that which concerns the future, we are obligated to note what we have observed regarding the end of philosophy as a speculative genre, historically dated and geographically localized." Humanity as a whole has now to produce a "post-philosophical" thinking.[6] Africans must pass beyond ethnic religions to the "scientific sociology of that which the people of black Africa" have produced.[7] As for the Negro-African philosophy, it is and cannot but be an "inverted representation having as a practical function the defense of class interests in contemporary African society."[8] It is concise, demagogic, but clear. Historical experience demonstrates that this kind of ultra-Marxist ideological inflexibility that pushes certain theses of Marx to the point of absurdity often constitutes a skillful manner of combating Marxism. It is always the true heirs of Marx, a Lenin, a Mao, who have continued to philosophize and consider dialectical materialism as an authentic philosophy. And in all the Communist countries, philosophy is to be found in educational programs.

THE METHODOLOGICAL CONDITIONS FOR THE UNBLOCKING OF AFRICAN PHILOSOPHY

The danger to which African philosophy is currently exposed is that of a real blockage. The ethnophilosophers strive to occlude and replace it with their concealed credo. If the ethnophilosophers have chosen to wear a mask to struggle against the awakening thought of Africa, scientists and epistemologists dismiss it overtly in the name of science or the commentary on science. It is therefore very important, in order to make an opening for African philosophy possible, to specify its concept by dispelling certain ambiguities that surround it, and to provide some methodological indications on the study of the constituted African thought and the exercise of a living African philosophical thinking.

In the expression "African philosophy," one should not see any essential link between the subject and the predicate. No civilization maintains such a relationship either with philosophy as such or with any particular philosophical conception. Heidegger thought that philosophy was Greek and Occidental in essence: "Philosophy," he affirmed, "is Greek in its nature [essence]," "[T]he West and Europe, and only these, are, in the innermost course of their history, originally 'philosophical.' "[9] We are not among those who share such a gratuitous prejudice. In the concept of philosophy, there is no essential link with any one particular civilization. The predicates Greek, German, European, or African that qualify philosophy relate to it only in a contingent manner. Philosophy is the thought of the essential, the methodical and critical examination of that which, in the theoretical order or in the practical order, has or should have for humanity a supreme importance. Such is philosophy in its abstract and entirely general essence. This general concept of philosophy is of a universal scope, and Africans have to respect it if they want to philosophize. We are not in agreement with those who think that Africans have to forge their own definition of philosophy. The expression "African philosophy" does not signify a particular philosophical conception that would specifically be African and would then team up with Africanity or negritude. Philosophy in the expression "African philosophy" does not have any particular content; rather, it refers back to the general concept of philosophy. When Tempels and Kagame speak about Bantu philosophy, they designate a system of categories, an ontology, a criteriology, which supposedly are proper to the Bantu and which could be extended to Africans in general, a system that Africans are invited to assume as their own, not because it is more fitting than other systems, not because it enjoys some kind of superiority that we are trying to establish, but due only to the single fact that it is African. When speaking about "African philosophy," we do not primarily envision a determined content of this kind. We want simply to designate an intellectual course of action that conforms to the purely formal definition of philosophy.

This point established, one has to see that any particular philosophy is always elaborated by philosophers who are not themselves abstractions, but are beings of flesh and bones who belong to a continent, to a particular culture, and to a specific period. And for a particular philosopher, to really philosophize is necessarily to examine in a critical and methodic manner the essential problems of his milieu and of his period. He will thus elaborate a philosophy that is in an explicit or implicit relation with his times and his milieu. He can then, going back to and based on principles, generalize and universalize. One can say of a philosophy that it is African or European, to indicate that Africans and Europeans have reflected on their fundamental problems.

In this sense, African philosophy is the exercise by Africans of a specific type of intellectual activity (the critical examination of fundamental problems) applied to the African reality. The type of intellectual activity in question is, as such, neither African, European, Greek, nor German; it is philosophy in general. What is African are the men of flesh and bones who are and who evoke the problems of supreme importance and on whom these same problems are applicable immediately.

This definition of philosophy seems to us reasonable. It is neither too broad nor too narrow. Defining philosophy only in terms of epistemology would lead us to exclude from the domain of philosophy works universally recognized as philosophical: works of ethics, ontology, political philosophy, aesthetics, etc. In this case, it would be difficult to speak of an African philosophy. The immediate consequence of this will be that Africans who are charged with the responsibility of teaching philosophy will turn away from works of the spirit [works of the mind] produced by Africans for thousands of years. I do not see what we stand to gain from such an amnesia, not even to consider the thought of our ancestors as worthy of being examined and discussed. If, on the contrary, we adopt too broad a definition of philosophy, we will certainly be incited to do so by our interest in our conceptions, but it is philosophy that we would risk losing and would no longer be practicing. We will exhaust our energies in a multitude of domains foreign to philosophy. In defining philosophy as the thought of the essential, we preserve the specificity of the philosophical approach [*demarche*] without excluding Africa from the kingdom of philosophical thought. This last point is important because it does not keep African thought from philosophers, who are the most qualified to grasp it and to appreciate it. We have an interest in studying and examining the conceptions and modes of thought of our people, whatever they may have been, simply out of a concern for knowing ourselves and in order not to fall back into the same mistakes again. Besides, there is nothing that says we could not find anything precious in their conceptions.

This definition of African philosophy implies some methodological considerations. The effort that Africans have to exert in the domain of African philosophy should aim at two main objectives—on the one hand, to seize the thought of Africans, to construct its history; on the other hand, to submit our actual problems to philosophical examination:

(a) The knowledge of the already established African thought belongs to the history of philosophy. And this approach [*demarche*] should, in our opinion, respect the methodological exigencies of the history of philosophy. Researchers should expect to find a great diversity of conceptions and of modes of thought. Contemporary Africans do not have the same conceptions and do not think in the same manner. There is no reason to think that it was otherwise in the past. We do not think like our fathers. There is no good reason to suppose that our fathers thought like our grandparents. In short, we should expect diversity both in a synchronic and a diachronic sense.

(b) The diversity of conceptions imposes on us a methodological *neutrality* and *objectivity* in approaching African conceptions. If Africans do not have one and the same conception of the world, nor only one mode of thought, it becomes impossible to adopt a single conception of the world for the sole reason that it is African—if, that is, one makes a choice, to philosophize. If the ethnophilosophers could demand adherence to Bantu philosophy due solely to the fact that it is African, this was because they supposed that all Africans have one and only one philosophy. And the supposition of a philosophy unique and common to all Africans itself had its roots in theological prejudices, in the unique credo of the ethnophilosopher that he surreptitiously slides into the analysis itself. The ethnophilosopher is a prisoner of his credo and wants to imprison us as well. Conscious awareness of the diversity of African conceptions presents itself as a liberation.

(c) On the other hand, the history of African thought, just as the history of philosophy in general, must be grounded essentially (but certainly not exclusively) on texts, whether written or oral. We are not in agreement with Hountondji, who wants to exclude oral texts. After all, Socrates did not write anything. This is not enough reason to pretend that he is not a philosopher. The ethnophilosophers, on the contrary, utilize any cultural element indiscriminately. They interrogate rituals, myths (without discrimination), art, poetry, language, social, political, and educational institutions, etc., on the pretext that philosophy is incarnated in the life of a people. It should also be noted here that it is not only philosophy that is embodied in all the compartments of the life of a society. Everybody is not a philosopher, and the culture of a people is not the work only of philosophers, but also of others—poets, artisans, workers, peasants, bureaucrats, politicians, priests, magicians, athletes, singers, etc. Since global culture is not only the work of philosophers, one cannot reconstitute without discrimination a philosophical system starting from any given cultural element. Suppose that the work of Sartre disappears—one cannot reconstitute Sartrian existentialism from the structure of the French language, the educational system, the political system, or the family life of France. But it is such an impossible reconstitution that the ethnophilosophers claim to have accomplished. Naturally, this is but a conception derived from their prejudices and from the convictions they thus produce.

Philosophy expresses itself essentially in discourse, oral or written, and it is from this discourse that one has to start, that is to say, from texts. The first task of the historians of African thought consequently consists in establishing a corpus of texts congruent with the adopted definition of philosophy and making this available to researchers.

(d) The study of the history of African thought is indispensable, as we have already emphasized. But it is only a preparation for the properly philosophical task that consists of discerning and examining the fundamental problems that pose themselves to us. This examination can result in the elaboration of a new philosophical system. It can also lead to the choice of an already established philosophical system. What remains then is to justify the options and the exclusions. The adoption of a preexisting system of thought should not lead us to dispense with thinking actively. No system of thought can foresee all situations and all problems. Inevitably, the thinker will find himself facing new situations, which he will have to examine personally and to which he must find solutions. He will have to internalize the maxim of Mao Tse-tung, according to whom right ideas come from practice and experience; they do not fall from the sky.

CONDITIONS OF AN INSTITUTIONAL AND MATERIAL KIND

What remains for us to do is to make some suggestions of a practical order capable of ensuring the development of philosophical thought in Africa.

The Augmentation of Enrollment

To increase the number of Africans who will devote themselves to philosophical studies, one can resort to a certain number of procedures, of which we will indicate only two. On one hand, one can diversify the educational formation of philosophers so that they can be oriented to areas of employment other than teaching: diplomacy, journalism, politics, etc. On the other hand, and above all else, it is necessary to extend the teaching of philosophy to the junior year and even to all the previous grades of high school. Our students study literature starting from elementary school. When they reach high school, it would be advantageous if certain philosophical works that also have great literary value and certain literary works that have an important philosophical significance (a large number of Platonic dialogues, the works of philosophical luminaries, such as Camus, Sartre, etc.) could be explained by philosophers.

Documentation

At the present time, those who are interested in African thought are confronted by the lack of works and documents. We have already emphasized the necessity of establishing those oral texts that have a philosophic import. This necessitates research that could be managed with relatively modest means. On this level especially, philosophers have lagged behind as compared with literati. The latter have to their credit numerous theses of oral literature that follow a tested and tried method: collections of oral literary texts published in the original language, learned translations and commentaries on published texts. This method could be adopted by researchers working in the domain of African thought. We should abandon the method, or rather the absence of method, of most ethnophilosophers, who speculate endlessly on African philosophy without texts of reference enabling them to check their affirmations. Nevertheless, numerous traditional and modern texts exist that are of great philosophic interest but are inaccessible to researchers. This is notably the case with the texts of ancient Egypt, without mentioning Meroeic texts not yet translated. Certain texts of Muslim Africans of the last century should be equally known and accessible. Even the translated Egyptian texts are worthy of being reviewed. Divergences that are at times considerable in the diverse traditions of "instruction" lead us to think that part of the work of translation still remains to be done.

Big centers of research in the principal regions of Africa should be created. They should be endowed with properly supplied libraries for advanced research. But all universities should also be endowed with libraries sufficiently supplied to enable works of research at the master's and doctorate levels. It is not easy to obtain research scholarships or paid missions of research for students at these levels.

Technical Equipment and Financing
An African researcher, in most countries, can hardly publish the results of his research even if they have a recognized theoretic value. But modern technology makes possible the obtaining of very presentable texts at a minimum cost. With ten million CFA Francs a philosophy department can obtain appropriate equipment (composphere, xerox machine, etc.) that will allow it to give a very acceptable presentation to its work. For publishing properly speaking, subsidies are necessary, and these are generally not available to the African researcher.

Periodic Colloquiums

African philosophers have an imperative need to discuss and to communicate their work. The best way of doing so is to hold periodic colloquiums. But such colloquiums are expensive. One has to have regular sources of financing. The Festivals of Negro Arts are very expensive. If one-hundredth of the expenses they incur were devoted to the project mentioned here, it would be infinitely more profitable for the future of the African culture.

Conclusion

We were only able to touch lightly on a subject as vast as the promotion of philosophic thought in Africa. I think that these few indications, if followed more or less, will help African philosophy avoid certain impasses and impress on it a vigorous and durable impetus.

NOTES

1. See our, *Essai sur la problématique philosophique*, (Clé, 1971), p. 26.
2. P. J. Hountondji, "Le mythe d'une philosophie spontanée", in *Cahiers Philosophiques Africains*, no. 1, January–June 1972, pp. 107–44, Lubumbashi, Zaire.
3. P. J. Hountondji, *Sur la philosophie africaine*, (Paris: F. Maspero, 1977), p. 125; [*African Philosophy: Myth and Reality* (Indiana University Press, 1983), p. 99].
4. Hountondji, op. cit., p. 246.
5. Ibid., p. 121.
6. J. Mbargane Guissé, *Philosophie, Culture et devenir social en Afrique noire*, N. E. A., p. 15.
7. Ibid., p. 18.
8. Ibid., p. 16.
9. Martin Heidegger, *Qu'est-ce que la philosophie?*, (Gallimard, 1957), pp. 14–15; [Martin Heidegger, *What Is Philosophy*, translated and introduced by W. Kluback and J. T. Wilde (College & University Press Pub., 1956), p. 31.]

OKONDA OKOLO (translated from the French original for this collection by Kango Lare-Lantone)

TRADITION AND DESTINY: HORIZONS OF AN AFRICAN PHILOSOPHICAL HERMENEUTICS

The birth and current revival of the hermeneutic movement seem to be linked to crises: the crisis of self-identity in German romanticism; the crisis of Europe confronted with a technicized [technicisés] world and language. Husserl was the first to echo this crisis, which was experienced by P. Ricoeur as a loss of language and felt by M. Heidegger as the forgetting of Being.[1]

In Africa, the interest in hermeneutics also arises out of the reality of crisis: a generalized identity crisis due to the presence of a culture—a foreign and dominating tradition—and the necessity for a self-affirmation in the construction of an authentic culture and tradition. This crisis, on the strictly philosophical plane, is the expression of a problematic that oscillates between a naive ethnophilosophy and an unproductive criticism.[2] To the imperious need for an authentic and African philosophy, hermeneutics seems to give a positive response. But is this response unique and definitive?

It is the African hermeneutic theory and practice that we need to question if we are to obtain a point of view that is a little more conclusive. Theophilus Okere has demonstrated in a magisterial way the possibility of an African philosophy in the approach of the factual interpretation of culture and tradition.[3] More recently, Professor J. Kinyongo has exhibited in a highly convincing manner, in the discursive mode proper to our folktales, proverbs, myths, etc., the fundament of the African philosophical discourse.[4] And already there are many who, with more or less success, are trying their hand at this philosophical hermeneutics.[5] For our part, we want to test the resources but also the limits of our hermeneutical models and practices, by examining the two notions that encompass our interpretative efforts in an unconquerable circle—the notions of Tradition and Destiny. These notions simultaneously define the object, the subject, the horizons, and the limits of interpretation. To interpret is always to close the circle of the subject and the object. We cannot, however, make this circle our own if we do not lay it out beyond the thought of the subject and the object, toward a thinking of our horizons and the limits of our interpretation defined by the reality of our traditions and the ideality of our destiny.

Our reading of the hermeneutics of P. Ricoeur, M. Heidegger and H. G. Gadamer[6] has lead us to formulate three propositions that, together, enunciate a general theory of hermeneutics:

1. Any theory of reading presupposes a theory of the text and vice versa.

2. Any reading (interpreting) presupposes some kind of "retake."

3. Any reading and any retaking involves a decision that starts from the reading and retaking subject's vision of the world.

From all this, what seems to be revealed is that all interpretation presupposes a tradition, and that tradition as such is always interpreted. Even more, all interpretation appears to be supported by a certain idea of destiny—destiny in the sense employed by the young Hegel, and found in Hölderlin and Greek tragedy. Interpretation is the space where tradition and an idea of destiny are deployed or unfolded.

But, what is tradition? One generally defines it as the matter that is delivered over and transmitted from generation to generation. We should, nevertheless, restore to this term its primitive meaning, which subsists within the law and the liturgy—i.e., the action of delivery and of transmission.[7] So defined, tradition finds itself fundamentally linked to the act of interpretation, which preserves and continues it. This act of interpretation is possible only when it is instigated and sustained by an idea of destiny, which, for every interpreter, summarizes the spiritual economy of a tradition.

Destiny, what is it? It is often defined as the mysterious power that determines the course of events, a certain kind of fatality.[8] As far as we are concerned, we take the term in the sense given to it by the young Hegel in the Frankfurt period. There, the idea of fatality is maintained, combined together with the idea of liberty and reason. The expression of a people's destiny, and of an individual's, inspired by Hellenism and by Greek tragedy, can already be traced in the works of Berne,[9] yet it is at Frankfurt that this notion receives its fullness and plays a central role in the philosophy of the young Hegel. During this period, his ideas are close to those of his friend Hölderlin, for whom the idea of the irrationality of life is dominant. The idea of destiny is the rational-irrational concept out of which Hegel elaborates the dialectics of life and of history. Destiny in general is, for Hegel, the effective reality; in brief, it is the history and judgment of the world. The destinies of peoples and individuals are particular forms taken by this general destiny, which correspond to the original passions of individuals and peoples. These passions are the means through which the universal spirit realizes itself. They are finite and particular and live out a characteristic tension between the finite and the infinite, between liberty and necessity. These passions define mankind and peoples, but they seem foreign to them and in struggle against them. Destiny is thus an implacable given of a people and of an individual, but it is also a task of the future for a people and for an individual.[10] It is the thread of tradition and of interpretations.

The idea of destiny that emerges from the hermeneutics of Ricoeur, Heidegger, and Gadamer rejoins that proposed by the Hegel of the romantic period. This hermeneutics participates in the Hegelian effort to render the tragic aspect of life and assumes the characteristic tension defining the Occidental tradition. It is known that Hegel went beyond and surpassed this *pantragisme* with a *panlogisme* that culminates in absolute knowledge.[11] Contemporary hermeneutists go back to and begin anew Hegel's effort of going beyond but refuse the closure of absolute knowledge. From this point of view,

European hermeneutics remains resolutely romantic and does not seem to have gone beyond the young Hegel. Shouldn't this idea of destiny be shattered so as to make possible a hermeneutics other than the European and Hegelian?

Our quest for a general theory of hermeneutics results in demonstrating that hermeneutics exists only in particular traditions. But, given the rapport between comprehension, interpretation, and application, and between reading and "retaking," the theory formulated here has, we believe, an exploratory virtue for African hermeneutics that is still not properly developed and adequately theorized. This theory, faced with a new tradition, instigates, as one will see, a recasting of an even greater generality.

"Any theory of reading presupposes a theory of the text and vice versa." Here, the African tradition is the text of our reading. But first, what is a text? One should not limit the text to a written text. We have to retain the lesson of contemporary hermeneutic theories and extend the sense of a text to include all verbal concatenations [*enchainement*] and all that offers itself to be read, that is to say, tradition as a whole. There is even a need to go beyond these theories. The ideality of meaning that appears more clearly in the text is not tied, as Gadamer affirms, to the text as that which is written, nor, as preconized by Ricoeur, to the text as the work, but very much so to the text as a fact of tradition. The written word, the work in itself, has nothing to say if it is not provoked, instigated, and recreated by tradition. It is the process of tradition-in-becoming [*devenir tradition*] that makes a text or a work autonomous from its author and from its initial destination; this same process of tradition-in-becoming extracts the text or work out of its quotidian ambient and offers it a propitious space from within which it can open up and recreate new worlds. Thus, the ideality of meaning proper to the text borrows from that more fundamental sense of the tradition.[12]

The tradition, essentially defined as transmission, constitutes a hermeneutic concatenation of interpretations and reinterpretations. To read our tradition is nothing like climbing the whole chain of interpretations all the way back to its originative starting point;

rather, it is to properly recreate the chain in actualizing it. We realize then that tradition and interpretation are intimately linked. Their dialectical relation ensures the inseparability of hermeneutical theory and practice. Hermeneutical theory is an integral part of hermeneutical practice. Here, theory is not added to practice as a luxurious supplement; it illuminates practice, which, in turn, provokes it in a dialectical manner. From all this, we can draw a rather important methodological consequence: A true hermeneutical practice must be one that can also be enunciated as theory.

Enunciating a theory enables the hermeneutist to properly assume his task of creation and actualization, and to be aware of the resources and the limits of the practice he is engaged in. The failure to enunciate a theory has led a good number of African and Africanist hermeneutists—among them, the ethnophilosophers—away from their proper task. They have ignored their resources, and their affirmations have gone beyond the limits permitted by their practice. A hermeneutical critique of ethnophilosophy still remains to be undertaken.

"Any reading is always oriented toward some kind of 'retake.'" This second proposition means first of all that appropriation is that which results from any reading. This "retake" is the recreation, the actualization, of what is being read. This actualization can take the form of differing epistemological statutes: From a reading, we can proceed to juridical, religious, philosophical, ideological, and scientific actualizations, and so on. The epistemological status of an actualization depends on its internal process and the implied basic postulates. For example, a philosophical actualization is possible only if we preserve unadulterated its requirements of rationality and if the order of questioning has adequate depth and is sufficiently defined.

The greatest threat, at the level of the "retake," is confusion and vagueness. African and Africanist "retakes" of African traditions would gain by being clearer and more precise. We have witnessed for a long time now "retakes" with dubious epistemological status; they promise philosophy, but deliver a theology or an ideology.

Our second proposition also means that reading is never innocent.

The impact of the "retake" we propose is always felt in the reading we undertake. The "retake" selects, at the moment of reading, susceptible aspects that enable it to be realized. It is up to the hermeneutist to properly define the problematic of the retake for which he is undertaking an interpretation. In so doing, we avoid falling into untruth— worse still, into mystification. This is so because the "retake" projects and delimits the role of creation in the reading.

Let us limit ourselves to the strictly philosophic retake. To be philosophical, the "retake" presupposes a problematic and a properly circumscribed philosophical course [*demarche*]. But to remain hermeneutical, it has to insert both the problematic and the properly circumscribed course into the tradition with the aim of effecting an appropriation. The examples of Heidegger and Ricoeur are extremely enlightening. Their philosophical "retakes" presuppose two well delimited philosophical problematics—the one pertaining to Being and the other to the *cogito*; as they themselves acknowledge, these problematics have their roots in the Occidental tradition. The ontological or reflective hermeneutics of Heidegger or of Ricoeur is therefore a hermeneutics of the Occidental tradition. Thus, a philosophical hermeneutics seems always to be a philosophical hermeneutics of a tradition.

From these last considerations ensues a problem for the African "retakes." Their contours are defined elsewhere than in the African tradition itself. It is, for example, Christianity that generally determines the problematic of a religious and theological "retake"; it is Occidental philosophy that often constitutes the basis of the philosophical "retake" of the African tradition. Whereas it is the African tradition itself that ought to assure the hermeneuticity, the philosophicity, and hence the Africanity of a determined practice.

The African tradition assures the Africanity of the African philosophical hermeneutics by providing the subject matter, the problematics, and its very own philosophical course. Now, at this point, the problem of the restoration of the past that we forgot because of our hermeneutical concern with appropriation poses itself. We should not only restore the monuments of the tradition but also the philosophies and orientations that occurred in our traditional past. The history of philosophical ideas is one of the conditions for an African philosophical hermeneutics. African hermeneutics, left to itself, must die as a hermeneutics if it is not sustained by a science of history applied to ideas—a science that will supply African hermeneutics with a subject matter, a problematic, and its own proper course [*demarche*].

How can we realize a history of philosophical ideas in an *oral* tradition? We will have to consider the phenomenon of orality, which is the only thing that can reveal to us the mode of transmission at work here and the possible forms of expression and of content.[13]

The concern with restoration has to go hand in hand with the concern for appropriation. Both concerns structure relations from "front to back" and define internally the process of the tradition and of the interpretation. The cultural memory is ceaselessly renewed retroactively by new discoveries. Our past, by continually modifying itself through our discoveries, invites us to new appropriations; these appropriations lead us toward a better grasp of our identity.

"Any reading and any retake decidedly starts from the reading and retaking subject's vision of the world." Before developing this third proposition, let us ask ourselves what the expression "vision of the world" could possibly mean. From all the definitions that we can give to this expression—vision of the world—we can retain three essential aspects: a descriptive aspect by which the vision of the world presents an image of the world, an existential situation; a justificatory aspect by which it reflects on and renders an account of what it is and what it has been; and a projective aspect through which it sketches the future of an individual or of a people.[14] Therefore, the vision of the world is itself hermeneutical and potentially contains other hermeneutical developments. It is expressed and summarized in the idea of destiny, in which it deploys the spiritual economy of an individual or of a people between the past and the future.

Our third proposition underlines the operative function of the vision of the world and of the idea of destiny in the hermeneutical process. The vision of the world does not only unleash the hermeneutical process; it also sustains it in its development and it is that toward which the latter tends tirelessly. The hermeneutics of Heidegger, of Gadamer, and of Ricoeur show us this, taken separately and as a whole. Their divergences reside at this level; but it is also at this level that an aspect of their convergence shows itself. They all share the vision of the world and the idea of destiny that stimulated Hegel's enterprise: destiny as a characteristic tension, rooted in Greek tragedy, and the view of life as both an implacable given and as a task that is always renewed. This destiny seems to culminate in a very precise mission, and a particular destination: Europe is called on if not to dominate, at least in some way to civilize, to liberate, to save, and to spiritualize other peoples. To do this, it has to preserve all of the spiritual weight that characterizes it. The retaking efforts that European hermeneutists deploy aim at preserving Europe from spiritual destruction and, with Europe, the entire world.

And what about us, what is our vision of the world, and what is our idea of destiny that directs our readings and our retakes? Can we align ourselves with the vision of the world, with the idea of destiny, secreted by European hermeneutics without implicitly negating our own tradition and our own history?[16] Can we simply reverse this vision of the world, this idea of destiny, and brandish our spiritual superiority in front of a technicized [technicisée] and materialistic Europe without falling back into a twisted Hegelianism?[17] We will have to, no doubt, explode the idea of destiny and recharge it anew starting from our hermeneutical situation. This hermeneutical situation is that of the formerly colonized, the oppressed, that of the underdeveloped, struggling for more justice and equality. From this point of view, the validity of an interpretation is tied to the validity of a struggle—of its justice and of its justness. Here, we affirm the methodological preeminence of praxis on hermeneutics, praxis understood in the sense of an action tending toward the qualitative transformation of life.[18] We do not share the opinion of those who think that praxis delivers a deadly blow to hermeneutics.[19] We affirm rather that, in a given situation, it is praxis that assigns to hermeneutics its place and its development. Praxis unleashes the hermeneutical process and gives it an orientation. Hermeneutics, in turn, offers praxis a cultural self-identity necessary for ideological combat.

* * *

By way of conclusion, we say that all these reflections on tradition and on destiny as horizons of a philosophical hermeneutics do nothing more than emphatically mark the recognition of tradition as the moment that decides the validity of the object, the methods, and the results of hermeneutics. We have to acknowledge that our efforts at theorizing interpretation and tradition are inscribed interior to the ways and means that tradition itself secretes and utilizes for its own preservation, renewal, and perpetuation.

NOTES

1. This text follows our doctorate thesis in philosophy entitled *Tradition et Destin, Essai sur la philosophie herméneutique de P. Ricoeur, M. Heidegger et H. G. Gadamer*, Lubumbashi, July 1979. "Crisis in German Romanticism: Dilthey," *Le Monde de l'esprit*, vol. 1 (Paris: Aubier, 1947), p. 19: "Its origin was the historically justified desire to found a conception of life and of the world in which the German spirit could find satisfaction." "Pour l'Europe: Husserl," *Krisis*, trad. fr. dans *Études philosophiques*, vol. 4 (1949), pp. 127–59, 229–301; Heidegger, *L'Etre et le Temps* (Paris: Gallimard, 1964), p. 17; Ricoeur, *La Symbolique du mal* (Paris: Aubier, 1960), p. 325.
2. We are borrowing this distinction from our colleague and friend Ngoma-Binda, "Pour une orientation authentique de la philosophie en Afrique: l'herméneutique," in *Zaire-Afrique*, no. 17 (1977), pp. 143–58.
3. Okere Theophilus, *Can There Be an African Philosophy?*, doctorate thesis, Louvain, 1971.
4. Kinyongo, J., "Essai sur la fondation épistémologique d'une philosophe herméneutique en Afrique: le case de la discursivité," *Présence Africaine*, no. 109, 1st quarterly (1979), pp. 11–26.
5. We are citing among others Nkombe Oleko, *Métaphore et métonymie dans les symboles parémiologiques tetela*, doctorate thesis, Louvain 1975.
6. Paul Ricoeur, born in 1913, is a French philosopher; Martin Heidegger (1880–1976), the most renowned of the contemporary German philosophers. Hans-Georg Gadamer, born in 1900, German philosopher, is the successor of Karl Jaspers at Heidelberg.
7. Lanlande, A. *Vocabulaire technique et critique de la philosophie*, 11th ed. (Paris: P.U.F., 1972), p. 1140.
8. Ibid., p. 219.
9. Among others, *L'Esprit du christianisme et son destin*.
10. Hyppolite, J. *Introduction à la philosophie de l'histoire de Hegel* (Paris: Marcel

Riviere, 1968), pp. 49–64; see also P. Bertrand, "Le sens du tragique et du destin dans la dialectique hegelienne," in *Revue de Métaphysique et de Morale*, 1940.

11. J. Hyppolite, cit., p. 15: "pantragisme" and "panlogisme."
12. We believe this has been demonstrated in our "Lecture et reprise philosophiques des traditions dans l'Afrique contemporaine," in *Rapport complet du Séminaire National des Philosophes Zaïrois*, Lubumbashi, 1976, pp. 132–42.
13. This study of orality we already have in progress.
14. The vision of the world is "simultaneously a perspective on the totality of the world, a way of making sense of human life in accordance with a scale of values, an approach to what is the fundament of all reality and the justification of all values, the transcendental . . . ," M. Dufrenne and P. Ricoeur, as quoted by Vancourt R., *La Philosophie et sa structure* (Paris: Bloud et Gay, 1953), p. 95. See also "Weltanschauung" in Dilthey, *Le Monde de L'esprit* (Paris, Aubier, 1947), pp. 378–405.
15. Martin Heidegger, *Introduction a la métaphysique* (Paris: Gallimard, 1967), p. 53: [*An Introduction to Metaphysics* (Yale University Press, 1959), p. 42.] "That is why we have related the question of [B]eing to the destiny of Europe, where the destiny of the earth is being decided—while our own historic being-there proves to be the center for Europe itself."
16. Indeed for Hegel: "[T]hat which we understand as a whole under the name of Africa, is an a-historical non-developed world, entirely prisoner of the natural spirit and whose place is still found at the threshold of universal history." (*La Reason dans l'histoire*, Paris, 10/18, 1965, p. 269).
17. We are thinking of negritude specifically in its Senghorian version.
18. Lalande, A., op. cit., p. 1271.
19. This opinion follows from Marx's 11th thesis on Feuerbach. We ask ourselves whether the Marxists, in their theories and practices, have come to terms with this interpretation.

E. WAMBA-DIA-WAMBA

PHILOSOPHY IN AFRICA: CHALLENGES OF THE AFRICAN PHILOSOPHER[1]

I. BANTU PHILOSOPHY, TRUE OR FALSE PHILOSOPHICAL PROBLEMATICS IN AFRICA

Theoretical work in Africa is developing, deepening, and being transformed. This is a theoretical expression of the profound socioeconomic, political, and cultural transformations Africa has been undergoing since the end of the last century, that is, since the beginning of the imperialist epoch, the highest stage of development of capitalist social formations. Through ideological struggles, these transformations give rise to different camps that are formed and that understand or grasp these transformations differently. Although the struggle took, in African history, various forms and contents, it has always had as a motive force of its tendential development the unity/struggle of contraries—imperialism and African national liberation. On the one side, one finds imperialist forces of domination that aim at the repeated defeat of the African resistance at all levels; and, on the other side, antiimperialist forces militating in favor of the strengthening, and the victory, of the African resistance up to complete national liberation.

The question of the defense or the negation (or denial) of African culture understood or expressed in different ways (African cultural identity, African personality, Africanity, African way of life, communalism, etc.) has in fact always been at the center of the African people's struggle against imperialist domination in all its forms. In their ideological aspects, these repeated struggles have given rise to several cultural trends or movements: pan-Africanism, negritude, search for an African philosophy, search for an African ideology, religious syncretic movements, authenticity or recourse/ return to ancestral sources/values, renaissance of the Egyptian Negro-African civilization, search for, or proclamation of, an African socialism, African theology, etc. Each of these trends or movements, in its tendential development, was essentially contradictory—an element of a radical ideological antagonism against imperialism went hand in hand with an element of an ideological collusion (of alignment—"against communism," for example) with imperialism. In its struggle against communism, imperialism sought and got some support from some aspects and tendencies of these movements. The stake of African philosophy emerged through these cultural battles induced or required by the African resistance against imperialist domination.

African resistance unveiled, very early, the mystifications of the European *civilizing mission*, which was based on a radical denial (negation and destruction) of African cultures. It was, in fact, to reflect on and to resolve the crisis of the Belgian *civilizing mission* generated by the cultural resistance of the Bantu masses that Father P. Tempels, intending to reexamine its philosophical presuppositions, discovered and co-opted the famous *Bantu Philosophy*. With the relative success of the Kimbanguist, Kitawalist, etc., ideological resistance, why should it surprise us that the ideologues of the Belgian colonial state reexamined the *ideological foundations* of the *civilizing mission*? It was with goodwill and intelligence that P. Tempels devoted himself to that work. But the ideological orientation that influenced his perception and epistemological awareness remained *colonialist* (or "colonizing"). As a matter of fact, P. Tempels wanted to boost the *European civilizing mission*, which encountered, in a period of grave socioeconomic crises, a persistent ideological resistance. To do exactly that, he intended following the example of his enemies, the Kimbanguists, who took some European cultural elements to use against colonialism, that is, to incorporate in the philosophical foundation of the civilizing mission even cultural elements of the natives to be civilized. More than that, he wanted to find in the very *inferior cultures* of the natives elements that could serve as a fertile ground for the seed of the *civilizing mission*. Tempels's concern is this—how to make the natives even just *hear* (let alone understand and act out) the *teachings* of the *civilizing mission* from the perspective of their own being-in-the-world, their world outlook, the native way of viewing the world. Of course, when it is raised by a colonialist—no matter how liberal or philanthropic he may be—the question is not *subversive* at all. It simply aims at making colonization more effective. The subversive Muntu would, on the one hand, have looked for, from within the Bantu way of living, elements that would prevent the Muntu from *hearing* the teachings of the *civilizing mission* and he would, on the other hand, find, from within the civilizing mission, European elements capable of canceling (or rendering void) the effectiveness on the Muntu of the *civilizing mission*. For P. Tempels, the challenge was to find a way of breaking, from within the cultures of the natives, their cultural resistance to the *civilizing mission*. In other words, it was necessary to rectify the angle and the line of sight of the civilizing aim (*"l'angle de visée du tir civilisateur"*) in order to hit the target (the natives to be civilized) at its fatal point. It was necessary, at the same time, to isolate from the native masses the rebelling "half civilized"—*évolués*—the Kimbanguists, for example. It was necessary to invest in the terrain of the enemy—to get the Muntu to swallow and internalize the idea that his own way of viewing the world, his own world outlook, has no other ultimate objective than the *European civilizing mission*. For him there is no other future history.

This fundamental revision of the *civilizing* mission has some risks: Baits (that the Muntu is a real human being, with a philosophy and a culture) could boomerang against the colonizing mission. Indeed, why would the Muntu as a human being have his own civilizing mission, even if it be a self-civilizing mission? Since no one can destroy what one is ignorant of, there is also in Tempels's attempt a recognition of the existence of the native's theoretical work—not as an element of the native's social practice but as a plausible object of colonial study. The Muntu, acting and guided by a philosophy, is incapable of systematizing his philosophy; this was the conclusion P. Tempels drew from his study. Such a systematization is possible only from the perspective of the highest level of the hierarchy of forces. Bantu philosophy became conscious of itself through the non-Muntu: P. Tempels is a savior of the Bantu already predicted, claimed, and announced by their own world outlook!

What is this if not a justification of the very foundations of imperialism?

It is the African resistance (taking several forms: cultural resistance, religious syncretic movements, etc.) against imperialism that forces imperialist ideologues to resort to cultural elements of the dominated natives to break up that resistance and give sound "rational" grounding to imperialism. Against such attempts at giving theoretical foundation to imperialism, African resistance must look for new and solid bases. Does resorting to the philosophical discourse emerging from the process of providing theoretical foundations to imperialism lead to, on solid theoretical bases, a theoretical arming of the antiimperialist resistance? From Nkrumah to Cabral, from Eboussi Boulaga to Towa, from Cheikh Anta Diop to Theophile Obenga, etc., attempts are being made, for better or for worse, to take up the challenge. Imperialism, in a specific conjuncture of its being challenged, works for a new philosophical justification. Does the African resistance against imperialism also need a philosophical justification to develop its momentum? African resistance is right against all the reasons imperialism can produce. One is, everywhere and always, right against reactionaries. Indeed, every systematization of the being-in-the-world of the Muntu cannot necessarily be imperialist. And the one produced by imperialism always misses its target: It cannot dry out the very source of the Muntu's resistance against imperialism. Initiative, even in this process, belongs not to imperialism but to the Muntu's resistance.

This is how, we think, philosophical problematics in Africa should be situated and grasped. Eboussi Boulaga, for example, tries to locate, in this very framework, the real stake of philosophical struggle in today's Africa, a struggle characterized by him as being a

desire to attest a contested humanity or a humanity in danger (or a threatened humanity) and that of being by and for oneself, through the articulation of having and making according to an order excluding violence and arbitrariness.[2]

Isn't this a very complicated way of talking about socialism? The articulation of relations of production (which determines property ownership or "having") and productive forces (which determines modes of acting or "making") constitutes a mode of production; the only one to give rise to a social order excluding violence and arbitrariness, isn't this the Communist mode of production? Doesn't the desire to reach that order imply a struggle for socialism?

Reactions—coming from all parts—to P. Tempels's work signaled the genesis and development of the modern form of philosophical struggle in Africa: Those who were confronted with P. Tempels's discourse (his treatise entitled *Bantu Philosophy*) were summoned to speak on the existence or nonexistence of Bantu philosophy as well as on its status as an important weapon in the ideological struggle in Africa. On the African side, the publication of *Bantu Philosophy*, in 1943, gave rise to the emergence of a new type of African intellectual or thinker. These are organic intellectuals of social classes that emerged through the historical process of imperialist penetration, domination, and the transformation of African societies. At a time when philosophy was still denied to the African people, still characterized by "primitive mentality," it is understandable why the book, initially at least, had such a powerful influence on these thinkers. On the imperialist side, by contrast, the inherent contradiction in every bourgeois ideology, opposing a philanthropic function or element to a repressive one, voiced by bourgeois philosophers, dropped its mask or was exposed. The hard ordeal of imperialist wars led to a considerable weakening of imperialist countries. In addition to the development of the socialist camp in the world, the movement of anticolonial struggles was increasingly gaining momentum. On the ideological

plane, the philanthropic function of bourgeois ideology was becoming dominant in the reproduction of imperialist domination.
About this time, talk of the crisis of European consciousness or
civilization started becoming fashionable. With the dominance of the
philanthropic function began the imperialist theoretical preparation
for neocolonialism. Bourgeois theoreticians of the philanthropic aspect of bourgeois ideology were extremely sympathetic to Tempels's
work, whose philosophical ambition (*visée*) was principally philanthropic. One should not interpret this bourgeois ideological sympa-
thy in terms of philosophical competence or incompetence.

The imperialist reform, to which P. Tempels devotes his work, is
required by imperialism to contain the rising momentum of the
anticolonial struggles. It also represents, for the anticolonial struggles, at the same time a partial victory (imperialism is obliged to
recognize its existence publicly) and a real danger of being ideologi-
cally co-opted and thus safely redirected away from its real target.

To those, on the African side, who saw in Tempels's work a real
cultural liberation of the African, a decisive blow against European
ethnocentrism—which always denied any genuine culture or philosophy to Africans—Fanon could certainly have addressed the following words:

Historically, the Negro steeped in the inessentiality of servitude was set free
by his master. He did not fight for his freedom. Out of slavery the Negro
burst into the lists where his masters stood. Like those servants who are
allowed once every year to dance in the drawing room, the Negro is looking
for a prop. The Negro has not become a master. When there are no longer
slaves, there are no longer masters. The Negro is a slave who has been
allowed to assume the attitude of a master. The white man is a master who
has allowed his slaves to eat at his table.[3]

Why can't one say the same thing about the African philosophers who
believed they had been truly liberated, without a fight, by P. Tempels?
For the Muntu, the white priest P. Tempels systematizes the former's
philosophy. Has there been, to tell the truth, any real philosophical
combat other than that of the cultural resistance of the Bantu that
compels P. Tempels to philosophize? As a representative of Western

philosophy (the very one that has always philosophized about the nonexistence of African philosophy), P. Tempels vis-à-vis the Muntu world outlook—serving as a partial ideological deep rooting to the Kimbanguist, Kitawalist, and Lukokist social contention, for example—although threatened, does not feel defeated. He only frees (against which enslavement?) the Muntu and uses the latter's vision to reinforce the hierarchy of forces (or powers) that places the imperialist West in the highest position of domination. (Since the West, in this hierarchy, is second only to the place occupied by God, who, precisely, is also revealed to the Muntu by the West.) This reminds one of a master who pretends to liberate his docile slave from the violence of the rebellious slave by giving the former his freedom. Isn't this the very reason P. Tempels cannot chew his words while speaking of the uprooted *évolués*? Through the publication of his book, P. Tempels, while proclaiming that "from now on, the Muntu has a systematic philosophy," still denies that the Muntu is capable of writing a treatise in philosophy.[4] What does this imply if not that Kimbanguist and similar Bantus cannot be genuine Bantu philosophers? But why doesn't Tempels call this philosophy *his* own philosophy?

A slave may refuse to accept the freedom given to him by his master—this would of course be the starting point of a rebellion by a docile slave—but to accept it would just confirm his defeat. Absolute indifference toward this gift—the possible position of a rebelling slave—would be more in line with real freedom.

As in the case of the slave who refuses to accept the freedom given to him by his master, are not those who deny that Bantu philosophy is a real (true, authentic) philosophy falling back into the imperialist ethnocentric problematic? Even if freedom was genuinely given, without the complete end of slavery as such, could this freedom, socially speaking, be real? Confronted with the co-optation of Bantu ontology by the imperialist camp, which attitude should the rebelling Muntu have adopted? Certainly it would have been more radical: It would have required him to leave the camp of the perpetual demand or begging for recognition and that of self-satisfaction under domination and to carry out his struggle to the very ranks of the *other*. He would have said *no* to any docility—even Bantu docility—and arming himself against the imperialist arrow (or bullet), he would have prevented, from within, this bullet from being fired. Imperialist ideologues, such as Tempels, were looking within the native cultures for cultural allies. The rebelling Muntu would have looked, also within the dominant culture, for a fertile ground upon which to establish firmly his rebellion and combat, to overthrow domination. Through Tempels's voice, imperialism asserts that Kimbangu, for example, is not an authentic Bantu philosopher for bourgeois philosophers. Kimbangu was preaching that:

the country, yes, the country will change Truly. The apostles of that idea will rise up on the day fixed by the saviour. The Whites have the sign of authority. But they no longer have authority. The power belongs to us from now on. It is no longer theirs.[5]

Moreover, the main doctrine of Kimbangu could be summarized in one sentence: "We want a civilizing mission of the Congolese by the Congolese and for the Congolese." And this is, of course, contrary to the Bantu philosophy, which claims the European *civilizing mission* to be its ultimate objective. Imperialism also asserts that Marx, for example, is not a true (authentic) philosopher. Should not the rebelling Muntu align himself with Marx and his like? But one needs to be well organized to invest victoriously in the terrain of the enemy. With no sound political organization, the Kimbanguists, for example, who tried to invest in the ideological terrain of the enemy, were, in their majority, finally co-opted by the dominant culture of the enemy. (Kimbanguists of today would find it difficult to understand Kimbangu—he is no longer an authentic philosopher perhaps?) Why would not the rebelling Muntu's philosophy and that of the internal rebel (i.e., Marx) of the imperialist camp—both philosophies being relegated by imperialism to the rank of nonphilosophy (if not antiphilosophy)—share a common enemy? Isn't to say yes (a jubilant yes) to imperialist recognition already to disarm oneself before the decisive battle against one's weaknesses has started? To transform an antagonistic contradiction into a nonantagonistic one is but the beginning of the resolution of a contradiction; its complete resolution requires that one of the contraries absolutely disappear and that the other as a consequence be profoundly transformed. Armed with Bantu philosophy, the *évolué* dominated by imperialism—to which he owes his very birth as a class, the systematization of his philosophy, that is, the genesis of his social consciousness—must pursue his struggle if he wants to free himself: Even his very social consciousness has not yet reached the level of sharpness reached by that of the rebelling Muntu. And would Bantu philosophy not be a useless extra weight to carry and one which would prevent him from seeing the real road to freedom?

Faced with P. Tempels's work, the African side, insofar as it did say something on the contributions of this philosopher, was divided—in favor of the work and its development (the stand of the gradualists and the allies of philanthropic imperialism), on the one hand; opposed to the very problematic inaugurated by that work and in favor of the systematization of the theoretical work of the dominated African people as required by their persistent resistance, on the other hand. In each African conjuncture, philosophical debate around P. Tempels's work is a good occasion that allows us to draw—if one can say so—a demarcation line dividing different camps: Tempels, Kagame, Senghor, Bohaken, Mbiti, A. N'Daw, B. J. Fouda, Lufuluabo, etc.; Nkrumah, M. Towa, Eboussi Boulaga, P. J. Hountondji, E. P. Elungu etc.; Cheikh Anta Diop, T. Obenga, Fode Diawara, etc.; Sekou Toure, F. Fanon, A. Cabral, etc.; African communalism (initiatory esoteric cosmogonies, etc.). These camps are not clearly delimited; there is not only complementarity and opposition among them, but there is interpenetration as well.

The history of the defeats of the African resistance is also seen in the institutionalization of the crisis (scission, split) of African nations: *évolués* vs. *non-évolués*, domesticated *evolues* vs. re-Africanized *evolues*, brutalized, silenced and beaten masses vs. resisting and rebelling African masses. This crisis, taking several contents and forms, provokes thought and offers itself as the object of African thought; it is also the motive force and the very essence of African philosophy. The latter appears at once as the arm of the continuation of imperialist domination, through reciprocal philanthropic participation (Tempels), if we may say so, and as the rhetoric or apology for the search of identity by *évolués* constantly appealed to or summoned, as African subjects, by imperialist philosophers. Only very rarely does African philosophy concern itself with the struggle against the African people's own weaknesses. As in the case of the slave freed by his master still looking for his identity (as a free man), some of our African philosophers are still looking for, in Africanity, an authentic African philosophy. The slave may not be aware that social conditions in the world forced his master to free him and not the goodness of his heart. P. Tempels, on the other hand, intends to provide imperialism with a weapon that may allow it to contain the natives on the basis of their own world outlook as the only means by which to continue and succeed in the *civilizing mission's* business. The *évolués* (mentally repulsed by imperialist cultural ethnocentrism) seized that work as a weapon allowing them to enter the Universal ("Universal history") and demand/claim ontological equality with their imperialist masters ("We too have something to bring with us to the Senghorian market of give and take—'*marche du donner et du recevoir*' "!). What does ontological equality mean under imperialist domination? Why should one not take seriously what Aimé Césaire has to say on this point?

If there is anything better, it is Rev. Tempels. Let them plunder and torture in the Congo, let the Belgian colonizer seize all the natural resources, let him stamp out all freedom, let him crush all pride—let him go in peace, the Reverend Father Tempels consents to all that. But take care! You are going to the Congo? Respect—I do not say native property (the great Belgian companies might take that as a dig at them), I do not say the freedom of the natives (the Belgian colonialists might think that was subversive talk), I do not say the Congolese nation (the Belgian government might take it much amiss)—I say: You are going to the Congo? Respect the Bantu philosophy!

"It would be really outrageous," writes the Rev. Tempels, "if the white educator were to insist on destroying the black man's own, particular human spirit, which is the only reality that prevents us from considering him as an inferior being. It would be a crime against humanity, on the part of the colonizer, to emancipate the primitive races from that which is valid, from that which constitutes a kernel of truth in their traditional thought, etc. . . ."

Now then, know that Bantu thought is essentially ontological; that Bantu ontology is based on the truly fundamental notions of a life force and a hierarchy of life forces; and that for the Bantu the ontological order which defines the world comes from God and, as a divine decree, must be respected.

Wonderful! Everybody gains: the big companies, the colonists, the government—everybody except the Bantu, naturally.

Since Bantu thought is ontological, the Bantu only ask for satisfaction of an ontological nature. Decent wages! Comfortable housing! Food! These Bantu are pure spirits, I tell you: "What they desire first of all and above all is not the improvement of their economic or material situation, but the white man's recognition of and respect for their dignity as men, their full human value". . . .

Tempels notes with obvious satisfaction "from their first contact with the white men, the Bantu considered us from the only point of view that was possible to them, the point of view of their Bantu philosophy" and "*integrated us in their hierarchy of life forces at a very high level.*"

In other words, arrange it so that the white man, and particularly the Belgian, and even more particularly Albert or Leopold, takes his place at the head of the hierarchy of Bantu life forces, and you have done the trick. You will have brought this miracle to pass: *the Bantu god will take responsibility for the Belgian* colonialist order, and any Bantu who dares to raise his hand against it will *be guilty of sacrilege.*[6]

That is how Aimé Césaire denounces the "trick."

Indeed, one cannot also say, as does Gatore Oswald, that "African societies were emptied of their potentiality for transformation in so far as colonialism had destroyed the seeds of their history."[7] It is the tenacious resistance of the popular African masses, apparently kept outside of the philosophical monologue/dialogue of the imperialist masters, a dialogue between the latter and the *évolués* (products of the *civilizing mission*), and finally, a dialogue regrouping the *évolués* together—against the imperialist domination reproduced even after political independence; it is this very resistance which forced part of these *évolués* to be re-Africanized. Through this mass resistance— now spontaneous, now organized, and always broken down and always resumed—under colonialism, Africa was always present. We cannot accept with Gatore Oswald that "Africa was absent because she lost her socio-cultural personality and that, victim of an arbitrary prejudice, she was considered to be a cold and immobile continent—outside history."[8] All those numerous mass uprisings, all those colonial wars and military operations that, under colonialism, they loved calling pacification operations, would have had no reason for being pursued had this been the case. Was it colonialism which was the subject of African linguistic productions, to take but one example? Indeed, what is meant by sociocultural personality? The colonized masses of African people, like the proletariat in capitalism, are structurally a piece of the colonial system but tendentially they are a heterogenous force to the colonial society and as such incarnate the very destruction of that society (as an anticolonial revolutionary force). This is a major difficulty in the revolutionary understanding of imperialism. Indeed, for example, if colonialism is studied as a system of absolute alienation, the only way to conceive of the abolition of alienation is from the outside of the system. Towa, for example, as we will see, reduces Africanity to colonizability (i.e., the specificity of African societies is to be colonizable). By so doing, he cannot conceptualize how colonizability is going to be transcended otherwise than through another outside form of imperialism.

The re-Africanization process of some *évolués* (this is a real transformation; some who did not even know native languages started learning them, etc.)—those who established some form of communion with the resisting masses of African people (the real source of the profound African aspirations for freedom)—having taken place, the very status of African philosophy as an arm of an ontological liberation removed from the mass, or even opposed to the real historical liberation that can only be achieved after violent, decisive, and difficult battles, was, indeed, put in serious doubt. In a real sense, it is about this very "crisis of the Muntu" that Eboussi Boulaga writes.[9] I feel that it is more correct to talk about the crisis of the "civilized or *évolué* Muntu"—the one who, after having mastered playing the imperialist game, is still not fully accepted as an equal of the imperialist masters. Other Bantus' difficulties are on a different level: how to develop their own organic intellectuals, or how to win over, or transform in their favor, the "civilized Muntu" as a condition of development to a higher level of the resistance movement against imperialist and alienated Muntu's dominations? (The Mau Mau mass movement, which entrusted leadership responsibilities to the Kenyattas, was finally co-opted by imperialism.) That is, given the continuous—but not yet complete—unmasking and overthrowing of imperialist domination by the persistent resistance of the popular African masses, even the most rigorous Muntu philosopher must settle accounts with his philosophical consciousness, which tries, through the concept (the arm of criticism), to get around the material antagonism opposing the African people to imperialism. (In other words, he just interprets this antagonism rather than transforming it.)

Only after such a settling of accounts can the arm of criticism of the re-Africanized civilized Muntu unite with the masses of the African people and be transformed into a material force in the hands of the latter. This arm of criticism will thus guide the criticism of arms held by the resisting masses of the African people. We are particularly thinking of the cult of rigor for rigor's sake and the cult of the universal raised to a principle by Hountondji and Towa, but also of the erudite refutation which does not lead to a theory of the organization of the African revolutionary struggle—in the sense used by A. Badiou[10]—of Cheikh Anta Diop, Theophile Obenga, and others. Scientific knowledge, too, has to be put correctly into the hands of the masses—who make history—to be able to guide the process of social transformation. Indeed, without such a transformation of the philosophical consciousness, which devotes itself completely to metaphysical preoccupations that ignore the present moment of the real relations of power in Africa, the African philosopher's deep rooting in the African people is constantly called into question. After all, for whom does he ultimately philosophize?

African philosophy also confronts the following important and crucial question: Who is the subject (or the maker) of history in today's Africa? One cannot get around this question by claiming that it is not scientific. To say that history is not made by anybody in Africa (that history is a process without a subject) lets imperialism pursue its domination of the African people undisturbed. "In summary," says Laleye, "the essential finality is, without any doubt, again truth, but in its existential relationship to man who therefore appropriates it in historical dimension, and which is consequently always incomplete and to be continuously conquered."[11] Isn't that a too complicated way of trying to say to what ultimate end philosophical work is done? It is, indeed, the protracted struggle for the complete liberation of the entire African people, that is, the struggle to destroy every form of exploitation of man by man, of African nations by other nations, of the African masses of people by one section of the African people, of African women by African men, etc., which is at stake. That is ultimately what the African philosophical struggle for truth aims at.

Since its beginning in many places, has not philosophy been the process of becoming aware of, and a desire to overcome or transcend, scission (all forms of cleavage)? Idealist or materialist reaction to science, in its practice and its theoretical results, is only one aspect of such an awareness and of a desire to transcend. It is important to grasp philosophy dialectically from the perspective of class struggles in theory, as Althusser often insists on in his works, but also from the perspective of theory in class struggles. We must not restrict *African philosophy*, as Hountondji invites us to do, only to a reaction toward the African science to come.

It is, I think, in the sense of transcending or overcoming scission through the concept that philosophy was, for Hegel, identical to idealism—that is, transcending, through the concept, scission, which is material. And since the material overcoming of scission is understood as the condition of genuine "theoretical transcendence"— which is but a reflection of the material resolution of the scission— materialist philosophy stands as a sharp contestation of idealism. Materialism is first and foremost a struggle against idealism.

Indeed, it is as true idealists that African philosophers want to get around the materiality (the material conditions of existence) of what they call the "crisis of the African consciousness," to resolve the latter by mere concepts. Thus, it is asserted that, despite the present material conditions of African inauthenticity, the simple interpretation of African realities through hermeneutics will provide us with the true authenticity of the Negro-African. An acrobatic spatial take-off with no landing in sight, an absolute detachment from the present situation in its daily life movement, external interpretations of the world, and so forth characterize the history of philosophy in its speculative idealist mode.

Looking more closely into things, Eboussi Boulaga's book *Crise du Muntu* begins an analysis very much similar to Marx and Engels's critique of the dominant ideology in *The German Ideology*. The three propositions that delimit Eboussi Boulaga's problematic[12] bring him very close to Marxist thought. The latter, as is well known, is a protracted struggle against idealism through a clear conceptualization of the articulation of proletariat/materialism/revolution/science.[13] Eboussi Boulaga seems, in this book, to have gone up to the very limit of what is philosophically at stake for the thrust or vision of the Muntu; he does not, however, succeed in going beyond it by clearly problematizing the question of the material transformation (and not only interpretation) of the world of the Muntu within the present context of Africa and the world. Without doing some work of social transformation will the Muntu be able to resolve his crisis of consciousness? How is the new consciousness, that of real clarity, achieved? Should not the Muntu first get his feet wet, as Walter Rodney used to say, before he can gain clarity?

In this book, however, Eboussi Boulaga is quite close to Amilcar Cabral, who very clearly (both theoretically and practically) raised the issue of transformation through the conceptualization of the articulation of the resisting or struggling African masses/the weapon of theory and the culture of resistance/the national liberation movement/national independence and the development of the African masses or the return of the African people to their own proper history under the new and specific conditions they now face. The weapon of theory must find an anchorage in the culture of resistance.

Rigor for rigor's sake, rigor derailed from its historical foundations, "abstraction which ignores conditions of time, place, morality, relationships and objects . . . ," says Eboussi Boulaga, this rigor leaves the real world where domination and exploitation prevail unchanged, intact. This overgrown (strange) rigor is even unable to deal with the question: How did this Muntu, so preoccupied with the exercise of rigor for rigor's sake, emerge?

As it is well known, scission, in the history of philosophy, took various forms of philosophical expression: One and Many, Being and Nonbeing, Nothingness and Becoming, Matter and Spirit, Knowledge and Non-Knowledge or Ignorance, Truth and Falsity, Infinite and Finite, Sameness and Otherness, Essence and Phenomenon, Chief and Sorcerer, Yin and Yang, Sense and Nonsense, Science and Magic, Freedom and Necessity (fatalism or determinism), God and Satan, Good and Bad, Beautiful and Ugly, etc. Theoretical work in its philosophical aspect, in today's Africa, is struggling very hard to grasp and comprehend divided *Africanity*. The African theoretical (ideological) struggles against European ethnocentrism, for example, are dominated by the dialectics of several of these forms of the philosophical expression of scission. Negritude, for example, opposes against the devastating imperialist universalism, African or Negro-African exceptionalism.

Indeed, most of the African thinking on this topic gravitates around issues of the following sort: How will the uprooted, alienated, civilized African and the African masses relegated to the inessentiality of servitude again form or constitute an organic whole? How are they going to become one again? Who has to exercise dominance and who must exercise determinance in an organic whole that excludes violence and arbitrariness? What should hold together an organic whole in which the vital needs of everybody are taken up without default? Which element of the scission (i.e., of the divided Africanity) is the potential carrier of a better future (free from exploitation and domination)? Am I truly other than what imperialism says of me? Am I a primitive man moved by emotions and specialized only in dancing and sex? Am I any different from what the African masses say of me? Am I a house nigger, a Mundele Ndombe (a black that is white through and through)? Is the fact that I prove myself to be *educable* a confirmation or a refutation of the pretensions of the *European civilizing mission*? What makes it possible for me to be dominated by the other? Why am I colonizable? Why am I fearful of the masses of the African people? Why am I so attracted to white beauty? Why do I envy the wealthy or the poor? These questions and many more arise from, and are provoked by, the scission.

The idealist thesis, which solves the problem by calling for a return to the situation prior to the scission, for example, identifies (equates) the movement leading to the scission and the one transforming the movement toward the scission. This is, of course, the position of Hegelian dialectics.[14] It leaves out the whole story of colonization and capitalist underdevelopment of present-day African societies. The "traditional" (communalist) conception of change, in which the possibility that an ancestor can be reborn on the conscious and collective request of the community does not make this error: The ancestor who comes back is, at the same time, the same and different (i.e., he/she is but a reproduction in a different and similar context). In the present situation of the postcolonial scission, how do we go beyond it and create a new organic *whole*, and which elements within the divided African present moment incarnate the disalienated future? In the perspective of the constructivist logic,[15] how can such a future be constructed from present elements? How should the futurity inscribed in the present decision be conceived and conceptualized? From where does the Muntu get his philosophical and philosophizing thrust?

The cult of the permanent[16] Negro-Egyptian cultural synchrony, presented or conceived as the anchor of disalienation and of the struggle against ethnocentrism, does not exactly have a hold on the present moment of the African concrete situation. How indeed, did the reproduction, if it did take place, of such a synchrony take place in African communities, if not through the cultural resistance of the African masses against every external form of domination? From King Alfonso to Emperor Haile Selassie or that other, most ridiculous, Emperor Bokassa the First, and even going back to the epoch of the pharaohs, the dominant ruling group has always distinguished itself through acculturation, that is, through the conscious adoption of the cultural practices of (foreign) dominant groups. The rise of Alfonso the First to the throne of the Kongo kingdom was associated with the attack and destruction of the Negro-African family structure (and its legal and material foundation), and the family structure of the northern cultural cradle was promoted. Even today, the members of ruling groups in Africa are rare who are still masters in speaking African languages in their purity (and not in their colonialist transformations into patois). What is the leading core of the cultural resistance that makes it possible for the *Negro-Egyptian Geist* to be reproduced in present African cultures? What is new in this resistance movement?

It is the new element that circumscribes the present movement of the African concrete situation. How does this new element incarnate the liberated African future? To what extent is this new element the forerunner of the future complete liberation of Africa? According to the constructivist perspective, instead of postulating the authentic *meaning* of *Africanity* as a primordial given (and taken for granted), meaning should above all else be conceived as a process of constructing, acquiring, or historically building meaning. Consciousness of division in the African community captivates African philosophers, as a social category produced through the imperialist process of African socioeconomic transformations. Their thought, as it aims at getting around such a division, is in fact a thought of division, that is, a reflection and reproduction of division. Isn't African philosophy the religion of the African neocolonial intellectual? This is the origin of the "malaise of the African philosopher [who] gets to a more or less confused awareness of the problematic character of his status, not simply as a philosopher, but as an 'African philosopher.' "[17] "What does 'African' mean in 'African philosopher' "? The very possibility of a communalist or collective philosophy, for example, terrorizes Hountondji. Is an individual philosophy, a philosophy of an individual, more liberating than a collective one? To philosophize is thus, in Africa as well, learning to die, not just through the movement through which the African who becomes a philosopher cuts his/her ties from the rest of the people, but also through the opposite movement of his/her union with and immersion in the African people as well. Cabral refers to this dialectic as de-Africanization and re-Africanization or class suicide. Like any real dialectical process, this movement is not completely voluntary, as Cabral tends to see it.

The socioeconomic status of the African philosopher is the very foundation of the malaise of her/his discourse: She/he is foreign or marginal to the power that requires (or solicits) her/him to produce its philosophical foundations, that is, to give a "nationalist coloration" to the Western-produced thought sustaining the neocolonial power, and he/she is at the same time foreign to the people who struggle against that same power. Despite his/her rhetoric of the *autonomy of the concept*, he/she becomes increasingly conscious that the pursuit of rigor for rigor's sake cannot be realized elsewhere but inside the very power that marginalizes him/her, and that the rationality of this power hardly internalizes the one practiced or aimed at by the African philosopher.

How does one get around the neocolonial power's rigor with the sole use of the concept's rigor? The African philosopher is never tired of making speeches for the crucial importance of the concept's rigor. Marxists, on the contrary, conceptualize the necessary articulation of the critique of arms and the arm of criticism. In their majority, African philosophers refuse such a position. Why? Kwasi Wiredu, for example, finds that articulation unscientific and authoritarian.[18] Hountondji, loyal to Althusserian theoreticism (idealism) proclaims, "I assert, on the contrary, for my part, the autonomy of the political level, and I ask that it be given its proper coherence."[19] To Caesar what is Caesar's! The problem is not the assertion of the autonomy of this or that, but that of the articulation of autonomous fields. And since the neocolonial power is very preoccupied with development, the philosopher Elungu, more slyly than Hountondji, proclaims: "Philosophy, [is the] condition of development in today's Africa."[20] If the neocolonial power really wants development to actually be the priority of priorities, then it must not marginalize the philosopher: Long live the philosopher-king! After all, Plato was also right for Africa!

Hountondji, who demands that political actors be left to their coherence (their integrity), assigns to philosophy in Africa, as the number one problem to deal with, the task or obligation to know how (philosophy) can help (contribute to) the development of science.[21] Philosophy must thus provide a foundation for science; the latter does not have its own coherence (integrity). But, how is science related or articulated to politics? What stand does Hountondji take on this debate? What position does he hold in the ideological struggle around the problem of the transfer of science and technology? The African philosopher is now neither an organic intellectual of the masses of African people who resist imperialism (a possible meaning of the term African philosopher), nor quite exactly an organic intellectual of imperialism (which is also a possible meaning of the term philosopher in Africa). He is neither because philosophy is an "attribute of power,"[22] which, in today's Africa, is principally imperialist or rooted in imperialist processes/structures of domination. The discourse of the African philosopher is but the wisdom of a class which is not yet sure of its power, that is, which does not exercise its own ideological and political leadership or any economic domination as of yet. Does the identification of set purposes (partisanship?) of African philosophers and those of the theoreticians or philosophers who orient (influence) public opinion in imperialist countries not imply a similarity in their socioeconomic status? Don't our African philosophers feel more at ease in the metropolis than in Africa, in cities or other Europeanized centers within Africa than in rural areas? Don't they express themselves better in metropolitan than in African languages? Jammed between the neocolonial power's rigor and that of the African mass resistance movement, don't African philosophers emigrate most often to the metropolis?

The masses of African people have, most often, only *heroes* who have *died* in struggle against imperialist domination. Why, indeed, are hermeneutics, phenomenology, Althusserianism, logical positivism, Hegelianism, structuralism, pragmatism, dialectical materialism, Thomism, etc., all products of specific material and symbolic conditions (specific ideological struggles), understood by our African philosophers as so many correct responses to the philosophical question in Africa? Why do African philosophers think of these philosophical orientations as being indispensable to the effort of clarifying the mode-of-being or African being-in-world, the African way of life? Is this solely a logical consequence of the fact that Africans are part and parcel of universal humanity? What is in the *Africanity* which they claim to have that allows them to find *meaning* in the above-listed philosophical orientations, which are not and cannot be neutral? What is in these *attributes of power* or in us, daughters and sons of the dominated African people, which allows us to practice these attributes of power and be so concerned with them? Why is it that it is Husserl, who makes it possible for Laleye, in his *De la personne comme histoire*, to discover the *evocative* phenomenology practiced, since long ago, at Ife by Yorùbá initiates?

Isn't the imperialist recognition of the philosophy of the Bantu, without any real prior struggle, the sign of the possibility of class alliance? The real issue is to find out between whom and which section of the native (indigenous) society such an alliance takes place. Are the Bantu masses really the core of the subject of Tempels's work or are they just used as a simple decoration. Who is the real "interlocutor" of Tempels? In front of whom does he make his discourse? Is it just a mere accident, a mere contingent fact, that most of the African philosophers are either priests, former seminarists, or organic intellectuals of Christian and Islamic churches? Is it not necessary to examine the effects of those material conditions of emergence of our philosophers on their philosophical discourses?

II. THE PLACE OF PHILOSOPHICAL WORK IN ANTI-IMPERIALIST STRUGGLES

It would be suitable and even necessary to do a historical study of the theoretical work of Africans before, during, and after colonialism, and to do so from the point of view of the African resistance movement (and thus of the national liberation movement). The historical or rather epochal, question, "Who have been, in each stage of African history, the authentic organic intellectuals of the African people in the struggle against external or foreign domination?" would lead us to the very core of the problem. Indeed, it is precisely resistance or rebellion that unveils domination and it is at the same time the motive force of its transformation. African philosophy is first of all the search for a theory of organization and/or of the destruction of the movement of African national liberation and of the authentic social development or the economic asphyxiation of Africa.

The discourse of *authenticity* in all its moving rhetoric, made where there is an effective imperialist domination (which does not mean that the people have been completely defeated and subjugated)—made, in other words, where there is an absence of a liberating relationship between power and the masses of people—is actually a demand (if it is not simply a mystification pure and simple) for the overthrow of such a domination and a call to arms for the struggle for complete liberation. Its philosophical foundations cannot conjure away the question of the theoretical requirements of the victory of such a struggle. He who lives *authentically* does not feel the need to proclaim his authenticity. As an old principle has it, a fish is not aware that it lives in water until it is out of water. Unless, of course, we agree with the imperialist opinion that the masses of African people—or *primitives* in general—are foreign to theoretical work, we should very much seek to know how theoretical work was organized and carried out by our ancestors prior to the Asiatic and European penetration of Africa, and how it was transformed by, and after, those penetrations. Through such a study, we may find out how and why those "Africans [who are] indifferent to reflection," as Hountondji says, have emerged. Such an indifference to thinking cannot be more natural (physiobiological) than historical. And those today who do nothing else except reflect, meditate, contemplate, or just dwell in abstractions, as a socially recognized function; how did they get to that, socially and historically speaking? The same way that the process of the emergence of free labor (i.e., the proletarianization process in Africa) is historically studied, we must also study the history of theoretical work increasingly becoming *autonomous* (i.e., we must examine the process of the separation of intellectual labor from manual labor in Africa) as a systematization of a socialized practice.[23]

We could then know why the mode of thinking, determined and required by capitalism (often taken as the model of rationality) serves as the standard for evaluating other possible modes of thought. Why, for example, do functionaries of our public administrations fail to make any effort to engage in creative theoretical work? And what about our political leaders? Don't they often, if not always, seek recourse from imperialist services (technical assistance, international cooperation, etc.) for the necessary theoretical clarification of problems raised by their own political actions? There are even those who go as far as imitating De Gaulle's phraseology (rhetorical style) to give themselves a token of pertinence.

Moreover, it is not enough to take for granted the idea that Africans are foreign to reason: "Emotion is Negro as reason is Hellenic," declares Senghor following Vergiat; it is indispensable to show how the African Negro has arrived at this condition. How is it, for example, that the Negro Senghor could have mastered "reason which is Hellenic"?[24] A really creative African thinker has become a real embarrassment, "an institutional analyst," as Loureau would say, of the sociopolitical system in place in today's Africa.

Why is it that worker and peasant producers are not in a situation to engage themselves, at least in the immediate process of capitalist production, in creative theoretical work? Why is it that, for the so-called African worker, trade unionism is less of a freeing of the African worker's creative theoretical work than the very centralist and oppressive restrictions of it—that is, a specific oppressive form determined by the separation of intellectual labor from manual labor? How then can the philosopher Hountondji write that a "dreadful theoretical void . . . is continuously spreading out into a weary population, indifferent to theoretical problems whose interest it cannot even see."[25] Isn't it thanks to this weariness and indifference required by the system of production and power in place that P. J. Hountondji, among others, can specialize in philosophical acrobatics to help society clearly formulate its standards of production (often called rationality) and the rules of good conduct?

Even if Hountondji recognizes that the "theoretical liberation or freeing (the 'conceptual takeoff' of F. Crahay) of philosophical discourse implies political liberation (or freedom),"[26] he does not however, examine the real implications of such a liberation: the indispensable and preliminary transformation of the relations of production, power, and hegemony that prevent a theoretical freeing from developing. Hountondji feels, nevertheless, content to launch his

directive for theoretical work in Africa: "[F]ree the theoretical creativity of our peoples, free it by providing it with the necessary means
through which it can become operative."[27] To whom is he addressing
himself? Who must free the theoretical creativity of our peoples?
Would it be France with her alphabetization programs well conceived
for and adapted to Africa? Could it be the African states that are
afraid of the African people's theoretical creativity? Isn't Hountondji
calling for a real cultural revolution? Aren't cultural revolutions based
on the crisis of ideological/cultural hegemony? Who is capable in
today's Africa of provoking such a crisis and of organizing a cultural
revolution? What do we know, historically speaking, about the sociopolitical conditions of a cultural revolution? How should philosophers
and *others* be acting in order for a cultural revolution—attacking/
reversing/overthrowing imperialist cultural hegemony in Africa—to
take place?

When Hountondji says that free discussions are the motive force[28]
of philosophy, that big "public debate in which the commitment of
each participant's intellectual responsibility is called for,"[29] one feels
as if one is listening to the Young Hegelians criticized by Marx and
Engels. What is it, in today's Africa, that blocks such a free discussion? Indeed, I fail to see in what sense a free philosophical discussion involves the commitment of each participant's intellectual
responsibility or honesty more than the African communalist palaver
or proletarian public self-criticism sessions. And why, in today's
Africa, don't other people besides the philosophers participate in this
"free public debate"? Is it only the lack of familiarity with the
esoteric philosophical language on the part of the African masses that
excludes them from participating in the debate? What is the historical
origin of such an esoteric language, on the one hand, and of that lack
of familiarity, on the other hand? Obviously, the masses of people are
not part of this "public" debate, but who are its members and where
do they come from and where do they get their philosophical creden-
tials?

It is thus necessary to study the genesis and development of the
"philosophical element" (*Le philosophique*) in Africa. And if, as
some claim, Greek philosophy is the result of "the West having stolen

ancient Negro-African philosophy,"[30] then one has to show why Negro-Africans alienated themselves from their own product and why they have since been unable to reproduce it in an extended way. To present the case of the Ghanaian A. G. Amo—one of Kant's teachers—to prove that black Africa also has had her philosophers, is meaningful only from the perspective of the European ethnocentric (and racist) problematic. Imperialism presented "the absence of philosophy" in African cultures as a proof of African exceptionalism understood as a "genetic default" of human nature, that is, the claim that African human nature is necessarily incomplete, different from and thus inferior to the European "universal" human nature.

The African philosopher's claim to ontological equality requires that philosophy be a part of the black people's creations. Aside from the sentimentalist support for the Negro-African thesis—and this makes sense only from a class perspective, that of those Africans ultimately concerned about "ontological equality"—the very existence of the philosopher Amo had no real weight in the development of the movement of African resistance.[31] From the point of view of that resistance, wasn't Simon Kimbangu a better philosopher than Amo? How, in African history, does the autonomy of the philosophical discourse that Hountondji proclaims become not only possible but realizable as well? As a theoretically concentrated expression of social antagonism, philosophy will always be difficult to grasp as an object of a rigorously materialist historical study.[32] The chronology of philosophical systems and works presented as the history of philosophy does not teach us much about the "social contentions"—to use Kwame Nkrumah's expression—which served as the anchorage and the motive force of those works. Ideas denote practical and historical realities, class relations, and not imaginary/ideal relations; they are governed, as far as their process of transformation is concerned, by forces external to the thought process. These external material forces, though aimed at in philosophical systems, cannot be deduced from them. There is always a high possibility of "ideological illusion"[33] in doing a history of philosophy through a simple chronology of works; intellectual production may be taken to be autonomous. Indeed, if the material base is recognized as determinant, the so-called autonomy of ideas and the claims to universality of those ideas become a serious problem to contend with. The paradox in philosophy is that the selection of a conception or the definition of philosophy one makes is necessarily an expression of one's philosophical position, stand, and outlook. And even to philosophize against philosophy—as empiricists do—is also to do philosophy.

Moreover, each philosophy, philosophical system, or stand in philosophy implies a definite conception of history. Studying the history of philosophy from a Hegelian position is very different from—and even opposed to—studying it from the Marxist point of view.[34] This is also why it is so difficult to compare two or more philosophical systems of thought outside of the historical class struggles that gave rise to and motivated them. To be able to compare their respective social contentions, a comparative criterion or index must be found.

Roberto Miquelez tried to resolve such a difficulty by devising a "conceptual scheme through which compared philosophical systems appear, in their particular organization, as being cases or variant forms."[35] Without being so rigorous, I think that it is necessary to study African philosophers in relation to the theoretical requirements of the self-organization of the African masses for the social transformation of their dominated societies and for real national liberation in Africa. It is necessary to study, from the point of view of dialectics, the position of African philosophers, for example, of those mentioned in the preceding pages. Indeed, dialectics is the theoretical expression of the process of transformation as such.

In the case of Africa, the problem is even more complex. The history of the simple (imperialist) diffusion of philosophy as an expression of imperialist domination (and thus the assimilation to this domination) must be differentiated from that of the complete Africanization of philosophy in Africa. In the epoch in which Amo lived, his philosophical pertinence was not quite a conscious expression of the process of self-organization of the African national liberation movement. The question that we could raise is thus: How have some African philosophers become authentic African philosophers? But also: How have African thinkers such as Ogotommeli, Fukiau, etc., Africanized appropriated Western and Eastern philosophical currents, forms, or trends? And, lastly, we will need to raise the question of whether or not there is a specifically African form of philosophy.

For us, Amilcar Cabral is an example of an authentic African philosopher of today's Africa: He expresses consciously the unconscious historical process of self-organization and struggle of the African masses against imperialist exploitation and domination and for complete national liberation. Immersed in that process, which forces him to engage in real struggles against his own weaknesses, Cabral is able to grasp the movement leading to the overthrow of imperialist domination, and through various attempts at summing up the lessons of those struggles, formulates correct theoretical guidelines to raise the movement to a higher level. Theoretical work is here no longer an ideological apology for the division but a contribution to the development of correct theoretical guidelines for a concrete practice emerging through that same practice.

Had Cabral lived to battle in the struggle for the postindependence national social reconstruction, he would have realized that class struggle should no longer be subordinated to the productive forces as the motive force of history.[36] He would also have helped to provide a conscious theoretical expression of the unconscious process of the working people's self-organization for the overthrow of capitalist relations of production. That is, if he had remained immersed in the movement of struggle for the complete liberation of Africa. Cabral is a real hero of the African people. Contrary to the philosophers of *nègritude* and *authenticity*, who ally themselves with imperialist leaders and ideologues of capitalist countries to struggle, as they claim, against imperialist domination in Africa, Cabral took the side, being rooted as he was in the African masses of which he became an organic intellectual, of the antiimperialist and anticapitalist popular masses of those [African] countries. He thus did not hesitate to take advice from the organic intellectuals of those African popular masses organized around the proletariat. We are, with Cabral, much closer to the "theoretical liberation" that Hountondji talks about than with the speculative cantors of the "universal rigor" that lacks any anchorage and rooting in the popular masses of the African people.

When assimilation is but an alignment with the positions of those who dominate/exploit, then it implies a defeat of a fraction of the dominated people. The desire that motivates and haunts that fraction is never that of the complete liberation of the entire people, but more that of becoming part of the camp of domination, even if only as a marginal element of that camp. Indeed, we should always ask: "For what real interest is every theoretical work—even the one geared toward rigor for rigor's sake—undertaken?" Moreover, the exercise of rigor for rigor's sake is but the *form of persuasion* of a class. P. Raymond has shown this in his study[37] of the ideologies of rigor for rigor's sake: these ideologies use logico-mathematical rigor to give some pertinence to ideological positions. "As regards to dissimulating, under the veil of the universal, class interests which (bourgeois ideology) legitimates, this is in fact a particular speciality of any philosophy of exploitation."[38]

The reinforcement of colonial states—which became neocolonial after the defeats of the attempts at their radical transformation by the popular movement of the anticolonial struggles—calls for the development of ideological apparatuses capable of dealing with imperatives of ideological struggles and supporting the reproduction of the conditions of the defeat of the African people's resistance. The increasing use of repressive apparatuses required by the exacerbation of the contradiction world revolution/imperialist wars and helped by the practices of arms merchants, proves to be more and more costly and less effective for the long-term proimperialist political stability of neocolonial regimes and countries. Imperialist economic-military domination of Africa, developed in reaction to the protracted popular armed struggles, must increasingly be complemented by imperialist ideological leadership; thus, policies of cultural assistance, technology transfers, philanthropic aid, etc.,—besides missionary and "peace" corps work—have been developed. The creation and development of departments of philosophy and theology, often claimed to be indispensable for development, are also required by the neocolonial reinforcement, as a phase in the development of the contradiction between imperialist domination rooted in the structure of every neocolonial state whose development coincides with the formation of principally *compradore* social classes, and national liberation struggles rooted in the structurally most oppressed and state-marginalized popular masses. (The emergence of the bureaucratic state class said to be defined by its ownership or privatization of the state as a means of production does not alter this development.) The nationalist revolutionary upsurge (Lumumba, Mulele, etc.) in Zaire, for example, forced church ideologues to shift their evangelical thrust to the hysterical attack on communism ("communists eat children and make of their wives a collective property" became part of the evangelical rhetoric). Moral Rearmament, Opus Dei, Rose-Cross, and Christian Science quickly dispatched their agents on the terrain.

In the period of relative peace, the so-called "prerevolutionary" period or conjuncture, neocolonial state structures develop themselves as simple extensions or imitations of the state structures of the imperialist metropolis. They develop under the blessings of our *civilizers*, who have become our partners in *cooperation* for our development. In the official ideological language, this is also called national development. To organize one's national university, etc., along the lines and models of state universities of the imperialist metropolis is, in this perspective of social development, to catch up with developed countries and thus to wipe away one's historical backwardness. This is why the expatriate personnel, from imperialist countries, are more at ease in these national state structures, functioning as if they were made by, and for, that personnel, than are the majority of the natives who have to bear these structures' repressive hierarchical weight. In these conditions, to be intelligent, reasonable, rational, civilized, etc., is to be receptive to, and to function according to, the logic and rationality governing these structures.

The masses of African people, structurally marginalized and closed off to the logic and rationality of these structures, are said to be ignorant, stupid, uncivilized, irrational, illogical, etc. The films of Africa's great son Ousmane Sembene (*El Mandabi*, *Xala*, etc.) say much more on this question than what could be said in an article or a book. The structures of marginalization thus reproduce tendentially the social division of labor similar to the one operating in the imperialist metropolis—in their most savage stage. The solution to underdevelopment caused principally by imperialism is again said to lie in the imperialist spreading of models of development deemed safe (produced, or entertained) by imperialism—thanks to the *compradore* classes for which these models are significant and "revolutionary."

African philosophers emerging from this social division of labor (i.e., from the social materialization of the separation of intellectual labor from manual labor) are principally the ideologues of neo-colonial states. Nevertheless, since the essence of these same neo-colonial states is the unity of opposites (dominant/ruling classes vs. dominated/exploited classes), the philosophical structure (philosophers, philosophies, philosophical institutions, etc.), is contradictory in its very essence. Professors Gabembo and Tsibangu-Wamulumba of Zaire are very clear on the ideological role played by African philosophers, when they write:

But since the situation of *tabula rasa* is no longer possible, who must now give us intuitive guidelines for a new philosophy which, we as philosophers, must systematize? It is the political actors. These [political actors] have already given us those insights, it is our duty . . . to systematize them as we are masters (of theoretical work) and [can] create a new system.[39]

Thus, African philosophy gives grounding to and systematizes the fundamental ideological insights of the political actors of neocolonial states. But why are the masses of African people not seen as the real political actors, insofar as they struggle, step by step, against the repressive hierarchization of power up to the overthrow of every state? This conception of political actors is absolutely out of the question for the theoreticians of *authenticity*. Hence we can see the implicit cult of the separation of theory from practice by these theoreticians: They alone are masters of theory!

In today's Africa, a philosophy department, where only the teachings or the thinking of the great masters of the West are taught, is principally an oppressive, and thus proimperialist, structure. In such a structure, the African masses' cultural resistance through administrators, office workers, students, and teachers against imperialist cultural domination is almost nonexistent. In some countries, such a resistance was able to become actualized only through the creation of resolutely non-Western parallel educational institutions. To philosophize in such a department is to try hard to become a disciple of the great ideologues of the Western imperialist states—even when one is a "bad student," as Laleye says.

Given the radical transformation of Hegel's problematic in Marx's thought, as a consequence of Marx's class suicide, one cannot say that Marx (unlike Feuerbach) was a "bad student" of Hegel. And everyone knows how seldom in this type of philosophy department the teachings of philosophers defending and systematizing the insights of the political actors struggling against imperialist states are taught: Marx, Engels, Lenin, Mao, Badiou, etc. What is the task of a philosophy department if not to guide real/concrete thinking and to help improve correct thinking in the perspective of the unity of theory/ practice? If the starting point is the assumption that creative and correct thinking is foreign to the African masses, a philosophy department's teachings cannot but be oppressive. The social contention inherent in the teachings of philosophers trained in these departments is far from being African since it is not rooted in the African masses' cultural resistance. (From the point of view of this resistance, to understand Plato is to take the point of view of the ancient Greek slave, since that point of view is closer to that of the African masses.) And after all, it is this protracted resistance against imperialist domination that expresses and develops authentic Africanity. Fashion— and fashion is very often a sign of class membership—often serves as a criterion of choice of the philosophical doctrines to assimilate among those that are fashionable in the West or elsewhere.

In contemporary Africa, the essential relation takes the form of a struggle against imperialism (in all its types and forms). On one side, one finds imperialism as inscribed first of all in economic state structures that are fundamentally colonial and as internalized by social classes determined by these structures—classes whose deepest desire and interests are aimed at maintaining and reinforcing these same imperialist structures—on the other side, one finds the popular masses of workers and poor peasants as well as their organic intellectuals and tactical allies. Ideas that emerge through this struggle reflect their fundamental antagonism. Even the one who makes a cult of the universal—if the content of this universal is reduced to what imperialism says of it and teaches—is thus expressing one's contempt for the native masses and the negation of their theoretical creativity, whose specificity precisely must be the anchorage, in Africa, of the authentic universal. Covering any *particularity* under an imperialist universal veil is the specificity of any and all exploiters' philosophy.

He or she who builds a cult of the *particular*, raised to the status of a static monument, and who thereby refuses to the African people access to the *authentic universal*, is an oppressor as well. Neither (bourgeois) oppressive domination nor (petit-bourgeois) anarchism will bring true liberation, but proletarian dictatorship, that is, the systematic organization of popular struggle against every oppressive hierarchization of state power leading to the genuine human community. Every *universal* must contain (or must be incarnated in) a *particular* and vice versa. Every *universal* also has a *particular.* Every universal—money, for example—is the externalization, under the form of the particular, of essential social relations. The human essence of man is the true human community. In that sense, the proletariat and oppressed nations are carriers of the universal liberation of man. Each philosophical work is marked by this fundamental antagonism, which takes, in the history of philosophy, the form of a protracted struggle opposing idealism to materialism. Its real content depends on its social environment and its historical conjuncture, which only historical materialism can clarify.

The whole system of technical assistance to neocolonial states (military and cultural advisers, missionaries, peace corps members, etc.) in its very contradictory essence is, first of all, a structural *interiorization* of imperialism. From the church minister—foreign missionary or native—to the village deacon, they are all part of structures capable of reproducing cultural imperialism against the workers and peasants' cultural resistance. They are there tendentially ready to undercut the work of the organic intellectuals of the masses of workers and peasants. And when they fail to do that, as in the case of Kimbangu and his allies/disciples, organic intellectuals and ideologues of the neocolonial state, dispatched among the popular masses at all levels, seek advice from the repressive structures of the neo-colonial state; it was the missionaries who first demanded and obtained Kimbangu's arrest and deportation.

As a corpus of doctrine used and usable in the ideological struggle against the African masses and their intellectuals, philosophy arrived in Africa as an attribute of the imperialist power; it was an integral part of the ideas serving as a justification for, and as guidelines to, imperialist penetration into Africa. In other words, philosophy was and remains an important element in the ideological struggle, as a real reflection of the material relations of the struggle for imperialist domination. Philosophical discourse was a demonstrative discourse of European cultural superiority and a grounding for the *civilizing mission*. The philosopher in Africa was a missionary and the missionary a philosopher. P. Tempels was the physical incarnation of that double role. He was spreading, in Europe as well as in Africa, a worldview conforming to bourgeois interests expressed in their generality. Locally, that is, in Africa, against the cultural resistance of the native masses and their intellectuals, he undertook to provide a new philosophical foundation for that worldview. One of the results was *Bantu Philosophy*. In the face of the immense task accomplished by missionaries to soften, modify, and transform the mentalities of the African masses, the work of African revolutionaries is less than a drop in the sea.

The theory of resistance against imperialism is often expressed as antiphilosophy, a permanent critique of philosophy by the masses of African people who view philosophy as the theory justifying the oppressive hierarchization of the colonial state power. "When you go to paradise," said a peasant to a missionary preaching in a church, "just take the ladder with you so that you will know for sure that I won't be following you; I will remain right here on Earth." Isn't this against the entire Christian philosophy? Doesn't this permanent critique of philosophy tie in very well with the Communist point of view (i.e., the project of liberation against all forms of domination?). Theoretical work that emphasizes the unity of theory/practice develops first of all the struggle against philosophy as idealism—that is, as the separation of theory from practice, as an autonomization of ideas and of claims to universality—it seeks thereafter to conceptualize and clarify the relation proletariat/materialism/revolution/science.

As we saw, Cabral is one of those African theoreticians who worked for that liberating perspective. Either philosophy unites with the popular masses, who make the authentically national history, and is thus liberating; or it is separated from them—idealizes itself—and loses its creative foundation and thus becomes oppressive. In today's Africa, to think is increasingly to think *for* or *against* imperialism. Indifference, neutrality, and even ignorance only strengthen imperialism. Any discourse on objectivism, or cognitive noninvolvement as the condition of truth and science, is nothing but an imperialist form of persuasion. Which side or camp is every African philosopher on?

It is in this general context of a history of African struggles against imperialist domination and its real or potential local sociomaterial roots, in all its aspects (including philosophical ones), that philosophical work in Africa can best be grasped. I firmly believe it. Nevertheless, the production of such a history, as well as the reconstruction of the sociomaterial and symbolic conditions of philosophical/ideological/theoretical productions in their very antagonistic lines of demarcation, goes beyond the framework of this article. So this article is but the beginning of an introduction to the immense task of settling one's accounts with one's philosophical consciousness, from which African philosophers must no longer retreat.

NOTES

1. This is a translation (by the author) of an article written in French and published in the *Canadian Journal of African Studies*, Vol. 13, No. 1–2, 1979 and as a chapter in the book edited by A. Schwarz, *Les Faux Prophètes de l'Afrique ou l'Afr(eu)canisme*, (Québec, Presses de l'Universite Laval, 1980). Of course, some necessary modifications have been made here and there. [Because of the numerous, clearly typographical, errors of the translation I have taken the liberty of *minimally* intervening in the text. (T. Serequeberhan)]

2. F. Eboussi Boulaga, *La Crise du Muntu*, (Paris: *Présence Africaine*, 1977); "desir d'attester une humanité contestée ou en danger et celui d'être par et pour soi-même, par l'articulation de l'avoir et du faire, selon un ordre qui exclut la violence et l'arbitraire," p. 7.

3. Frantz Fanon, *Black Skin, White Masks* (New York: Grove Press Inc., 1967), p. 219.
4. Placide Tempels, *Bantu Philosophy* (Paris: *Présence Africaine*, 1959), p. 36.
5. Martial Sinda, *Messianismes Congolais* (Paris: Payot, 1972), p. 65.
6. Aimé Césaire, *Discourse on Colonialism* (New York, Monthly Review Press, 1972), pp. 37–39.
7. Gastore Oswald, "Theophile Obenga et las paradoxes de l'ethnocentrisme," *Présence Africaine*, no. 103 (1977), p. 112.
8. Ibid.
9. Eboussi Boulaga, *La Crise du Muntu*, op. cit.
10. A. Badiou F. Balmies, *De L'Ideologie* (Paris: F. Maspero, 1976), pp. 17–18.
11. Issiaka Prospero Laleye, *La philosophie? Pourgoui en Afrique?* (Berne: Herbert Lang, 1975), p. 10.
12. *La Crise du Muntu*, op. cit., pp. 11–24.
13. Georges Labica, *Le Statut marxiste de la philosophie* (Bruxelles: Editions Complexe, 1976), p. 370.
14. Pierre Raymond, *Materialisme dialectique et logique* (Paris: F. Maspero, 1977), pp. 43–71.
15. Y. Gauthier, *Fondements du Mathematique* (Montreal: Les Presses de l'Université de Montreal, 1976).
16. Cheikh Anta Diop, "Dr. Cheikh Anta Diop" (Interview), *Black Roots Bulletin*, vol. 4, no. 4 (Winter, 1976).
17. I. P. Laleye, *La Philosophie*, op. cit., p. 13.
18. Kwasi Wiredu, *Philosophy and an African Culture* (London: Cambridge University Press, 1980).
19. P. J. Hountondji, *Sur la philosophie africaine* (Paris: F. Maspero, 1976), p. 245.
20. Elungu Pene Elungu, "La Philosophie condition du development en Afrique aujourdu'hui," *Présence Africaine*, no. 103 (1977), p. 3.
21. P. J. Hountondji, op. cit., pp. 246, 124–27.
22. Eboussi Boulaga, op. cit., p. 8.
23. Alfred Sohn-Rethel, *Intellectual and Manual Labour* (London: The Macmillan Press Ltd., 1978); Yannick Maignien, *La Division du travail manual et intellectual* (Paris: F. Maspero, 1975); Lyn Marcus, *Dialectical Economics* (Lexington, MA: D.C. Heath and Co., 1975).
24. Antonim M. Vergiat, *Les rites secrets des primitifs de l'Oubangui* (Paris: Payot, 1951), p. 113.
25. P. J. Hountondji, op. cit., p. 36.
26. Ibid., p. 37.
27. Ibid., p. 50.
28. Ibid., p. 73.
29. Ibid., p. 50.
30. J. B. Jackson, *Introduction to African Civilization* (Secaucus, NJ: Citadel Press, 1974); Henry Olela, "The African Foundations of Greek Philosophy," in

Wright, ed. *African Philosophy: An Introduction*, (Washington DC: University Press of America Inc., 1979), pp. 55–68; George G. M. James, *The Stolen Legacy* (New York: Philosophical Library, 1954).

31. I do not minimize Amo's important theoretical work of defending, against slavery, the rights of Africans in Europe. Amo wrote in 1792 a book entitled *The Rights of Africans in Europe*. The fact remains that it is only now that Africans are becoming aware of this work.

32. On this point, see for example, Pierre Raymond, *Le Passage au meterialisme* (Paris: F. Maspero, 1973); Theodor Oizerman, *Problems of the History of Philosophy* (Moscow: Progress Publishers, 1973); and Pierre Macharey, "L'histoire de la philosophie consideree comme une lutte des tendances," *La Pansee*, no. 185 (February 1976), pp. 3–26.

33. Nguyon Ngoc Vu, *Ideologie et religion d'apres Karl Marx et F. Engels*, (Paris, Aubier-Montaigne, 1975), p. 30. On this important question, see also, Alain Badoiu and F. Balmes, *De L'Ideologie*, op. cit., pp. 21–37.

34. See Yuon Belaval, *Histoire de la philosophie*, III, *Encyclopedie de la Pleiade* (Paris, 1974), especially pp. 902–20.

35. Roberto Miquelez, *Sujet et histoire* (Ottawa: Editions de l'Université d'Ottawa, 1973), p. 8.

36. See Amilcar Cabral, "The Weapon of Theory," *Revolution in Guinea* (New York: Monthly Review Press, 1969), pp. 90–111.

37. P. Raymond, *Materialisme dialectique et Logique*, op. cit., pp. 121–77.

38. A. Badiou and F. Balmes, op. cit., p. 13.

39. Quoted by Ngoma Binda, "Pour une orientation authentique de la philosophie en Afrique: l'herméneutique," *Zaire-Afrique*, no. 113 (March 1975), p. 151.

SELECT BIBLIOGRAPHY

The following is a limited selection of texts in English on African philosophy. For a more extensive bibliography on African philosophy and related subjects, please see the entries for Mudimbe and Wright given below.

Abraham, W. E. *The Mind of Africa*. Chicago: University of Chicago Press, 1962.

Anyanwu, K. C., and Ruch, E. A. *African Philosophy*. Rome: Catholic Book Agency, 1981.

————. "Cultural Philosophy as a Philosophy of Integration and Tolerance." *International Philosophical Quarterly*, vol. 25, no. 3, issue no. 99 (September 1985).

Apostel, Leo. *African Philosophy*. Belgium: Scientific Publishers, 1981.

Beattie, John. "Understanding Traditional African Religion: A Comment on Horton." *Second Order*, vol. 1, no. 2 (July 1973).

Blocker, Gene. "African Philosophy." *African Philosophical Inquiry*, vol. 1, no. 1 (January 1987).

Bodunrin, P. O., ed., *Philosophy in Africa*. Ile-Ife: University of Ife Press, 1985.

Césaire, Aimé. *Discourse on Colonialism*. New York: Monthly Review Press, 1972.

————. *Return to My Native Land*. New York: Penguin Books, 1969.

————. *Letter to Maurice Thorez*, English translation. *Présence Africaine*, Paris, France 1957.

Crahay, Franz. "Conceptual Take-off Conditions for a Bantu Philosophy." *Diogenes*, no. 52 (Winter 1965).

Diemer, Alwin, ed. *Philosophy in the Present Situation of Africa*. Wiesbaden: Frantz Steiner Verlag, 1981.

Diop, C. A. *The African Origin of Civilization*. Mercer Cook, ed. and trans. Lawrence Hill & Co., 1974, Wesport.

Etuk, Udo. "Philosophy in a Developing Country." *Philosophy*, vol. 62, no. 239 (January 1987).

Fanon, Frantz. *The Wretched of the Earth*. New York: Grove Press, 1968.

Floistad, Guttorm, ed. *Contemporary Philosophy: A New Survey*, vol. 5, *African Philosophy*. Dordrecht Netherlands: Martinus Nijhoff Publishers, 1987.

Grialue, Marcel. *Conversations with Ogotemmeli*. New York: Oxford University Press, 1970.

Gyekye, Kwame. *An Essay on African Philosophical Thought*. New York: Cambridge University Press, 1987.

————. "African Religions and Philosophy." *Second Order*, vol. 4, no. 1 (1975).

Hallen, B., and Sodipo, J. O. *Knowledge, Belief, and Witchcraft*. London: Ethnographica, 1986.

Hart, A. W. "The Philosopher's Interest in African Thought: A Synopsis." *Second Order*, vol. 1, no. 1 (1972).

Horton, Robin. "Traditional Thought and the Emerging African Philosophy Department: A Comment on the Current Debate." *Second Order*, vol. 6, no. 1 (January 1977).

————. "African Traditional Thought and Western Science." In *Rationality*, Bryan R. Wilson, ed. Britain, Worcester: Basil Blackwell, 1984.

Hountondji, P. J. *African Philosophy*. Bloomington: Indiana University Press, 1983.

Jahn, Janheinz. *Muntu*. New York: Grove Press, 1961.

Keita, L. "The Debate Continues: A Reply to Olabiyi Yai's 'Misère de la philosophie speculative.' " *Présence Africaine*, no. 120, 4th quarterly (1981).

_____. "African Philosophical Systems—A Rational Reconstruction." *The Philosophical Forum*, vol. 9, nos. 2–3 (Winter, 1977; Spring, 1978).

Makinde, Akin M. *African Philosophy, Culture, and Traditional Medicine*. Athens, Ohio: Ohio University Center for International Studies, 1988.

Mbiti, S. John. *African Religions and Philosophy*. London: Heinemann, 1988.

Momoh, C. S. "Modern Theories in African Philosophy." *The Nigerian Journal of Philosophy*, vol. 1, no. 2 (1981).

Mudimbe, V. Y. *The Invention of Africa*. Bloomington: Indiana University Press, 1988.

_____. "African Gnosis: Philosophy and the Order of Knowledge." *African Studies Review*, vol. 28, nos. 2–3 (June and September 1985).

_____. "African Philosophy as an Ideological Practice: The Case of French-Speaking Africa." *African Studies Review*, vol. 26, Nos. 3–4 (September and December 1983).

Nwala, T. U. "Philosophy and Its Relevance to African Society." *The Nigerian Journal of Philosophy*, vol. 1, no. 1 (1981).

Okere, Theophilus. *African Philosophy: A Historico-Herméneutical Investigation of the Conditions of Its Possibility*. New York: University Press of America, 1983.

_____. "The Relation between Culture and Philosophy." *UCHE* (Journal of the Department of Philosophy, University of Nigeria, Nsukka), vol. 2 (1976).

Oruka O. H., and Masolo, D. A., eds., *Philosophy and Cultures*. Nairobi: Bookwise Limited, 1983.

_____. "The Fundamental Principles in the Question of 'African Philosophy,' " *Second Order*, vol. 4, no. 2 (1975).

Outlaw, Lucius. "Philosophy in Africa and the African Diaspora: Contemporary African Philosophy." *Philosophical Perspectives in Black Studies*, no. 3 (papers presented at the 6th National Council for Black Studies Conference, Chicago, 1982).

Ruch, E. A. "Is There an African Philosophy?" *Second Order*, vol. 3, no. 2 (1974).

Senghor, L. S. *On African Socialism*, Mercer Cook, trans. New York: Frederick A. Praeger, Pub., 1964.

Sodipo, J. O. "Philosophy in Africa Today." *Thought and Practice*, vol. 2, no. 2 (1975).

Tempels, Placide. *Bantu Philosophy*. Paris, France: *Présence Africaine*, 1969.

Udoidem, I. S. "Wiredu on how not to Compare African Thought with Western Thought: A Commentary." *African Studies Review*, vol. 30, no. 1 (March 1987).

Wiredu, Kwasi. *Philosophy and an African Culture*. New York: Cambridge University Press, 1980.

_____. "On an African Orientation in Philosophy." *Second Order*, vol. 1, no. 2 (1972).

_____. "An African Concept of Nature." Paper presented at the Boston Colloquium for the Philosophy of Science, 1985–1986.

Wright R. A., ed. *African Philosophy*. New York: University Press of America, 1984.

Yai, Olabiyi. "Theory and Practice in African Philosophy: The Poverty of Speculative Philosophy." *Second Order*, vol. 6, no. 2 (July 1977).